T0330230

A World in Emergence

A World in Emergence

Cities and Regions in the 21st Century

Allen J. Scott

University of California, Los Angeles, USA

Edward Elgar

Cheltenham, UK • Northampton, MA, USA

Published by
Edward Elgar Publishing Limited
The Lypiatts
15 Lansdown Road
Cheltenham
Glos GL50 2JA
UK

Edward Elgar Publishing, Inc.
William Pratt House
9 Dewey Court
Northampton
Massachusetts 01060
USA

A catalogue record for this book
is available from the British Library

Library of Congress Control Number: 2012941549

MIX
Paper from
responsible sources
FSC
www.fsc.org   FSC® C018575

ISBN 978 1 78100 930 7 (cased)

Typeset by Servis Filmsetting Ltd, Stockport, Cheshire
Printed and bound by MPG Books Group, UK

Contents

Figures

Tables

Preface

The present moment is one in which the relatively stable economic and social arrangements of the post-War decades are now only a dim memory but in which the outlines of an alternative order remain strikingly in flux. The last couple of decades have been marked by great economic and political turbulence all around the world. On the one hand, a dynamic capitalism has been insistently globalizing, bringing more and more territory and people into its scope of operations. On the other hand, this same process has been attended by enormous and continuing instabilities. Many efforts and experiments to deal politically with the threats and opportunities offered by these instabilities are under way at every spatial level from the local to the global. The First, Second, and Third Worlds, as such, have gone. Nor can we even talk any longer about the contemporary world as though it were marked by a binary split between a core group of developed nations and a periphery of underdeveloped nations doomed to permanent economic stagnation. Rather, a continuum of national (but rapidly integrating) capitalisms at diverse levels of average income and political transparency is now in play. This is also a world in which two main ideologies, namely neoliberalism and one version or another of social democracy, contend with each other as sources of regulatory prescription for the capitalism of the 21st century. Capitalism itself has changed dramatically since the demise of high fordism in the 1970s, for while it is still greatly dependent on the electro-mechanical technologies and manual labor that characterized that era, it is now more and more characterized by computerized production processes and by an associated proliferation of highly qualified human capital. Hence, the capitalist system today is dependent more than it ever has been in the past on a labor force endowed with finely honed cognitive and cultural skills. In addition, it is an arena within which increasing numbers of workers in low-wage, precarious forms of employment struggle to eke out a living. All of these changes are exerting potent effects on geographical outcomes across the entire surface of the earth.

These are some of the elements of the world that is in emergence as we move more deeply into the 21st century. In this book, my goal is above all to try to work out how these elements are constituted and how they shape the formation of the contemporary economic landscape. My chief concern here is with the enormous resurgence of urbanization all over the world in the last few decades, in large degree as a function of the revivification and spread of capitalism since the 1980s. This resurgence and the new regionalism that accompanies it will almost certainly come to be one of the defining features of the geography of global capitalism in the 21st century. It is manifest above all in a still-unfolding system of global cities, or better yet, a cosmopolitan network of city-regions representing the main economic engines of world capitalism, each enchained with the others in intensifying relations of competition and cooperation. At the same time, there is a real sense in which terms like "urban" or "city" themselves are rather inadequate for the purposes at hand. Especially in today's world, cities do not represent finite bounded tracts of territory, even though municipal boundaries may give the impression of closure. To the contrary, while cities indeed represent relatively dense inflections of economic, social, and political activity, they are also protracted indefinitely outward in extensive systems of relationships that in the final analysis encircle the globe. Yes, there are definite and localized emergent effects that we equate with urban phenomena at specific geographic locations where these inflections reach a level of maximum intensity, but they are also in every sense continuous with what we might call the wider space-economy of contemporary capitalism. A corollary of this remark is that while any sharp distinction between the urban and the rural has long been questionable, it is especially problematic at this moment in history. The latter point is all the more forceful because, as I shall show at a later stage, the new capitalism of the 21st century is producing restructuring effects in many of the interstitial spaces between large cities that significantly redefine what it means to be rural.

In spite of the above strictures about the city as a finite territorial entity, it still assumes substantive if nebulous form as a system of spatial and other relationships that take on a special kind of social significance by reason of their extreme density, both in terms of land use and interaction, and the multiple emergent effects that flow from this state of affairs. By the same token, I take it as axiomatic that any viable theory of the urban must at the outset be able to answer the fundamental question as to why it is in the first instance that large numbers of people come to live clustered together in this way. Of course, a viable urban theory must also be able to answer very many more questions than this. For example: How is the internal spatial structure of any given cluster likely to be arranged? What is the nature of urban social stratification? What is the impact of urbanization on the formation of human mentalities and vice versa? How are cities governed? How are they distributed over geographical space? And many more. Indeed, any inquiry into the genesis of cities can only be fully dealt with in the light of the answers we give to these other questions and their implications for the ways in which cities evolve. But the first question has a special privilege because it goes to the heart of the urban process, as such; and moreover carries with it the implication that we need to look at the wider system of social and economic relationships in order to construct a meaningful answer. By the same token, it is open to the possibility that radically different combinations of these relationships may give rise to generically different kinds of cities, as in the contrasting cases of, say, feudal Kyoto, traditional Yogyakarta, precolonial Ifè, or modern Los Angeles. I am using the notion of genesis here not only in a historical sense but also in an analytical or process-oriented sense, and it is in the same sense that we can think of cities as being continually regenerated on top of and articulated with older structures as social context changes.

In this book, my focus is exclusively upon cities as they emerge in capitalism, and, in particular, as they materialize in relation to the peculiar form of capitalism that has been taking shape since the last quarter of the 20th century. My approach is based on the fundamental point of departure that the origins of the urban process in capitalism can be ascribed primarily to the dynamics of productive activity in the context of profitability criteria in capitalism, and the ways in which the social reproduction of capitalism is secured through the mediation of spatial agglomeration. From this point of departure, and making use of the idea that we are moving into a new capitalism that actively induces and thrives on definite forms of spatial and social differentiation, I attempt to explain how it is that the world that is in emergence all around us is not only preeminently urban but is also ushering in many new kinds of geographical division and variegation. In this respect, my argument goes sharply against the grain of those frequently-encountered statements to the effect that globalization involves a process of spatial homogenization.

I fully recognize that some of these preliminary remarks will be seen as controversial in a number of quarters. Some will object at the outset that they do not promise to make enough of cultural or political factors in the formation of modern cities (though as the discussion proceeds, I increasingly pick up on factors of these sorts). Others will feel that they are much too general or suspiciously Eurocentric and are liable to foreclose examination of important differences in contemporary forms of urbanization in different parts of the world, especially in "postcolonial" situations. Certain neoclassical economists and their fellow travelers can also be expected to object that I make too much of production as a key element in the genesis of cities and not enough of the role of individuals' tastes and preferences in relation to the physical and social amenities of cities. I argue my own case at length in the chapters that follow, and those who demur will have an opportunity then of dealing with the details of my approach. For the present, I simply want to advance the following main point. Whatever the specific historical and geographical circumstances that have attended the formation of cities at different locations around the world, all forms of urbanization today are being shaped and reshaped under the aegis of global capitalism. This is not the same as saying that cities are all converging toward some universal set of empirical specifications. As a matter of fact, the contrary is the case. In the first place, as already mentioned, capitalism itself produces significant forms of spatial differentiation, and most especially under current conditions of production, exchange, and consumption. In the second place, numerous hybrid urban forms appear as the logic and dynamics of capitalism encounter different local circumstances in different parts of the world. These hybrid forms are certainly well worthy of study in their own right, but my preeminent focus in this book is on basic and generalizable urban responses to capitalism, and especially to the new capitalism of the 21st century as it consolidates its hold on the global economy. A warning of *caveat emptor* is in order at this point. My theoretical ambitions in this book are fairly general, but in the chapters that follow, most of the detailed statistical work refers specifically to the United States. This bias of course reflects my own interests and experience as well as the availability of detailed data, but it is in no way intended to function as a surreptitious claim that the empirical complexities of American cities stand in, in any kind of direct substantive sense, for the complexities of non-American cities. Nevertheless, as I shall argue out more fully later, the theoretical framework on offer in this book is designed to cover a great though not unlimited diversity of possible empirical outcomes. Those that we observe in the United States are not only important and interesting in their own right, but also – and despite the preceding caveat – help us to cast enormous light back onto the wider theoretical question that is central to this book of the interrelations between capitalism and the configuration of geographic space.

Almost all of the presented textual material has been prepared explicitly for the present volume. All of it, of course, is infused with ideas and analytical conceits that I have laid out in journal articles on a number of prior occasions. From time to time, but in a very limited way, I have incorporated text directly from these articles into this book. This, however, is almost entirely an original compilation with a distinctly new narrative. I offer it as a description of some of the most important geographical shifts that are now taking shape before our eyes as the new capitalism runs its course, and as a general guide to some of the theoretical ideas that I consider to be essential for dealing politically with this world in emergence.

1. A brief historical geography of capitalism

SOCIETY AND SPACE

One of the major accomplishments of social science over the last half-century or so has been the recognition of the deepening significance of geographic space in the working out of human affairs. There is, at first glance, something paradoxical about this proposition, for the last half-century has also been one in which geographic space has seemed to shrink steadily as improvements in transport and communications technologies have brought far-flung parts of the world into ever deeper contact with one another. In a very real sense, we live in an age in which the exotic is fading away as a meaningful category of human experience. Yet at the same time, the increasing accessibility of any given place to every other place on earth is actually making it possible for new and ever more subtle differentiations of geographic space to occur, above all in regard to the urban and regional foundations of economic life. Rising levels of accessibility are assuredly responsible for the elimination of many kinds of human diversity across the world, especially those that are linked to pre- or extra-capitalistic forms of social existence; but, all the same, the drive in modern capitalism toward the proliferation of multiplicity and variety (in regard to sectors, inter-firm relations, market niches, and so on) is associated with the formation of a system of increasingly specialized locations harboring many different forms of production and associated patterns of settlement. The mechanism underlying this trend is the pervasive urge to agglomeration within specialized fragments of the capitalist production system. This basic drive in capitalism means, too, that the social and economic geography of the world today is in a constant state of evolutionary change. To an ever-increasing degree, we live a world that is in an endemic state of emergence, and nowhere is this more the case than in regard to its underlying urban and regional arrangements.

Space, like time, is a dimension in which events occur and take on individuality. There is a sense in which space can be represented as an absolute geometric system, definable in terms of an unchanging set of Cartesian coordinates. There is also another more relative kind of space that is written, as it were, onto these coordinates, but that is constantly being re-written in other shapes and forms with the passage of time. This latter form of spatial variation is social in origin; it represents the shifting geographic expression of organized and evolving human activity; and its distance metrics are constantly changing. The critical observation I want to make here is that this relative space is not simply a dependent outcome of pre-existing social relationships, but is intimately bound up with the reproduction of social existence as such. In other words, social relationships unfold over space and take on locational attributes, but then the specific spatial configuration of human activity acts back reflexively on the structure and dynamics of the same relationships. A modern city, for example, is not simply a dense internally-differentiated agglomeration of social and economic existence; its very density and internal structure constitute conditions without which modern society could not continue as a viable going concern. In this sense, space, like society itself, is a political construction, and these two phenomena are intertwined with one another in what Soja (1980) has called a "socio-spatial dialectic." In today's world, the motions of this dialectic are in the final analysis animated by the logic of capitalism and its central motif of accumulation. The point here is not that every detailed geographic occurrence we observe is directly and mechanically explicable in terms of capitalism as such; rather, the claim is that the large-scale dynamics – and hence the broad geographic outlines – of modern society are regulated in some fundamental way by capitalism, even if many intimate details of social reality have at most a contingent relationship to this state of affairs.

Certainly, a broad understanding of capitalism is a basic requirement for any overarching investigation of the geographic landscape of the contemporary world, for one of the principal outgrowths of the socio-spatial dialectic is the overall configuration of urban and regional development (Harvey 1982). Capitalism, at its core, is a system of production involving the search for profit by means of investment in physical assets and the employment of workers so as to turn out sellable goods and services. These arrangements are structured by competitive markets, which, among other things, ensure that the profits raised in any given round of production are reinvested (that is, accumulated) in the quest for yet more profit, thereby securing future rounds of production. Reinvestment itself proceeds both directly, by ploughing profits back within the firm in which they were raised, and, if they cannot be usefully deployed at once in this manner, indirectly, via the system of banking and finance that is also an intrinsic part of the whole system. The consequence of this process of accumulation is incessant change in the economic sphere in the form of new products, new technologies, new divisions of labor, new managerial strategies, new kinds of financial instruments, new locational outcomes, and so on. For more or less extended periods of time, however, certain relatively stable configurations in the overall structure of capitalism can be discerned and these are often referred to in the literature as "regimes of accumulation" (Boyer 1986; Lipietz 1986). In its simplest formulation, a regime of accumulation can be represented in terms of a composite model of capitalism as structured by the leading sectors of the economy, the technological bases of production, the dominant forms of labor relationships, and prevailing modalities of economic competition. We can usefully add a fifth main variable to this conventional description, to wit, the spatial and locational character of the economy.

For present purposes, one especially critical aspect of the capitalist economic system, depending on the prevailing regime of accumulation, is its irregular but persistent tendency to promote continual deepening and widening of the division of labor. Societies where the division of labor is highly developed are typified by a corresponding form of social integration that Durkheim (1893) described as organic solidarity, namely the intimate dependence of every individual on every other individual in the pursuit of economic well-being. Capitalist societies are intensely organic in this sense, and with globalization advancing apace under the pressures of economic expansion we can say that organic solidarity is now beginning to materialize at the level of the entire world. Equally, the ever-deepening and widening of the division of labor in modern capitalism means that the geography of production is subject to endless readjustments, at both the intensive and extensive margins of the system. Another way of saying much the same thing is that with advances in the division of labor, the spatial footprint of capitalism tends over time to become more differentiated in its internal structure and more far-flung in geographic extent. This twofold trend is expressed in both the economic specialization and the spatial proliferation of cities and regions in capitalism. At the same time, the cities and regions of modern capitalism are increasingly interlinked with one another in a great diversity of global relationships.

More generally, we can say that the time–space pattern of economic growth and development in capitalism over different regimes of accumulation entails both an intensive front (that is, rising productivity due to improved production methods), and an extensive front (that is, an increase in the volume of output due to the spread of capitalism into new geographic spaces). In fact, the territories that compose the extensive margins of contemporary capitalism are shrinking at a rapid pace, for there are few places in the world today that are not directly under its sway thanks to steadily diminishing costs of transport and communications. Or, at least, if they are not under its direct sway, they are apt, more likely than not, to be indirectly articulated with it as sources of critical resources or migrant labor. This same insistent expansion of capitalism is one of the principal forces pushing globalization forward, not only in the sense that increasing amounts of geographic space are incorporated into the capitalist system with the passage of time, but also in that different national capitalisms are embroiled in a continuing and still incomplete process of amalgamation into a comprehensive world-wide system of production, exchange, and consumption. At some hypothetical end point, such a system would presumably be marked by fully integrated markets, price systems, wage and profit rates, financial arrangements, and so on; though, obviously, many different localized interests and political barriers stand in the way of any smoothly operating trend in this direction. Even in a European Union that is explicitly committed to increasing levels of integration, this commitment repeatedly comes up against political obstructions, as witnessed dramatically in recent years by the inter-state disagreements sparked off by the crisis of the Euro.

URBANIZATION AND REGIONAL DEVELOPMENT IN HISTORICAL PERSPECTIVE

As capitalism emerged historically in North America and Western Europe, so very distinctive forms of urbanization and regional development started to spring up, and these represented radical departures from anything that had previously been observable on the geographic landscape of those parts of the world. The economic functions of the traditional cities of pre-capitalist Europe, were based for the most part on their role as market centers for the surrounding countryside, and on simple forms of craft production. Some of the more important of these cities also functioned as bastions of feudal political power. Social organization at this time could be more accurately described, not in terms of organic solidarity, but in terms of Durkheim's complementary idea of mechanical solidarity – that is, a state of social organization where most of the population is composed of socially undifferentiated individuals, held together as a whole by political authority rather than by functional interdependence. Marx (1852 [1935]) alluded to a classic case of this phenomenon in his account of the mid-19th century French peasantry, which he described as resembling disorganized "potatoes in a sack." By the same token, spatial differentiation in much of pre-capitalist society was less a function of economic dynamics related to the division of labor than it was of basic contrasts in physical geography such as soil, topography, climate, and so on, which in turn set the parameters for variation in patterns of agriculture and simple craft industry.

Mercantilism and Early Capitalism

The advent of full-blown industrial capitalism was heralded by the system of mercantilism that emerged in the 17th and 18th centuries. Mercantilism represents a system of political economy based on the pursuit of national prosperity by means of trade; and in the late pre-capitalist period that meant, above all, long-distance trade by sea among the North Atlantic countries, and to a somewhat lesser degree, trade between the North Atlantic region and the rest of the world. Much of this trade was composed of basic commodities like minerals, timber, wheat, sugar, hides, furs, spices, tobacco, and most notoriously, slaves. Cities on both seaboards of the Atlantic grew vigorously from the proceeds of this trade as well as on the basis of simple processing of the raw materials that passed through them. In North America, port cities like Quebec, Baltimore, Boston, New York, Charleston, and New Orleans, among others, flourished notably at this time; as did Bristol, Liverpool, London, Le Havre, Amsterdam, and Hamburg on the European side of the Atlantic.

Through the 18th century, and most insistently in Britain, rising investment in productive enterprise in the guise of factories and workshops started to overshadow investment in trade. By the same token, mercantilism steadily gave way to capitalism proper, and eventually to a dominant factory and workshop regime of accumulation. Some of the new investment in production was directed to the coastal cities that had flourished under mercantilism, but to an increasing degree it was channeled into emerging manufacturing towns in hinterland areas where many of the critical resources for early industrialization were readily available. Among these resources, water power was initially of the first importance. Subsequently, coal and iron ore became essential foundations of more extended capitalist industrialization and urbanization. In Britain, by the end of the 18th century, major inland manufacturing regions or districts were springing up, as exemplified above all by Lancashire, Yorkshire, the Midlands, Tyneside, and the Central Valley of Scotland. These regions became concentrated foci of urban development as factories and workshops multiplied in number and as displaced agricultural workers flocked to the towns in search of employment. The classical industrial town of this period was marked by an inner zone of factories surrounded by a more extensive zone of dense working-class housing, often in a state of extreme dilapidation; though as the 19th century wore on, general urban conditions steadily improved as a function of rising prosperity and the introduction of basic urban planning services (Benevolo 1971). The spatial structure of these centers of productive activity and working-class settlement was in turn complemented by the formation of suburban rings where the rising middle class staked out its main residential bases.

Throughout the 19th century, the continued expansion of capitalism underpinned sustained development and growth of the manufacturing regions and cities that had come into being over the previous century not only in Britain, but also in the rest of Europe, notably in France, Germany, and the Low Countries (Pollard 1981), as well as in the United States. As these developments occurred, extended geographic belts of manufacturing activity began to emerge in both the northwest of Europe and the northeast of the United States. For example, by the end of the 19th century, industrial capitalism in the United States had stretched far beyond its original geographic base in New England, New York, New Jersey, and Pennsylvania, and now, in a new and more dynamic phase of development, was consolidating its grip over places as far west as Ohio, Indiana, and Illinois, where, by the turn of the century, Chicago was starting to function as its main western hub. The Manufacturing Belt of the United States, as it came to be known (De Geer 1927), rapidly developed into a hive of innovation with regard to mechanical technologies and factory organization, the most revolutionary of all being the automated assembly line that in its turn functioned as the essential foundation of the 20th century mass production system.

Fordism and Mass Production

The mass production system along with the labor-management accords and other social arrangements that sustained it is nowadays, following Gramsci (1975), commonly referred to as "fordism," or the fordist regime of accumulation. The term *fordist*, of course, directly conjures up the spirit of Henry Ford, who launched his great River Rouge car assembly plant in Detroit in 1917. The River Rouge plant was seen as the paradigmatic expression of the most advanced forms of industrial development at the time of its establishment, and the mass production system that it helped to usher in laid the foundations for the economic primacy of the great manufacturing belts of both North America and Western Europe over much of the 20th century. The plants that stood at the pinnacle of this system, whose outputs consisted of metallurgical products, chemicals, cars, industrial machinery, farm equipment, processed foods, and the like, were sustained by tiers of subsidiary industrial establishments forming networks of direct and indirect input providers. Moreover, the locational pull of selected nodes within these networks toward their common center of gravity stimulated massive rounds of urbanization in the shape of growth-center development. These trends were complemented by the expansion of selected older primate cities, like New York, London, and Paris, that played important roles as major banking, financial and corporate centers of the fordist system as a whole.

The American Manufacturing Belt represented the unchallenged leading edge of industrialization and urbanization over this period, and its main metropolitan centers, such as Chicago, Detroit, Cleveland, Buffalo and Pittsburgh, functioned as the preeminent engines of the US economy. The internal structure of the large fordist metropolis of the early to mid-20th century can be represented by a schematic composite model that is in part (but only in part) based on classical Chicago School ideas about urban spatial structure (Park et al. 1925). On the one hand, and at the outset, this structure can be described in terms of a central business district surrounded by a massive conglomeration of industrial establishments (though as the century wore on, many of these establishments steadily abandoned the central city for locations in the suburbs and yet further afield); but on the other hand, the internal structure of the fordist metropolis was also characterized by an extended space of residential neighborhoods riven along diverse lines of social segregation. The mass production system generated immense demands for blue-collar workers, who provided basic manual labor, and for white-collar workers, who maintained the engineering and bureaucratic functions that were an essential element of the mass production system. These two different strata were significantly segregated from one another in their places of residence. Blue-collar workers lived in dense neighborhoods in inner-city areas with ready access to workplaces. White-collar workers formed residential communities in low-density suburbs that became, in turn, repositories of a kind of normative vision of middle-class American family life (Walker 1981). This, at least, was the dominant pattern in North America over much of the first half of the fordist era; but in many continental European cities, the spatial ordering of blue-collar and white-collar communities was largely reversed, mainly because the old historical cores of these cities were markedly resistant to intrusive industrialization. However, with the passage of time, the original layout of social space in the American fordist metropolis started to move in some degree toward a more European-like pattern. After the Second World War, in particular, increasing numbers of industrial establishments began to migrate from the inner city to more suburban locations in search of cheap land, and this turn of events was predictably followed by a corresponding outward shift of large numbers of blue-collar workers from inner-city neighborhoods to new working-class communities in the suburbs.

In parallel with these changes, a number of broad spatial transformations could be discerned at the level of the space-economy as a whole in each of the major fordist countries. These concerned a set of symbiotic

relations between the industrial–urban core of each national territory and a
wider, less-developed periphery. As Hirschmann (1958) and Myrdal (1959)
argued, the essentials of the dynamic that flowed from these relations
entailed a threefold set of variables. First, growth of the industrial–urban
core was secured on the basis of economies of scale in production and
economies of agglomeration in the local milieu; second, and as a corollary,
streams of migrants moved steadily from the less developed periphery to the
more developed core in search of jobs and higher wages; and third, as the
process of decentralization spilled over beyond the suburbs of large cities,
there was an accelerating dispersal of branch plants from the core to locations in the periphery where cheap land and labor were available (Norton
and Rees 1979). This dispersal mainly involved plants with standardized
production technologies that were no longer dependent on the agglomeration economies of the core and that could be operated by unskilled and
inexperienced workers. By the late 1950s, decentralizing industrial facilities
were starting to move even beyond the national periphery and to adopt
off-shore locations in the wider global margins of capitalism where production costs could be reduced yet further, and this trend accelerated greatly
over the subsequent decades. Selected countries in Asia and Latin America,
some of which came to be known as newly industrializing countries, or
NICs, were the main recipients of these facilities. By the same token, many
individual cities in the world periphery, like Seoul, Hong Kong, Singapore,
Taipei, Mexico City, and São Paulo, now expanded greatly on the basis
of the corresponding inward flows of foreign direct investment. Toward
the end of the 1970s, the internationalization of the production systems of
the advanced capitalist countries was advancing at such a rapid pace that
Fröbel et al. (1980) felt sufficiently confident to declare that a "new international division of labor" was coming into being under the aegis of the
multinational corporation. Their specific prediction was that the core capitalist countries would henceforth function as centers of industrial research,
innovation, and management while the rest of the world would steadily
become a specialized reserve of blue-collar labor. The severe economic
crisis of the mid-1970s in North America and Western Europe lent credence
to this prediction, and all the more so as the crisis was accompanied by the
rapid descent of the American Manufacturing Belt to the status of a waning
"Rust Belt." As usual, however, events on the ground turned out to be
rather more complex than the predictions advanced by theoreticians.

Postfordism and Beyond

In 1956, Bardeen, Brattain and Shockley were awarded the Nobel Prize
for their invention of the transistor, a device that became the main basis

of the digital revolution that is still running its course today. In the years following its invention, the simple transistor technology evolved into a very much more complex array of semiconductor devices with enormous implications for computing and communications. Out of the many far-reaching effects of this revolution, one of the most dramatic concerns the production system of capitalism at large, for industrial technologies as well as manual and mental labor processes are subject to significant reshaping by the ever-expanding range and power of digitization and the high-technology machines it sets in motion.

Even as fordism was forging ahead through its so-called golden age in the 1950s and 1960s, some of the first stirrings of a "postfordist" system could already be detected on the landscape as the first rounds of production of digital devices and associated high-technology equipment were secured, largely under the auspices of the US Department of Defense (Markusen et al. 1986; Scott and Angel 1987). One important manifestation of this state of affairs was the growth of new high-technology industrial agglomerations in a number of peripheral regions in the United States. Indeed, the periphery as a whole was shortly to be recast as the Sunbelt and to emerge decisively over the 1970s as a flourishing focus of industrialization in its own right. Silicon Valley was the geographic epicenter of this new phase of industrial development, but many other Sunbelt centers, from Orange County in California to Dallas–Fort Worth in Texas, also participated in the same trend. Analogous trends were making their appearance in Europe, though at a less dramatic pace, while additionally, Japanese manufacturing industry in the 1970s was rising rapidly to international standards of competitiveness due to its revitalization of mass production (sometimes referred to as neofordism) based on pioneering just-in-time production methods and increasing digital control of the assembly line.

At an early moment in the transitional period between fordism and postfordism, Bell (1973) had declared that the advent of "post-industrial society" was in the offing. While there was much that was genuinely prescient about this claim, especially regarding Bell's further contention to the effect that a service economy was now supplanting industrialism, it was in a sense premature, and nowhere more so than in regard to its erroneous underestimate of the continuing role of physical processing, fabrication, and assembly work in contemporary capitalism. It was also considerably off the mark in its pessimism about the deterioration of the work ethic among white-collar workers. Still, Bell's analysis pointed generally in the right direction, and by the early 1980s, there was a growing consensus that an alternative version of capitalism, radically different from fordist industrialism, was indeed coming into being. In brief, a new regime of accumulation was again beginning to assert its preeminence in the capitalist system at large.

One of the defining features of this new *postfordist* version of capitalism was its turn away from the rigidities of classical mass production, and, with the aid of digital technologies, its adoption of flexible specialization (Piore and Sabel 1984). As its name suggests, flexible specialization involves greatly enlarged variability of the product designs that any given firm can bring to market, and this, concomitantly, helped to sharpen the winds of competition that were also unleashed as the new regime came to the fore. Of course, despite significant and continuing spatial and technological reorganization across large swaths of the economic landscape, mass production industries have by no means disappeared. That said, as postfordism continued its rise, the leading edges of the capitalist economy became more and more clearly focused on sectors like high-technology production, software, business and financial services, and a growing array of cultural industries like film, television program production, music, electronic games, fashion, sports, and so on. In addition, labor markets moved toward significantly less rigid and more competitive configurations than was the case under fordism, and this in turn was underpinned by the dramatic decline of blue-collar trade unionism, a trend that has continued down to the present day. Similarly, the keynesian welfare-statist policy apparatus that had been put together as an overarching system of social regulation in fordist capitalism was steadily dismantled in its essentials as market-driven neoliberalism came in the 1980s and 1990s to dominate policy practice in country after country across the world (Brenner 2004a).

The geographic foundations of the postfordist economy appeared most dramatically, in the first instance, in a series of so-called new industrial spaces that sprang up outside the established spatial margins of fordism, and that began to grow with special force after the 1970s. Silicon Valley and other major technopoles, as already indicated, were one expression of this remark, but many other geographic shifts occurred as the new economy gathered momentum. An early instance of this trend was the rise of the so-called Third Italy over the 1970s and 1980s and its development as an internationally-important center of revivified craft industry and fashion-oriented production (Bagnasco 1977; Becattini 1987b; Scott 1988b). Another was the accelerated growth of business and financial services in major world cities like New York, London, and Tokyo, especially as the financialization of the emerging system of global capitalism steamed ahead. The same cities along with other established major centers, such as Los Angeles, Paris, and Milan also played important roles as centers of an expanding range of cultural industries, frequently grafted onto more traditional activities such as theatrical and media production.

Moreover, developments like these were by no means restricted to the most advanced capitalist countries, but were also starting to occur in major metropolitan areas of the world periphery, where significant stocks of advanced human capital assets were now beginning to accumulate. At the same time, growing numbers of unskilled migrant workers were flocking from the periphery into major cities of the core where they were and are in large degree incorporated into the bottom rungs of the labor market, and especially into low-wage sweatshop and service industries. Both of these developments sounded the death knell of the theory of the new international division of labor that had been put forward by Fröbel et al. (1980). To be sure, manufacturing employment continues to shift offshore from the core countries of world capitalism and into repositories of cheap labor on the periphery. A great many parts of the periphery – or, more accurately, the former periphery – are now, however, moving rapidly up the scale of capitalist development, and in many instances (the so-called BRICs, for example, or OECD countries like Chile, Korea, Mexico, and Turkey), have succeeded in mastering much of the technological and managerial know-how of the core capitalist countries. Still, many left-behind parts of the world remain comparatively untouched by these developments. In particular, several countries in Africa stand to a large extent outside of these currents, and are only tenuously linked into the wider global economy through a few cities acting mainly as entrepôt centers for the export of raw materials.

The world of postfordist capitalism that is sketched out schematically above, is now, I would argue, moving into a new phase of development in which the trends already described are taking on greatly augmented intensity, both in regard to their economic scope and their geographic impacts. Something of this turn of events can be deciphered in recent theoretical work that has sought to characterize contemporary capitalism in terms that are very much more affirmative than "postfordism," for the latter term expresses itself only by reference to what it is not rather than what it is. The label "postfordism" has served its purpose well but is now due for honorable retirement; and among the alternatives on offer are terms like the "knowledge economy" (Cooke and Piccaluga 2006), the "information economy" (Drennan 2002), "cybercapitalism" (Peters et al. 2009), the "creative economy" (Franke and Verhagen 2005; Markusen et al. 2008), and "cognitive capitalism" (Moulier Boutang 2007; Rullani 2000). These terms all capture something real about the nature of the current regime of accumulation, but in the remainder of this book, I shall use a number of variations on the formulation "cognitive–cultural economy" as a way of referring to the regime that is so strongly in emergence all around us today. The explicit reasons for this choice will become apparent in due course.

EMERGING CITIES OF THE THIRD WAVE?

The preceding discussion characterizes historical–geographic trends in capitalism as being marked by three major regimes or episodes, namely the 19th century factory and workshop system, fordist mass production, and an emerging cognitive–cultural economy whose opening phases have commonly been described under the rubric of postfordism. In the context of these three episodes of capitalism, we can also identify three distinctive waves of urbanization and spatial order. I am not proposing to reduce the whole of the history and geography of capitalism over the last two centuries into this scheme – far from it – and neither am I suggesting that there are clear and unambiguous points of separation between each episode, especially as many elements of one regime tend to linger on even after it has been superseded by another. As I suggested earlier, each episode can be described in terms of an ideal type focused on a leading collection of sectors, a central technological dynamic, a peculiar set of labor relations and labor market outcomes, and a given state of market competition, together with an associated pattern of urban and regional development; but each is also realized in empirical reality in a diversity of hybrid forms that reflect previous rounds of capitalist development as well as idiosyncrasies rooted in local and historical circumstances. The crux of the matter, however, is that this point of departure helps us to establish a system of analytical preliminaries for dealing with the complexities of empirical outcomes on the ground, and hence to spotlight some of the central dynamics of the geographic landscape at key articulations of the socio-spatial dialectic.

Most importantly, for the present, I argue that current rounds of capitalist development focused on the central sectors of the cognitive–cultural economy are bringing into existence a distinctive third wave of urbanization and spatial development. The main expressions of this third wave are to be found in a network of large metropolitan areas that span the whole globe; though as I shall also show, a number of interstitial spaces between these metropolitan areas are similarly undergoing major transformation as the new capitalism runs its course. In this emerging world, the logic of urban and regional development can no longer be meaningfully described in terms of purely national models but must be analysed directly in the context of an insistent process of globalization in which metropolitan areas in many different countries are increasingly caught up in an overarching system of competition, collaboration, and social interaction. Major cities all over the world, both in the Global North and in the Global South, participate in this developmental wave, though far from equally and far from uniformly in their responses. Table 1.1, which

Table 1.1 The largest 45 urban agglomerations in the world (2007)

Urban agglomeration	Country	Population (millions)		
		1975	2007	2025
Tokyo	Japan	26.6	35.7	36.4
New York–Newark	United States of America	15.9	19.0	20.6
Mexico City	Mexico	10.7	19.0	21.0
Mumbai	India	7.1	19.0	26.4
São Paulo	Brazil	9.6	18.8	21.4
Delhi	India	4.4	15.9	22.5
Shanghai	China	7.3	15.0	19.4
Kolkata	India	7.9	14.8	20.6
Dhaka	Bangladesh	2.2	13.5	22.0
Buenos Aires	Argentina	8.7	12.8	13.8
Los Angeles–Long Beach– Santa Ana	United States of America	8.9	12.5	13.7
Karachi	Pakistan	4.0	12.1	19.1
Cairo	Egypt	6.4	11.9	15.6
Rio de Janeiro	Brazil	7.6	11.7	13.4
Osaka–Kobe	Japan	9.8	11.3	11.4
Beijing	China	6.0	11.1	14.5
Manila	Philippines	5.0	11.1	14.8
Moscow	Russian Federation	7.6	10.5	10.5
Istanbul	Turkey	3.6	10.1	12.1
Paris	France	8.6	9.9	10.0
Seoul	Republic of Korea	6.8	9.8	9.7
Lagos	Nigeria	1.9	9.5	15.8
Jakarta	Indonesia	4.8	9.1	12.4
Chicago	United States of America	7.2	9.0	9.9
Guangzhou	China	2.7	8.8	11.8
London	United Kingdom	7.5	8.6	8.6
Lima	Peru	3.7	8.0	9.6
Tehran	Iran	4.3	7.9	9.8
Kinshasa	Democratic Republic of the Congo	1.5	7.8	16.8
Bogotá	Colombia	3.0	7.8	9.6
Shenzhen	China	0.3	7.6	10.2
Wuhan	China	2.7	7.2	9.3
Hong Kong	China, Hong Kong SAR	3.9	7.2	8.3
Tianjin	China	4.9	7.2	9.2
Chennai	India	3.6	7.2	10.1
Bangalore	India	2.1	6.8	9.7
Bangkok	Thailand	3.8	6.7	8.3
Lahore	Pakistan	2.4	6.6	10.5
Chongqing	China	2.4	6.5	8.3
Hyderabad	India	2.1	6.4	9.1
Santiago	Chile	3.1	5.7	6.3
Miami	United States of America	2.6	5.6	6.3
Belo Horizonte	Brazil	1.9	5.6	6.7

Source: United Nations (2009).

provides population data on the largest 45 cities in the world in 2007, gives a very preliminary sense of what is at stake in these remarks. Not all of the cities listed in the table participate unequivocally in the cognitive–cultural economy, and those that do so differ greatly from one another in terms of both the levels of production that they are able to achieve and the qualitative features of their outputs. Obviously, cities in the Global North like Tokyo, New York, Los Angeles, Paris, and London are major centers of cognitive–cultural production. But many of the cities in the Global South as listed Table 1.1, such as Mexico City, Mumbai, São Paulo, Bangalore, Beijing, Shanghai, Seoul, Hong Kong, and Bangkok are also important foci of the new economy in sectors like finance, business services, cultural products, fashion, and technology-intensive industry. Even less obtrusive cases like Lagos, or Karachi, or Bogotà are making decisive moves in the same direction.

Alongside these developments we can also trace out some important shifts in the geometry of space, and, in particular, the appearance of what is now often referred to as a "new regionalism" (Scott 2008a; Soja 2010). By this I mean a situation in which, as part of the ongoing reconstitution of social being and economic activity at diverse scales of spatial resolution, large and powerful city-centered regions are now decisively entering onto the world stage as important actors in global affairs. In fact, the third wave, as such, is in part definable in terms of a peculiar combination of the local and the global, for one of its most outstanding features is the formation of the great global city-regions of the contemporary world. Each of these city-regions is composed of an extended urbanized area (often comprising more than one metropolis) and a widely-ranging hinterland that may itself contain multiple urban settlements, virtually all of which are assertively inserted into the wider global economy. As such, modern city-regions function as the principal productive engines of the entire capitalist system at the present time. Above all, they are the privileged sites of the new cognitive–cultural economy, and this means in turn, as we shall see, that they are also characterized by many novel features of social organization, internal spatial structure, and built form.

2. On urbanization and urban theory

WHAT IS A CITY?

The world that is coming into emergence in the 21st century is preeminently a world of cities. More than half of the population of the earth now lives in urban areas according to a recent report by the United Nations (2007). The trend toward increasing levels of urbanization is one that will certainly continue for the foreseeable future, despite predictions in some quarters that the digital revolution will rapidly undermine any continuing benefits to be obtained from geographical proximity (Cairncross 1997; O'Brien 1992). So it is well worth returning, at the outset, to the perpetually contentious question as to what cities are and why they remain such a prominent element of the geographic landscape.

An initial but not very informative approach to defining a city is to fix on its dominant empirical form and to say that it comprises a large, dense settlement of people. This answer is formally correct but evades the central issue of the essential social dynamics that account for the existence and internal configuration of large, dense settlements of people in the first place. We can certainly say, with support from Childe (1950), that there must be an agricultural surplus before cities can come into existence, but this proposition does not carry us very far either. We can point, too, to factors like defense, religion, or political centralization as providing incentives for the formation of cities, but while these considerations may account for some types of urban development, they are obviously not of much help in the effort to pinpoint the nature of the large-scale forms of urbanization that prevail today. This remark implicitly raises a further definitional issue. Large dense settlements of people are historically-specific in the sense that their bases and attributes can only be understood in relation to prevailing social arrangements and the ways in which they induce spatial agglomeration of population and shape associated forms of life. Therefore, any attempt to define the city must be overtly sensitive to notions of historical periodization. If we focus our attention on urbanization in some relatively limited historical period, then at least some of the definitional issues will be apt to come into somewhat sharper perspective; or, to put it another way, the definitional issues can in this manner be more readily tailored to the specificities of the tasks at hand. In the present discussion, these tasks are very explicitly concentrated on achieving an understanding of urbanization in capitalist society.

Accordingly, the point of departure for our investigation here is to inquire how capitalism – founded as it is on a system of production revolving around the imperative of accumulation within a regime of private property and economic competition – could engender and sustain large-scale agglomeration. In fact, we can conveniently initiate the analysis by considering certain proto-capitalist social formations in which primitive types of urbanization (or "central place" systems) emerge on the basis of simple markets serving the local countryside. As early theorists like Christaller (1933) and Lösch (1940) showed, central place systems can be described in terms of three main elements, comprising: (1) the *aggregation* of selected market operations at discrete locations or centers; (2) the limited spatial *range* or reach of the different types of goods supplied by each center; and (3) the consequent development of a *hierarchy* of market centers over the landscape. What Christaller entirely neglected to deal with, and what Lösch considered in only a perfunctory way, but which is needed in order to cement the argument, is that localized economies of scale, or agglomeration economies, must be present in order for the essential aggregation process to occur. Specifically, agglomeration economies in simple market systems flow from things like shared infrastructure, the pooling of market information, and the joint attractive power of multiple sellers; and it is phenomena like these that ultimately underpin the formation of clusters of market activity over geographic space.

If we introduce production as well as exchange into the analysis, we will find that the incentives to agglomeration are multiplied many times over, and the scene is now set for a vastly expanded and intensified urban process. In particular, the forms of industrialization characteristic of capitalism give rise to extended social divisions of labor in the specific form of complex networks of interdependency between specialized units of production. Some of these units are under considerable pressure to condense out on the landscape as interrelated clusters of economic activity (Scott 1988a; Storper 1997). Thus, on the one hand, if groups of producers within these networks are closely interlinked, at least some of them are likely to locate in close proximity to one another so as to reduce the costs of transferring inputs and outputs across geographic space and to expedite other kinds of interactions such as face-to-face meetings of personnel from different firms. On the other hand, as producers cluster together in geographic space, they will also tend to generate additional streams of agglomeration economies, hence reinforcing convergence around their joint center of gravity. In complex industrial systems, these agglomeration economies will not only be of the sort already alluded to, but will also derive from processes like enhanced local learning and innovation dynamics, place-based reputational effects, shared labor markets, and overall risk reduction due to the multiplicity of alternative providers of inputs and buyers of outputs (Duranton and Puga 2004; Storper and Scott 1990). At the same time, every agglomeration of producers will call a local pool of labor into being, so that a complementary system of residential activity will form in proximity to employment places, and further growth effects will flow from this state of affairs, including the formation of retail and personal service functions. Of course, there are at least temporary limits to this sort of localized growth. One limit is set by the extent of external markets for the goods and services produced in any center. Another makes its appearance as agglomeration *dis*economies set in due to factors like congestion, pollution, rising land values, and the like.

Even if we agree on the discussion up to this point, we are still very far from answering our initial question about the origins and character of urbanization because so far we have only dealt with a very general and rather abstract process of locational concentration. This point of departure nonetheless provides a durable anchor for the rest of our discussion. Indeed, we can say as a matter of first principle that competitiveness, profitability and accumulation depend so intimately on agglomeration – among other things – that there is no hitherto realized form of capitalism that is not also associated with urbanization; just as we can also say that so far in human history the onward march of capitalist economic development has always, with only minor interruptions, engendered rising levels of urbanization (see Figure 2.1). All the same, agglomerations of productive activity together with a rudimentary residential space are not yet fully urban in and of themselves. We may call them proto-urban forms in that they are the skeletal foundation of full-blown urbanization. They only become fully urban when the logic of their intra-urban spatial structure is addressed and when the multiple emergent effects, reflexivities, and conflicts set in motion in the wider urban sphere start to come to life. This is not to reduce the latter phenomena *en bloc* to mere reflections of the proto-urban foundation stones – for they have their own particular logics – but only to point to their situatedness in a specific kind of geographic context in a specific system of social and property relations. Moreover, cities are not just dependent variables in relation to capitalist social dynamics, for they also constitute critical sites for the reproduction of capitalism as a whole by reason of their complex efficiency-preserving and productivity-enhancing qualities and their functions as social collectivities. Their status as *sui generis* phenomena is underlined by the formation of local political apparatuses and other institutions of collective order with capacities for

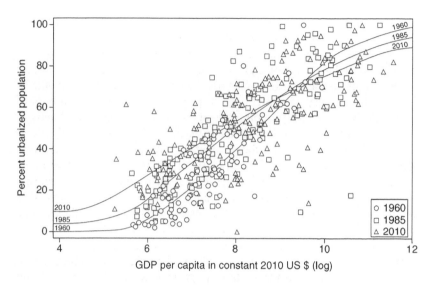

Notes: Hong Kong and Singapore are omitted. Lines represent logit regressions for 1960, 1985 and 2010. The adjusted values of R^2 for these regressions are 0.68, 0.55 and 0.49, respectively. Note that for poor and middle-income countries rates of urbanization for a given level of GDP per capita are accelerating over time; by contrast, for the richest countries with already high percentages of their populations living in urban areas, rates of urbanization for a given level of GDP per capita are decelerating over time.

Source of data: World Bank, *World Development Indicators*, http://databank.worldbank. org/ddp/home.do?Step=12&id=4&CNO=2.

Figure 2.1   Percentage of total population living in urban areas in relation to the logarithm of GDP per capita (in constant 2010 US $) by individual country, for the years 1960, 1985, and 2010

remedial action in regard to recurrent economic limits on growth and to social disruptions due to the endemic political conflicts of urban life.

All of this is consistent with the observation that even within the overarching structure of capitalism cities are subject to considerable historical and geographical differentiation, a point that is illustrated (but not exhausted) by the three waves of capitalist urbanization as identified in Chapter 1. Still, and to re-phrase a point that has been made already, if cities in capitalism invariably comprise an enormous range of different empirical relata they cannot effectively be defined in terms of these relata alone. The factories, warehouses, office buildings, utilities, shopping centers, transport networks, schools, houses, neighborhoods, and all the rest that are to be found in any modern city are not necessarily or even in the first instance urban phenomena. The urban does not reside in any single occurrence of heterogeneous phenomena like these but only in their mode of spatial integration within a dense nexus of interacting locations and land uses. Even the psycho-cultural theories of the city developed by writers like Benjamin (1969), Simmel (1903 [1950]) and Wirth (1938) are in essence derived out of this process of spatial integration, with its concomitant attributes, in Wirth's formulation, of density, heterogeneity, and size. In this context, Saunders (1981) was correct to warn against the temptations of eclecticism in "urban studies" but was also surely mistaken in his assessment (p.15) that "the city in capitalism does not constitute a theoretically specific object of analysis."

The urban is a relational phenomenon more than it is a simple sum of its discrete empirical parts. Recent attempts to seize the nature of urbanization based on assemblage theory are hence quite apposite to the degree that they repose on notions of relationality (Farías and Bender 2010; McFarlane 2011), but they miss much of what is crucially important here by de-emphasizing the specific shape and logic of this relationality within the wider system of a spatialized capitalism. Amin and Thrift (2002), too, rightly point to the importance of the multiple extra-local linkages of cities, but they then undermine this promising line of argument by claiming that the city is "not a place of meaningful proximate links" (p. 27) just as they do when they reject the idea that the spatiality of cities (or, in their terms, "agglomeration, density, proximity" (p. 53)) generates specific economic and social effects. Modern cities, to repeat, are in the first instance relational entities composed fundamentally out of dense agglomerations of capital and labor. As such, cities are privileged locational structures in capitalism and are sites where unusually large masses of profits and wages are generated. In addition, and as a result of their internal spatial interconnections, cities generate huge quantities of land rent, and this, too, is an important sign of their specificity, for land rent mechanisms are anchored in the formation of intensely polarized centers and subcenters in urban space. These mechanisms also engender sharp contrasts between different types of intra-urban land use, of which perhaps the most notable is the imperfect but virtually always observable separation between the production spaces and residential spaces of the city. From this separation springs the single most important daily rhythm of the city in capitalism, namely, the journey to work.

This insistence on the notion of the urban as an essentially relational phenomenon raises the ever-recurrent question as to where the outer boundaries of the city should be drawn. In fact, there are no determinate outer boundaries of the city in capitalism, no line drawn in the sand that can encompass any modern city in its entirety. Even local government boundaries have a very specialized character and do not represent any kind of real functional limit of the city as a going concern. From this point of view the city can assuredly be described as a local articulation of the space-economy as whole. The city's functional range, in other words, spreads outward asymptotically in a system of relationships whose extent nowadays encircles the globe. But again, with apologies to Amin and Thrift, these statements do not mean that the city dissolves away either as an identifiable assemblage of human activity or as a meaningful object of study. From the same relational point of view, the city emerges as an assertive spatial entity in its garb as a dense polarized nexus of differentiated land uses and locations. It is this polarization, or gravitational pull, even in the absence of clearly delineated outer boundaries, that makes it possible to talk in meaningful terms about distinctively urban agglomerations at distinctive locations in geographic space, in contrast to randomly demarcated tracts of territory.

AGGLOMERATION AND URBANIZATION IN CAPITALISM

The Mainsprings of Agglomeration

The clustering of economic and social phenomena in geographic space is a basic outcome of the play of agglomeration economies in the twofold sense of (a) reduced transactions costs due to the co-location of interlinked activities, and (b) localized externalities reflecting the synergies that come from size and multiplicity. In combination with one another, these factors beget gravitational effects at particular locations; and in favorable circumstances, these can be sufficiently strong and multidimensional as to lead to behemoth cities of the sort that now flourish on every continent.

Much of the theory of agglomeration stems from the original ideas of Marshall (1890; 1919) on the formation of specialized industrial districts in Britain at the end of the 19th century, and in recent decades, this theory has been elaborated into a highly sophisticated body of concepts. The core of the theory, as we have seen, resides in the observation that certain groups of actors will tend to cluster together in geographic space so as to minimize the costs of their mutual interactions and to take advantage of jointly determined synergies, where the latter phenomena refer variously to rising productivity, falling costs of production, and intensifying know-how as a consequence of the size, scope, and density of the economic and social order in any given locality. These synergies can be further unpacked by reference to their socio-economic genesis, most notably in relation to inter-firm relationships, local labor markets, and learning and innovation processes, but other variables also play an important role, including capital-intensive infrastructures and the institutional arrangements that are constructed to deal with the constant and endemic breakdowns inherent to the urban system.

To begin with, then, wherever we encounter extended social divisions of labor in the guise of vertical disintegration, networks of specialized but complementary producers will also make their appearance, reflecting the flows of inputs and outputs through the system of production. Transactions of this type will incur a series of spatially-dependent costs, including direct transfer costs on the inputs and outputs themselves, interest payments on the immobilized capital represented by goods in transit, and personnel costs associated with the labor entailed in setting up and monitoring the arrangements needed to maintain the transactional system, especially where this entails face-to-face contact between high-wage managerial workers. For these reasons alone, selected groups of producers have strong inducements to agglomerate together in geographic space, though the inducements will obviously vary depending on the kinds of products at issue, and, *ceteris paribus,* will tend to diminish over time as transport technologies become more and more efficient. That said, the effects of falling transport costs may be neutralized by countervailing pressures emanating from within the system of inter-firm transactions itself. One source of pressure is related to the size of the transactions at issue. Where transactions are small in scale and frequently changing in their content, transfer costs will often be quite high per unit of distance as compared with those incurred by large standardized transactions where economies of scale in shipping are frequently available. This means that small and variable transactions will tend to be relatively constrained in their feasible spatial range, thus requiring high levels of proximity between firms that interact in this manner; by the same token, small entrepreneurial firms with variable transactional interrelationships are precisely one of the mainstays of the urban economy (Hall 1962; Hoover and Vernon 1959; Scott 1980; Struyk and James 1975). Another source of pressure concerns the degree of repetitive transacting between firms. For example, where a firm's production schedules are variable with regard to timing or product specifications, both its upstream and downstream transactions will be apt to change rapidly, leading to elevated unit costs (including search and setup costs) that may well make production uncompetitive unless many and varied input providers and output users are located nearby. Agglomeration thus also provides a kind of insurance against supply and demand blockages or uncertainties in production systems marked by high levels of instability and product diversity.

The local labor markets that form within and around these

agglomerations of productive activity are additional potent sources of agglomeration economies and productivity enhancements. At the outset, the concentration of work-places and residence-places within a narrow spatial compass means that the daily activity system of work, commuting, and family life can proceed in regular and relatively low-cost rhythms. The same concentration reduces the search costs both of individuals looking for work and of employers looking for workers, and these costs will fall even further as local labor markets increase in size. These relationships are captured in a statistical study by Jayet (1983) who shows that large local labor markets are typified by relatively high turnover rates and short periods of unemployment whereas small local labor markets are marked by long job tenure but also by long periods of unemployment. In addition, labor markets in urban areas are arenas within which significant processes of socialization and training of workers go on. Workers become habituated into local production norms and sensibilities through immersion in the flow of work and life in specialized production complexes; and they also acquire agglomeration-specific skills through on-the-job-learning and local training programs. Moreover, the educational and research programs of schools and universities are frequently tilted in ways that serve local production needs. In this manner, important pools of human capital necessary for the economic success of any agglomeration are created and sustained by the logic of urban development and economic specialization.

These benefits of agglomeration are reinforced by the role of the city as a locus of creativity, learning and innovation effects (Franke and Verhagen 2005; Hall 1998; Scott 2010a). Because so many of the core functions of cities revolve around transactions-intensive economic activity there is constant interaction between many individuals as they go about the daily business of production and work, and as a consequence large amounts of information flow constantly through the urban system (Acs 2002; Camagni 1991; Storper and Venables 2004). Much of this information is no doubt of little value, but some of it will from time to time combine with other bits of information in the minds of various intermediaries, and this will often initiate innovative insights that can be applied in process and product improvements. For the most part, these mechanisms operate at a rather small scale and rarely give rise to earth-shaking innovations, but cumulatively, over the passage of time, they can result in continual forward advances in the productive capacities and competitive advantages of any given agglomeration (Russo 1985). A large amount of empirical evidence has accumulated to suggest that these processes are quite pervasive in modern capitalism and they in part explain the continued creativity and competitiveness of certain places over long periods of time. Silicon Valley is a celebrated example of this phenomenon (Saxenian 1994). In line with these remarks, a seminal paper by Jaffe et al. (1993) has shown that specialized types of patents tend to originate within correspondingly specialized agglomerations in the United States and that definite genealogies of patenting activity are observable in the same agglomerations.

Parallel bursts of innovative energy and intensifying agglomeration are observable in the entrepreneurial capabilities that are so frequently to be found in large urban areas. These capabilities are commonly manifest in spin-off processes giving rise to generation after generation of new firm formation in an evolutionary spiral of development. Klepper (2010) has described processes like these in the context of the Detroit car industry in the first half of the 20th century and the integrated circuit industry in Silicon Valley in more recent decades. However, whereas Klepper sees spin-off processes as leading unproblematically to spatial clustering, an alternative view, in the light of the arguments laid out here, is that consistent spatial concentration of spin-off firms cannot be guaranteed in the absence of a complementary system of agglomeration economies. We might say that spin-off processes reflect the opportunities for vertical and horizontal disintegration that exist in any given production complex, so that as they occur they replicate something of its latent temporal structure; but that agglomeration economies are essential prerequisites if it the complex is to survive and persist as a durable spatial cluster.

From Agglomeration to Urbanization

Agglomerations of the sort alluded to above are the basic building blocks of the city in capitalism. They are the glue that holds many different units of capital and labor together in geographic space and that sustain the full-blown emergence of the city as a very special kind of collectivity within the wider collectivity of society as a whole. This urban collectivity functions as a system of intricate interdependencies between production, work, and social life within a narrow spatial orbit and in daily and weekly cycles of activity. In capitalism, with the privilege it accords to private property, the individual, and competition, most of this activity is coordinated by markets. Yet, as already suggested, markets of all kinds in the urban sphere have a tendency to fail, which means that some sort of collective decision-making and action must also be present in order to prevent costly malfunctions of urban space. More importantly, the urban collectivity comprises much more than simply a system of market arrangements with occasional flaws that call for extra-market correction. It is at once a phenomenon that generates outcomes far in excess of the sum of its parts, and that also, irrespective of the need to deal with technical market failures, has a necessary and deeply-rooted public or political dimension.

¹ To be sure, even the technical market failures of urban space call for robust institutional arrangements with powers of remedial action. The very spatiality of the city leads to numerous predicaments with high social costs like agglomeration diseconomies, negative spillover effects, free-rider dilemmas, lock-in problems, and supply breakdowns in regard to many kinds of infrastructural artifacts and services. These generic types of predicaments are manifest in a multiplicity of familiar urban problems like sprawl, congestion, pollution, deteriorating neighborhoods, persistent land use conflicts, and lost developmental opportunities, as well as in the widespread necessity for public investment in road systems, garbage disposal services, street lighting, and so on. The presence of such market failures is one reason why cities have administrative apparatuses. However, these apparatuses are not merely an unfortunate circumstance made necessary by the existence of market failures. As Hardt and Negri (2009) suggest, any analytical maneuver like this concedes far too much ground to the idea that markets and the war of all against all are not only normal but represent the supreme end point of rational social organization. We need to acknowledge that the city is a many-dimensional commons, or a set of common-pool resources and synergies, and that these phenomena are not only irreducible to private property and market logic, but are liable to costly disruptions where markets are allowed to operate unhindered. In other words, markets themselves are part of the recurrent crisis of urbanization in capitalism at large.

The urban commons is a field of immense complexity and social importance. For one thing, agglomeration economies and diseconomies are a product of joint but at the outset uncoordinated action; they evade any sort of private ownership and hence in whole or in part are intrinsic constituents of the public estate. Accordingly, in the absence of coordination and management, severe irrationalities in the levels and range of the agglomeration economies and diseconomies generated in any given city are likely to develop. Certainly, economists have devised market simulacra to deal with some kinds of agglomeration diseconomies, as in the case of pollution or congestion pricing mechanisms. These simulacra may bring about some semblance of efficiency in specific instances, but they, too, are dependent on underlying public initiatives and supervision, and, moreover, by invoking purely market-oriented solutions they evade many wider questions of social or environmental justice. For another thing, problems involving social reproduction of the labor force and social overhead capital pose many severe threats to urban viability if left to the play of markets. Competitive market structures are simply unable to secure many different kinds of basic social outcomes in requisite quantities and with the right qualitative attributes that are essential for the continued effective functioning of capitalist urbanization. Education, housing for the poor, public health, recreational opportunities, unemployment benefits, crime control, and so on, are all liable to severe undersupply – relative to socially rational levels – in the absence of collective action. Again, market simulacra have been devised (school voucher systems, for example) to deal with some of these matters, but once more, this is only a mask for a necessary policy process that, in addition, is unable or unwilling to confront fundamental questions of social justice or fairness, including issues of income redistribution. Whatever our normative inclinations may be in regard to these matters, the conclusion follows that purely individual decision-making and behavior in the urban realm must be complemented by some mechanism of collective coordination and governance, not as an optional extra, but as a fundamental condition of urban viability. The urban can never be simply conflated with a system of private property and competitive markets but calls imperatively – in indicative and normative ways – for diverse institutional arrangements both to deal with technical market failures and to manage the common pool resources of the city as a whole. Intertwined with this minimal role for governmental arrangements in the city is the yet more difficult task of mediating the endless political collisions that occur between different interest groups over the appropriation and use of urban resources and urban space (Cochrane 2007).

These general processes of agglomeration and urbanization and the contingent outcomes that are associated with them have always operated in capitalism, though with markedly different empirical effects in different times and places, and we need to acknowledge, in particular, that the endemic tendencies to agglomeration in the capitalist economic system are always complemented by countervailing forces which are sometimes relatively dormant and sometimes quite powerful, depending on a variety of circumstances. Obviously, if external markets for the products of any agglomeration shrink then urban stagnation or decline are likely to ensue. Also, the advantages of agglomeration do not always outweigh the attractions of more decentralized locations. In the fordist era, for example, standardized and deskilled branch plants with routinized external linkages were often able to attain higher levels of efficiency when they dispensed with the agglomeration economies of major manufacturing centers altogether and relocated in peripheral areas where cheap land and labor were available. Over the crisis years of the 1970s, this process of industrial decentralization became rampant, leading to severe economic and social dislocations in many cities of the US Manufacturing Belt. In today's capitalism, by contrast, trends to agglomeration are once again intensifying. These trends and the forms of urban resurgence that have accompanied them are in significant ways related to the burgeoning of the sectors at the dynamic core of the cognitive–cultural economy. As I argue more fully in Chapter 10, the advent of globalization has not only not undermined this tendency but has actually accentuated it.

THE GROWTH OF CITIES

If the preceding theoretical commentary is correct, it follows that the growth of cities is likely to be best explained in terms of the development of the central production apparatuses and agglomeration processes that give rise to their existence in the first place together with the institutions of urban governance that help to maintain competitive advantages and social order. There seems to be little controversy that the growth of cities in 19th century and much of 20th century capitalism can reasonably be accounted for by invoking the primacy of production, but an alternative narrative has come into prominence over the last few decades suggesting that we are now entering an era marked by "consumer cities" and that a new way of thinking about urban growth is necessitated by this alleged turn of events. The main exponent of this alternative view is Glaeser and a number of co-workers (Glaeser and Gottlieb 2006; Glaeser et al. 2001) who have suggested that amenities such as moderate winters and the "playground" assets of cities now account for much if not all of the recent urban growth in the United States. With reference to large-scale urbanization in the US Sunbelt, Glaeser (2011, p. 63) writes that "over the last century, no variable has been a better predictor of urban growth than temperate winters," though even if we accept the causal potency of temperate winters, extending the time period back over the last hundred years is a bit of a stretch. Analogous views to those of Glaeser are expressed by Clark (2004; see also Clark et al. 2002) who likens the modern city to an "entertainment machine," and by Florida (2002) who claims that members of the creative class are now thronging into cities that can satisfy their supposedly overriding appetites for social diversity, tolerance, and a generally agreeable urban environment. Many of these arguments are propped up with elaborate regression models that purport to show a statistically significant and positive relationship between amenities and urban growth.

The basic mechanism that amenities theorists invoke to explain their findings rests on two main pillars. One is that individuals with high levels of human capital are said to be "footloose;" the other is that these individuals will then optimize their utility levels by migrating to amenity-rich places. Partridge (2010) has recently reviewed the evidence for and against the amenities argument of urban growth and has concluded that the statistical evidence comes down heavily in support of an affirmative view. There is also a certain common-sense argument in favor of this view. People most certainly do have preferences for amenities of various sorts, and it may very well be that a majority of people have a strong partiality for mild winters over cold winters and for entertaining cities over boring cities. The question is, can we elevate this point of agreement into a theory of urban growth, and if not, how can we account for the observed statistical results that seem to support the arguments of the amenities theorists? The analysis of urban development in capitalism advanced at an earlier stage in this chapter already points in the direction of a reasoned skepticism in regard to the amenities theory, but we now need to make the critique much more explicit.

Consider, at the outset, the issue of livelihood. Urban dwellers and migrants to cities do not subsist on amenities; they need jobs in order to survive. Glaeser and Gottlieb (2006) suggest that as people arrive in cities in search of amenities, *ceteris paribus*, wages will go down and house prices will go up. This approach allows for a kind of urban equilibrium to occur, but, curiously, it does not embrace changes in employment levels. The implicit assumption seems to be either that local job generation will proceed as a matter of course so as to absorb increased population due to amenities-induced migration, or that new arrivals at any given locality will immediately and successfully mobilize (inherent?) entrepreneurial talents. In any case, the Glaeser–Gottlieb analysis provides no explicit mechanism to guard against the possibility that large numbers of amenity-hungry hordes in any city will end up in mass unemployment.

As it happens, there is a countervailing body of empirical evidence from a number of different countries suggesting that migration patterns are related preeminently to the geography of employment opportunities rather than to the geography of amenities (see, for example, Chen and Rosenthal 2008; Grant and Kronstal 2010; Greenwood and Hunt 1989; Niedomysl and Hansen 2010; Scott 2010b). Obviously, a critical proviso must be offered here to the effect that retirees and others with an independent income can and do migrate to places independently of local employment opportunities and there is in practice much migration of this sort into the US Sunbelt. Once this has been said, individuals who have spent considerable time and money acquiring advanced levels of human capital and formal qualifications are not likely to want to squander this investment by then selecting places in which to live simply on the basis of their amenity value. These individuals may be mobile, but they are emphatically not likely to be footloose in the sense of being indifferent to employment opportunities that will permit them to capitalize in some meaningful way on their talents and training. We can reinforce this remark by noting that not all forms of human capital are equally valuable in all cities, and that there is an important matching process on both the supply and demand side that must be taken into account. Actors and screen-writers are attracted to Hollywood, computer and software engineers to Silicon Valley, financial analysts to Wall Street, academics to centers of higher education, and country-music performers to Nashville precisely because these types of workers can have reasonable expectations of capitalizing on their specific talents and qualifications in these places, irrespective of any amenities that may or may not be present. With an analytical strategy like this, then, we can also begin to acknowledge processes of local economic specialization, a phenomenon that the sunshine or playground theories of urban growth are quite incapable of facing up to. Equally, the massive migration of low-wage workers from Asia and Latin America into the major metropolitan areas of the United States is directly related to the status of these areas as hotbeds of the types of jobs in manufacturing and services that are preferentially reserved for socially-marginal workers with low levels of formal qualification. One further critical point needs to be made in this context. As part of their justification for their amenities-based view of urban growth, Glaeser and Gottlieb (2006) refer to the case of New York, which lost population between 1970 and 1980, allegedly because of high levels of crime and violence. Glaeser (2011) further suggests that the substantial growth of New York after 1980 occurred because crime and violence had been greatly reduced and the "playground" facilities of the city had once more come into their own. But this account conveniently overlooks the fact that the 1970s was a period of deep economic crisis in the United States in general and in New York in particular (a circumstance that might plausibly explain the high crime rate), whereas the subsequent period has witnessed a great flourishing of the city's financial, business service, and information sectors and allied industries.

An alternative and to my mind a much more satisfactory explanation of the growth of cities must focus on their continuing function as the locomotives of the capitalist economic system. Thus, Sunbelt cities did not suddenly start to overtake Frostbelt cities in the 1970s for climatic reasons or because they offered superior amusements, but because, on the one hand, the dramatic crisis of fordist capitalism undermined continued urban growth in the Northeast, and, on the other hand, a window of locational opportunity opened up as the new technologies, new labor processes, new organizational structures, and new products of postfordist industrialization came to the fore, and made it possible for cities in the rest of the country to capture a large proportion of the employment opportunities thus generated. In view of this observation, the evidence from statistical models indicating that urban growth in the United States over the last few decades correlates positively with average winter temperatures is not in the least surprising, but is also clearly no more than a contingency. Any locational adjustment, like the shift of employment growth from Frostbelt cities to Sunbelt cities, will then be consolidated in a path-dependent process rooted in the increasing returns effects that flow from dense, local-ized pools of capital and labor, and expressed in continuing rounds of local employment expansion, inward migration, and city growth. Much the same kind of process can be observed in the readjustments now occur-ring as huge numbers of migrants move from western China to eastern China. In this alternative model, socially-constructed amenities assume their correct status, not as causes but as dependent outcomes of the growth and rising prosperity of cities.

CRITICAL URBAN THEORY: WHAT KIND?

I take it that a viable urban theory must provide at least the rudiments of an account of the origins, growth, and form of cities. A critical urban theory is one that accomplishes the same goals but that in addition opens up a space allowing for a progressive political perspective of the city. These desiderata have helped to guide much of the previous discussion, though at the same time I have insisted on the limits of meaningful theoretical gen-eralization about cities outside of given frameworks of historical time and geographic space. I have argued that any coherent theory of urbanization relevant to the current conjuncture must be derived by reference to the logic and dynamics of capitalism as a whole. By the same token, detailed adjustments to any theory like this must also be made depending on the versions of capitalism that prevail at specific times in specific places. The analytical challenges are made yet more complex because generic theoreti-cal accounts can never fully capture the mass of specific empirical detail that always accompanies any concrete instance of urbanization on the ground.

I make this point partly because there is a mounting sense of unease in much of the literature today about the application of "Western" theories of urbanization to situations in the Global South, and a certain skepti-cism as to whether one general theory will do justice to the full range of social-cum-urban outcomes across the globe (Escobar 2005; McGee 1967; Robinson 2006; Roy 2011). Special concern has been expressed about the Eurocentrism that often haunts contemporary urban studies as reflected in the uncritical transfer of concepts from the more economically advanced Global North to the Global South, and which, by the same token, tends to subdue subaltern, postcolonial voices from cities of the latter sphere. This concern is quite legitimate and insofar as it explicitly raises a protest against the wholesale transfer of Chicago School ideas to African cities (Robinson 2006) – or to any city for that matter – is absolutely on the right track. The unanswered questions raised by this literature remain, however: is there some single but as yet unformulated overarching theory that will get the job done (and if so, how)?; or do we need multiple theories to take account of the full panoply of urbanization in today's world (and if so, how many, and what should they look like)? Quite clearly, there are special questions that revolve around the cities of the Global South. Hyperurbanization is one such question; so is the deeply indurated poverty and the extensive slums in cities of the South as well as the related issue of the extensive informal economy in these cities. There are, too, many cultural idiosyncrasies that mark off cities in different parts of the world from one another, both within and between the North and the South. These and other particularities most certainly merit treatment on their own terms and in their own right.

Much of the postcolonial literature, however, takes its point of departure in a critique of the traditional tension between modernism and developmentalism, which is fair enough, but not very productive in a world that is nowadays increasingly in the throes of deepening social and spatial integration under the aegis of a pervasive global capitalism. This remark suggests that, far from being incommensurable splotches of uniqueness, most cities all across the world are actually arrayed in a grid demarcated by a number of common but extensively drawn-out axes. The implication in turn is that there is some reasonably comprehensive theoretical approach that captures crucial elements of urbanization in both the North and the South while simultaneously acknowledging the likelihood of wide variation in the range of possible empirical outcomes. Dick and Rimmer (1998) argue, no doubt correctly, that Southeast Asian cities are rapidly converging toward US patterns of urbanization. Nevertheless, a sensitive and comprehensive theory of urbanization is not necessarily committed to the notion of social and economic convergence. To the degree that urban forms wherever they may be in the world participate in capitalism, we can certainly invoke broadly similar kinds of theoretical ideas about their genesis and functions. However, we will patently have to nuance our account depending on the specificities of the form of capitalism that is in play, and by the same token, we also need to pay attention to the concrete historical and geographical circumstances that are inevitably present in any given instance. In particular, many poor cities of the periphery have internal social peculiarities that remain outside the main orbit of capitalism as such, but are nonetheless deeply articulated with it. The "Slumdog" conditions of Mumbai's shadow city of Dharavi as described by Roy (2011) are a case in point. So, incidentally, are the poverty, slums, and informal economic arrangements that blighted London in the 19th century, as described in Dickens' novel *Our Mutual Friend,* with its fictional account of the grotesque landscape of London's "dustheaps" and their human scavengers, who, in symbolic terms, are not only combing through the refuse of the metropolis but also through human excrement (see also Stedman Jones (1984)).

To sum up, Robinson (2006) is correct to call for a cosmopolitan and non-dualistic urban theory for today's world, though her claim that this can be based on a notion of the "ordinary city" remains enigmatic at best. The point is not to assert that cities everywhere are converging toward a common future destiny. The point is that cities in an increasingly capitalistic world can be understood by reference to a set of fundamental principles that are nonetheless accompanied by enormous divergence of empirical outcomes on the ground.

3.   Toward a new economy: technology, labor, globalization

Capitalism is endemically subject to a logic of evolutionary change. For greater or lesser periods of time relatively stable regimes comprising dominant sectors, technologies, labor relations, and forms of competition may make their appearance, but these are always superseded by other versions of capitalism marked by other organizational structures. The 19th century factory and workshop system developed in a climate of open economic competition and was able to produce a variety of output but at a limited scale. In 20th century keynesian–fordist society, the automated assembly line freed production from quantitative restraint, but at the expense of variety. Producers in the new globally competitive economy of the 21st century are able to achieve significant economies of scale, but are now also capable of combining scale with ever-shifting product variety. This latest version of capitalism is dramatically different from anything that theorists in the middle of the 20th century foresaw as the shape of things to come.

When Schumpeter (1942) wrote his great book on capitalism, socialism and democracy, he tried to deduce the future by extrapolating forward out of the condition of American mass production at the time, and accordingly he foresaw a never-ending continuation of capital-intensification, mechanization, and increasing internal economies of scale in corporate enterprise. His logical inference from all of this was that processes of industrial concentration would continue indefinitely into the future, leading in the end to effective monopolization of all the main sectors of the economy. He also averred that along the pathway to this state of affairs, market coordination of the economy would steadily give way to oligopoly and monopoly, and at some point government would find it necessary to intervene in order to ensure the maintenance of order and efficiency in the economy as a whole. In effect, this meant, for Schumpeter, wholesale nationalization of industry, and hence the socialization of the economy, not as a left-wing political objective, but as a structured outcome of the dynamics of capitalism itself. As brilliant and closely argued as Schumpeter's analysis may have been, events in reality have turned out quite differently. Like so many of his contemporaries (see for example, Giedion (1948)), the late Schumpeter could not conceive of economic progress in terms other than

mechanization and the Chandlerian multi-divisional firm with its hierarchical organization and standardized production. With the wisdom of
hindsight, we now know that industrial technology did not advance along
a smooth trajectory toward ever greater mechanical integration, but was
marked by a decisive rupture that took it, and the wider capitalist system,
onto a completely different evolutionary pathway.

THE POSTFORDIST MOMENT: FURTHER OBSERVATIONS

By the late 1970s and early 1980s, the Thatcher and Reagan revolutions
in Britain and America, respectively, were pioneering a new conservative
mode of social regulation in response to the crisis of the 1970s. Over much
of the period of fordism, and beginning especially in the 1930s, various
versions of a counter-cyclical policy system had been cobbled together in
virtually all of the advanced capitalist countries, and this was consolidated
after the Second World War into an overarching keynesian welfare-statist
apparatus. In its most basic expression, this system comprised deficit
spending by national governments in times of economic downturn in
order to revive flagging levels of production together with a set of welfare
arrangements, including unemployment insurance, public housing, health
benefits, and so on, designed to assist the less well-off, and especially to
provide a cushion for the working class in times of large-scale lay-offs.
The new Thatcher–Reagan dispensation sought to modify this political
bargain, most especially by means of severe cuts in welfare, while at the
same time taking actions to reduce the power of labor unions, thereby
undermining continued political support for the welfare state. The end
result of these interventions was a significant resurgence of market forces,
which, in the context of growing globalization, released strong new winds
of competition across the capitalist economic system. These neoliberal
winds continue to blow and have now spread far beyond their original
points of origin in Britain and the United States.

As these policy changes were occurring, the digital technologies that
had been force-fed by military demands over the 1960s and 1970s were
starting to make significant incursions into the broader economic system,
and these technologies were soon to facilitate very dramatic changes in
the organization of production and in basic divisions of labor. The watchwords of fordist mass production systems were routinization, repetition,
and standardization in the interests of cost minimization. These features
reflect the foundations of fordism in large-scale electro-mechanical equipment and the division of labor between white-collar (administrative

and technical) workers and blue-collar (manual) workers. White-collar workers maintained the bureaucratic and R&D functions necessary for fordist enterprise to conserve its competitive edge, though even some of these workers were employed in relatively routinized jobs in low-level office functions. Blue-collar workers were in large degree caught up in detailed technical divisions of labor – that is, the fragmentation of work tasks along an assembly line within the individual firm. The accelerated rhythm of the moving assembly line greatly heightened the productivity of these workers. However, large-scale electro-mechanical equipment is notoriously inflexible, and it can most effectively achieve cost minimization when output variations are suppressed. Still, not all forms of production in the era of fordism were organized in these ways. Many industries, like clothing and furniture, were marked by much more flexible labor-intensive methods, and, as such, they were sometimes regarded as archaic remnants of an earlier industrial age that would eventually be swept away by the full force of industrial rationalization.

By the late 1960s, as fordism was approaching its climacteric, early forms of lean production and industrial flexibilization were making it possible both to reduce the number of workers along mass production assembly lines, and to increase the flexibility of production. An early expression of these developments was the emergence of a new kind of mass production, often referred to as neofordism, involving continuing high levels of scale, but also increasing product variety, and, by comparison with the fordist/ chandlerian firm, greater levels of vertical disintegration. In the 1970s, rapid Japanese advances with neofordist technologies and the expanding export program that they underpinned contributed greatly to the deepening of the crisis of classical fordism in North America and Western Europe that was occurring at that time. The 1970s also witnessed the emergence or re-emergence of flexible specialization (Piore and Sabel 1984) where units of production specialized in a relatively narrow line of business while constantly changing the design specifications of their output. Flexible specialization is highly reminiscent of 19th century craft production, and indeed, in the wake of the crisis of fordism in the 1970s, revitalized forms of craft production were starting to flourish again in certain parts of the world, and above all in the specialized labor-intensive industrial districts of the so-called Third Italy (Bagnasco 1977; Becattini 1987a; Brusco 1982; Garofoli 1987). Equally, computerization was making possible an even wider resurgence of the flexible specialization model, not only in relation to existing craft industries, but also sectors like electronics, machinery, and metallurgical production. Flexibly specialized firms grew rapidly in number after the early 1980s in virtually all of the advanced capitalist economies, where they functioned as providers of low-volume inputs to other firms and as sources of high-quality consumer goods. This trend was accentuated by the great intensification of competition that occurred over the postfordist years, with its accompanying syndrome of increased risk, destabilized production systems, and vertical disintegration (Scott 1988a, 1988b).

The crisis of classical fordism together with the rise of a more flexible postfordist economy was a further factor in the erosion of the labor unions that had played so strong a role over much of the 20th century in helping to improve the wages and working conditions of blue-collar workers. This erosion was particularly severe because it was concentrated in traditional geographic centers of industry, whereas much of the new postfordist economy was making its appearance in more peripheral areas of North America and Western Europe. In these areas, there was little or at best limited historical experience of union organization, a factor that made them all the more attractive to the new and revitalized forms of economic production that were emerging with postfordism. One effect of the collapse of the labor union movement was the formation of increasingly flexible labor markets as reflected in greatly expanding levels of part-time and temporary work, especially for those in the bottom tier of the labor market. In this economic and political climate, the incomes of the upper and lower halves of the labor force now began to become markedly more unequal than they were in the period of fordism, and they have continued to diverge ever since. Piketty and Saez (2003) have shown, for example, that while the average wage in the United States in inflation-adjusted terms remained more or less constant at close to US $29 500 between 1970 and 1999, the salaries of top-ranked CEOs went up from an average of close to US $1.5 million to about US $35.0 million per annum in the same time period.

By the mid-1980s, these different developments were starting to be categorized by geographers and sociologists in a narrative to the effect that the previously dominant regime of fordist mass production was being superseded by a new postfordist model (Amin 1994). The main elements of this new model were seen as involving flexible production processes and increased product variety, a resurgence of production networks involving many small vertically-disintegrated firms, and deeply restructured labor markets. Of course, large firms and mass production methods continued to play an important role in the capitalist system, but even in these cases, and in line with the thrust of 1970s neofordism, flexibility was increasing and product variety widening thanks to computer-based automation. The changes in the US car industry from the 1970s to the 1990s dramatically illustrate this point. At the same time, the vertical structure of authority and control that characterized the large multiplant, multidivisional corporation of fordism steadily gave way to much flatter intra-corporate structures with each individual establishment inside the firm operating as a profit center in its own right and with considerable leeway regarding basic managerial decisions.

THE NEW DIVISION OF LABOR

Digital technologies, in the context of assertive political shifts toward neoliberalism, were one of the important factors in fostering the postfordist moment, and they have now spread far and wide throughout capitalist production systems. Out of all the ways in which they function in today's economic order, perhaps none is more important than their role in fostering a new division of labor. The old dominant division of labor based on blue-collar and white-collar fractions characteristic of fordism has by no means disappeared, but it has been giving way over the last few decades to an alternative principle of work organization with many important implications for urban and regional development.

A first major observation in this regard is that, with digitization, many kinds of routine labor tasks can be easily reconfigured and carried out by computers. Thus, with dramatically falling costs per unit of computation over time, computers have been steadily displacing purely repetitive work wherever it may occur in the economy (Levy and Murnane 2004). This displacement has been strongly evident in the realm of manual work, but it has also had important impacts in the office environment as well, where many routine tasks, like book-keeping, filing, record maintenance, and so on, have also been largely taken over by computers. Even an occupation like draughtsmanship has virtually disappeared from the contemporary economy as computer graphics programs substitute for paper and the drawing board. Conversely, computers can be used to enhance work processes that involve very high levels of mental (cognitive) and affective (cultural) labor involving human interaction, discretionary decision-making, problem-solving challenges, creative rumination, pictorial representation, and the like. In short, as Autor et al. (2003) suggest, computers not only *substitute* for routine labor, but also *complement* nonroutine labor of many different kinds. Accordingly, and as the new economic dynamics set in motion after the late 1970s have continued to advance there has been a notable decline in low-wage standardized work of all kinds, and a corresponding rise in high-wage nonroutine work. Admittedly, some of this nonroutine work was already present in the period of fordism (in the film and fashion industries, for example) but the creativity and productivity of these older industries have been enormously enhanced by digital technologies. These transformations have caught the attention of many theorists who have accordingly begun to ascribe new meanings to labor and the labor process in capitalism, as intimated in terminologies that strongly echo many of the alternative labels that have been suggested as replacements for "postfordism" (see Chapter 1). These terminologies include offerings like symbolic analysts (Reich 1992), immaterial labor (Fortunati 2007; Lazzarato and Negri 1991), knowledge workers (Kunzmann 2009), the cognitariat (Moulier Boutang 2007), and the creative class (Florida 2002), or what I have designated elsewhere as cognitive–cultural workers (Scott 2008b). In this connection, Hardt and Negri (2000, p. 29) have written, echoing the theories of immaterial labor propounded by Italian Marxists, that "the central role previously occupied by the labor power of mass factory workers in the production of surplus value today is increasingly filled by intellectual, immaterial, and communicative labor power." It is because of this prominent feature of modern capitalism, as an organizational structure that relies crucially within its central nervous system on mobilizing the cognitive and cultural capacities of workers, that (as indicated in Chapter 1) I prefer to substitute the term cognitive–cultural economy for the once useful but now essentially obsolete label "postfordism." The new division of labor that is being brought forth as this economy forges ahead can be identified at the outset in terms of an upper fraction of well-paid, highly qualified cognitive and cultural workers, and a lower fraction of low-wage workers, increasing numbers of them in services and most of them with minimal formal qualifications.

The upper tier of the labor force in this new cognitive–cultural economy differs in important respects from the old "white-collar" category – a term that should properly be used to designate the bureaucrats and technicians of fordism – and even more so from the figure of the "organization man" identified by Whyte (1956) in the mid-1950s. Today, the upper tier of the labor force (which now includes substantial numbers of women) is considerably less regimented than it was when the old hierarchical model of fordist corporate organization lay at the center of the capitalist system. This change was already intimated by Gouldner (1979) with his theory of the "new class" composed of technocrats no longer willing to submit uncritically to authority. Elements of the old hierarchical model can still be found, but the upper fraction of the labor force (made up in Reich's terms by symbolic workers) is nowadays increasingly called upon to exercise its personal talents and creativity in much more open-ended tasks that entail key skills such as analytical shrewdness, deductive reasoning, technical insight, inter-personal judgment, imaginative thinking, cultural sensibility, story-telling abilities, and so on. These tasks must frequently be undertaken in the context of shifting collaborative teamwork that in turn

Table 3.1   Employment in selected professional occupations in the United States (2000–2010)

Major occupational group	2000	2010	Percent change
11 Management Occupations	7 782 680	6 022 860	−22.6
13 Business and Financial Operations Occupations	4 619 270	6 090 910	31.9
15 Computer and Mathematical Occupations	2 932 810	3 283 950	12.0
17 Architecture and Engineering Occupations	2 575 620	2 305 530	−10.5
19 Life, Physical, and Social Science Occupations	1 038 670	1 064 510	2.5
21 Community and Social Services Occupations	1 469 000	1 901 180	29.4
23 Legal Occupations	890 910	992 650	11.4
25 Education, Training, and Library Occupations	7 450 860	8 457 870	13.5
27 Arts, Design, Entertainment, Sports, and Media Occupations	1 513 420	1 716 640	13.4
29 Healthcare Practitioners and Technical Occupations	6 041 210	7 346 580	21.6
Total	36 314 450	39 182 680	7.9

Source: Bureau of Labor Statistics, Occupational Employment Statistics, http://www.bls.gov/oes/.

requires special skills of social interaction and empathy so as to ensure smooth progress toward desired (business) goals (Grabher 2001b; 2004).

A rough empirical identification of the upper tier of the labor force in the United States can be made in terms of major occupational categories representing professional workers as shown in Table 3.1. Employment levels for each category are also laid out in this table for the years 2000 and 2010. The decade from 2000 to 2010 was one of considerable economic difficulty in the United States, and the US labor force as a whole actually declined by 2.0 percent over this period. In spite of this negative economic climate, employment in professional and allied occupations as revealed in Table 3.1 grew by 7.9 percent overall. Only two of the occupational groups given in the table showed a decline over this period, namely management occupations, many of which have been lost as manufacturing activities have moved offshore, and architecture and engineering occupations, which have been eroded at the edges by increasing automation. Notwithstanding the particularly difficult financial conditions that prevailed in the second

Table 3.2   Employment in selected low-wage service occupations in the United States (2000–2010)

Major occupational group	2000	2010	Percent change
31 Healthcare Support Occupations	3 039 430	3 962 930	30.4
33 Protective Service Occupations	3 009 070	3 187 810	5.9
35 Food Preparation and Serving Related Occupations	9 955 060	11 027 340	10.8
37 Building and Grounds Cleaning and Maintenance Occupations	4 318 070	4 175 550	−3.3
39 Personal Care and Service Occupations	2 700 510	3 425 220	26.8
41 Sales and Related Occupations	13 506 880	13 437 980	−0.5
43 Office and Administrative Support Occupations	22 936 140	21 503 800	−6.2
Total	59 465 160	60 720 630	2.1

Source: Bureau of Labor Statistics, Occupational Employment Statistics, http://www.bls.gov/oes/.

half of the decade, employment in business and financial operations occupations grew by as much as 31.9 percent.

The lower tier of the labor force has also been greatly transformed in recent years, and again the old fordist terminology ("blue-collar" in the present instance) needs to be used with caution. In fact, we must distinguish between two different fractions of the lower half of the labor force today. One of these consists of production workers who are mainly employed in manufacturing and for whom the blue-collar label still retains some validity. However, the number of production workers in the United States is rapidly dwindling. According to the Bureau of Labor Statistics, employment of these workers reached a historical maximum of 32.1 million in 1979. This number subsequently declined to 12.4 million in 2000 and to 8.5 million in 2010, a loss of 31.1 percent in just the last decade, much of it from large metropolitan areas. The other main fraction within the lower half of the labor force consists of workers in what Florida (2002) has referred to as the "service class," in contradistinction to the creative class. As shown in Table 3.2, this service class can be identified in terms of seven low-wage two-digit occupational categories ranging from healthcare support occupations to office and administrative support occupations. The number of workers in these occupations grew by 2.1 percent from 59.5 million in 2000 to 60.7 million in 2010. This sharp contrast between rates of change in the numbers of production workers and service workers

Table 3.3   *Median annual wages/salaries of workers in professional,*
production, and low-wage service occupations (2000–2010), in
constant 2010 US $

	2000	2010	Percent change
Professional occupations	58 472	61 913	5.9
Production occupations	25 999	25 929	−0.3
Low-wage service occupations	29 705	29 224	−1.6

Source: Bureau of Labor Statistics, Occupational Employment Statistics, http://www.bls.gov/oes/.

can in significant degree be explained by the relative resistance of service jobs to both automation and offshore relocation. In particular, proximity to the point of service is a common requirement for the latter jobs (Gatta et al. 2009).

The three main groups of workers recognized here – namely professional, production, and low-wage service workers – do not exhaust the whole of the US labor force, but together they accounted for 85.3 percent of the whole in 2010. As indicated by the wage/salary data in Table 3.3 the upper tier of professional workers earned more than twice the median earnings of either production workers or low-wage service workers in 2010. Even over the difficult decade 2000–2010 professional workers' median earnings increased by 5.9 percent while production workers' and low-wage service workers' earnings decreased by 0.3 percent and 1.6 percent respectively. These findings are all of a piece with the longer term trends of income bifurcation in the American economy observed by Piketty and Saez (2003).

COGNITION, CULTURE, ECONOMY

Capitalism has always displayed marked variations across the geographical dimension depending on local conditions with regard to production technologies, sectors, skills, and so on. This diversity is compounded, as the varieties of capitalism school suggests, by the diverse legal and political norms that prevail in different jurisdictions (Hall and Soskice 2001). Today, for example, we can find, at one extreme, highly sophisticated enterprises using the most advanced technologies and employing high-wage qualified labor; but we can also find, at the other extreme, low-technology, labor-intensive forms of production using low-skill workers to make simple outputs like pottery or cheap wooden furniture; and virtually every combination of possibilities between these two extremes is also observable. In spite of the diversity that intrinsically inhabits capitalism, we can almost always identify, at any given time, a peculiar configuration of technologies, sectors, and human capital characteristics that represent a rising, dominant, or waning core of best practice(s). In the early 21st century, an essential and still rising core of this sort can be described in terms of a combination of digital technologies and complex cognitive and cultural work tasks calling for wide discretionary decision-making on the part of individual employees. This cognitive–cultural economy, in general, is recognizable by its central dependence on high levels of scientific and technical labor, its wide array of knowledge-intensive and affect-intensive production processes, and its heavy focus on turning out aestheticized consumer goods and services. In turn, the cognitive–cultural economy can be represented in large part – though assuredly not entirely – by three main groups or ensembles of sectors, namely, technology-intensive industry, business and financial services, and the creative or cultural economy. Each of these groups can be briefly described as follows:

1. The technology-intensive industrial ensemble comprises a broad base of electronics sectors (computers, semiconductors, etc.) as well as industries like aerospace, communications equipment, pharmaceuticals, and biotechnology. These sectors represent important employment foci not only in the more advanced capitalist countries but increasingly in many of the countries of the Global South as well. Technology-intensive industry is also the sector that produces the hardware and software enabling much of the rest of the cognitive–cultural economy to function, and allowing so many other sectors of the capitalist system, from food processing to cars, to attain hitherto unmatched levels of process and product flexibility and thus to advance well beyond the stage of classical mass production.

2. The business and financial services sectors have grown by leaps and bounds in many different countries since the 1980s. They are a major part of the contemporary US economy, with the professional and business service sector accounting for 15.3 million employees in 2010 and the financial services sectors accounting for 9.4 million in the same year, according to the US Bureau of Labor Statistics. The notable expansion of these sectors in recent decades reflects in part the growing demand for knowledge-intensive services such as legal advice, advanced accounting, technical consulting, insurance coverage, commercial intelligence, and many other forms of professional expertise. Above all, there has been an enormous trend to financialization in the new economy which involves not just simple banking and investment

operations, but the ever more elaborate development of instruments designed to leverage capital assets and to manage risk. In spite of a widespread faith in certain quarters that financial markets are as close as it is possible to come to a perfectly self-equilibrating system (given their foundations in instantaneous electronic trading with information feeding into central computers from across the entire globe), these markets collapsed in the United States and in much of the rest of the world in the 2007–2010 period. The ensuing crisis points to some of the intrinsic instabilities built into the cognitive–cultural model and certainly calls into question the neoliberal policy environment within which much of the new economy has developed in recent decades.

3.   Our third major ensemble within the cognitive–cultural is focused on the creative or cultural economy, comprising numerous industries devoted to the production of symbolic outputs with high levels of aesthetic, semiotic, and libidinal content. In its purest form, the cultural economy, as such, comprises sectors like film, music, and television-program production whose outputs are entirely symbolic and have virtually no utilitarian value. These sectors are growing apace all over the world as evidenced not only by cultural products from the more advanced capitalist countries, but also by items like telenovelas from Colombia and Mexico, films from Bollywood and Beijing, and popular music from such widely dispersed places as South Korea, Senegal, or Jamaica. These cultural products, moreover, are rapidly penetrating global markets. Many forms of fashion-oriented and design-intensive production are also important elements of the cultural economy. They include, for instance, the clothing, furniture, jewelry, and architecture sectors. Despite the lack of any consensus about where the cultural economy as such begins and ends, the published evidence suggests that cultural products industries constitute an important and growing component of modern economic systems. Pratt (1997), for example, has shown for the case of Britain that a little under one million workers (4.5 percent of the total labor force) were employed in cultural industries in 1991. Power (2002) has indicated that 9 percent of Sweden's total employment is made up of a similar set of industries. Garcia et al. (2003) estimate that 4.5 percent of Spain's total GDP is generated by the cultural economy. More recent data would almost certainly reveal substantial increases in these values. At the same time, employment in cultural products industries appears to be overwhelmingly located in large cities. Thus, Pratt's data show that London accounts for 26.9 percent of employment in British cultural products industries; Power finds that most workers in the Swedish cultural economy are located in Stockholm; and Garcia

et al. estimate that Madrid is by far the dominant center of cultural production in Spain.

Wherever they may occur, these three core ensembles of the cognitive–cultural economy are almost always directly coupled with an adjunct penumbra comprising a flexible low-wage employment segment made up to an increasing extent by an underclass of service (and to a lesser degree sweatshop) workers. The low-wage service-oriented segment of the new economy is focused on jobs like housekeeping, child care, health care, food preparation and serving, janitorial work, taxi driving, and home repair, in which workers may not enjoy the same levels of autonomy as upper tier workers, but in which they are frequently called upon to exercise distinctive forms of discretionary judgment in relatively open-ended situations. If workers in these jobs lack formal qualifications, they are almost always endowed with useful types of cerebral and affective know-how that is deployed in tasks where they must make critical decisions with regard to time management, coordination with others, social and cultural interactions, styles of communication and address, equipment maintenance, vehicle operation, and so on. Hence, even in the low-wage service-oriented segment of the economy, workers must generally have real capacities for knowing how to go on in varying and unpredictable situations, including many that entail a direct human interface. I shall return later to the role of these workers in the new economy. For the present, we can simply refer to them as a new service underclass, or perhaps even a new servile class, not only because the work is systematically underpaid, but more particularly because so much of it is devoted to functions involving the social reproduction of the upper tier of the labor force and the maintenance of the urban services on which the upper tier depends for its livelihood and pleasures.

The emerging cognitive–cultural economy that reposes on these foundations is driving some of the most remarkable changes now discernible in leading global cities, a trend that is all the more striking in view of the fact that routine manufacturing employment is steadily declining in many if not most of these same cities. In its place, new and revivified agglomerations of technology-intensive, business and financial, and cultural industries are appearing. As I have shown, all of these industries have advanced by leaps and bounds in recent decades. The great growth of the cultural industries, in particular, can in part be accounted for in terms of Engel's Law, which suggests that consumption over and above that which is required for simple subsistence tends to increase disproportionately with rising incomes. In fordism, the operation of Engel's Law was evident in the formation of what we might label "consumer society mark I", where households accumulated masses of relatively standardized material products. Today, we are moving into "consumer society mark II" where households expend more and more of their budgets not only on material products, now relatively destandardized, but also on a large and constantly varying palette of goods and services that, for better or worse, have potent experiential significance, from electronic games and recorded music to tourism and sports events (Pine and Gilmore 1999). The new capitalism is typified in general by the injection of ever-increasing amounts of symbolic content into consumer products of all kinds, a tendency that even extends far down into the more utilitarian reaches of the economy, where products like cars, office supplies, sports shoes, and kitchen utensils nowadays appeal to consumers not only on the basis of price but also on the basis of complex aesthetic and semiotic values that complement or enhance their performance and appearance. As a corollary, while cognitive–cultural capitalism is marked by intense economic competition, this is not some sort of re-approximation to *laisser-faire*. On the contrary, competition today is increasingly Chamberlinian in character, in the sense that it is built on distinctive qualitative attributes peculiar both to individual producers and to individual places of production. One manifestation of this ever-widening process of product differentiation is the explosion in the number of branded products in contemporary capitalism.

GLOBALIZING CAPITALISM

The deepening and widening of relationships of trade and communication between different countries has been going on irregularly but persistently for centuries. This trend reached a peak at the end of the 19th century and was not surpassed again until well into the fourth quarter of the 20th century. The latter half of the 19th century was a time when institutional barriers to the movement of people and goods across international boundaries were notably few and far between, and we might well refer to this moment as a period of proto-globalization. The upheavals of the 20th century, including two World Wars, a major inter-war depression, and the outbreak of the Cold War, pushed these barriers upward again, choking off the levels of international interchange that had been previously established. After 1945, the division of global space into the First and Second Worlds, each vying with the other for influence over the emerging Third World, greatly sharpened the lines of division cutting through the international sphere. Even so, international trade between the countries of the First World gradually regained some momentum over the post-War decades though still at an aggregate rate relative to GDP that was far below late 19th century standards (Hirst and Thompson 1996; Thompson and Krasner 1989). Up until the 1970s, world trade still remained below the historical peak established three-quarters of a century earlier. The very selected nature of the return to international interaction in the immediate post-War decades (under the aegis of the *Pax Americana*) meant that this was not yet tantamount to any meaningful form of "globalization" as such. These decades, rather, represent a period of a widening but always circumscribed internationalism.

The collapse of the Soviet Union at the end of the 1980s marked a substantive turning point when we might say that globalization in the large sense of the term was re- launched as a continuing long-term trend, picking up again from the course of events at the end of the 19th century. This trend, moreover, is multidimensional. It reflects not only intense and expanding trade, communication, migration, and exchange of ideas between many different and widely dispersed countries, but even more dramatically, a gradual and persistent integration of the institutions of the capitalist economy across the globe. Price systems, rates of interest and profit, financial operations, corporate structures, input–output systems, and all the other detailed indicators of the capitalist economy are increasingly intermingling with one another across national boundaries to such a degree that it is now virtually impossible to say where one country's capitalism ends and another's begins. Of course, this process of cross-country integration of the arrangements of the capitalist economy is still in an incipient stage and could be reversed by any number of untoward events. Should the process continue, it portends the eventual consolidation of some sort of supra-national capitalist system, which in turn points to the urgent need for a very much more effective system of economic regulation and policy construction at the global level than the one that is currently in place.

Whatever further advances may be made in the direction of a more comprehensive supra-national regulatory system (for example, a coordinated system of hierarchical authority, or a diffuse network of loosely overlapping institutions à la Hardt and Negri (2000)), their ultimate shape and form remain matters of pure speculation. The currently emerging situation is marked by a mix of territorially-based administrations, cross-cutting institutions, and hierarchical arrangements operating at a variety of scales; but it is also one of considerable ambiguity and flux. Nation states certainly remain the dominant political and economic bodies within the global capitalist system, but even they are subject to significant restructuring as globalization proceeds. Thus, many of the traditional functions of the nation state are being reconstructed at more comprehensive political levels, such as the European Union, NAFTA, ASEAN, or MERCOSUR. Some of these functions are also being assimilated into global or quasi-global institutions such as the OECD, the G8, the G20, the World Bank, the International Monetary Fund, and the World Trade Organization. Of special pertinence for the discussion in this book is the fact that many regulatory functions are also drifting downward from the level of the nation state to be reconstituted at the local level where global integration and competition are now pushing municipalities and other local authorities to take energetic proactive stands with regard to attracting capital, promoting economic development, responding to migratory in-flows, and numerous similar issues. This concern is reflected in many of the changes now proceeding in urban governance systems all over the world, and, in particular, by the search for new kinds of political order to deal with the burgeoning phenomenon of the mega city-region (see Chapter 10).

All of this economic and political ferment is activating notable adjustments in the geography of the contemporary world. These are expressed above all in the world-wide patchwork of globalizing economic and political spaces that is now emerging at very different levels of development and scale. Some of the more striking constituents of this patchwork correspond to the growing city-regions around the world where the main concentrations of the cognitive–cultural economy occur. Others are to be found in intervening areas where traditional rural economies are undergoing major transformation at the present time (see Chapter 9). Others, again, coincide with the dynamic new industrial and urban spaces that have appeared since the 1980s in parts of Asia and Latin America and above all in the so-called BRICs (Brazil, Russia, India, and China, together with South Africa). Yet others are coming forth in parts of the world that have sometimes been thought of as left-behind residuals, especially, but not exclusively, in many parts of Africa, where signs of new developmental stirrings are evident. To be sure, this patchwork is marked by great unevenness in levels of wealth and social well-being, both between and within the individual spaces out of which it is composed, but it also certainly represents a radically altered situation by comparison with the old core–periphery system (with its inner syndrome of the development of underdevelopment) that some theorists had described as an indurated fixture of world capitalism (see, for example, Frank 1978). Today, many parts of the world that were previously thought of as being endemically resistant to development are integral elements of the resurgent capitalism of the 21st century.

4. Economic geography and the world system

Space has always represented a barrier to the onward flow of capitalist development, though one whose potency has tended to decline steadily over time. This does not mean that the forces of agglomeration and urban growth are waning – they have, if anything, been reinvigorated by the economic changes of the last few decades – but it does help to explain why individual urban clusters all over the world are increasingly becoming bound up with one another in relationships of trade and social exchange. In addition, as the old fordist regime has waned, and the new economy has advanced, so the world-wide core–periphery spatial order has undergone significant erosion. As the finale of the present chapter will show, these intertwining trends, involving renewed agglomeration, ever-extending spatial interlinkage, and a fading core–periphery system, are manifest in the emergence of a new macro-geography, one of whose most visible components is a far-flung network of global city-regions. The main physical expressions of the new capitalism in general, and the cognitive–cultural economy in particular, are concentrated in these city-regions.

LOCATION AND TRADE

The most obvious and elementary starting point for an investigation of large-scale economic variation across geographic space is to look at the physical landscape and to ask how the opportunities and constraints built into its ecological conditions may have helped to shape a system of human responses. The location of mineral deposits, differences of climate, accidents of relief, and so on, all leave their mark on the geography of human existence, though considerably less so today than was the case a few centuries ago. Even where these factors remain in play, moreover, human responses never simply appear as unmediated outcomes of the physical environment, but are also shaped by many different kinds of social and economic variables, one of which is what Ricardo (1817 [1971]) referred to as "comparative advantage."

The Ricardian theory of comparative advantage provides an account of national economic specialization and international trade based roughly on the notion that countries will tend to concentrate their production and export efforts on commodities they can turn out relatively cheaply while making up for deficits in their overall needs by means of imports. Consider a simple situation involving two countries, a and b, both able to produce two given commodities, x and y. One country has an absolute advantage in the production of either of these two commodities if it can produce it more cheaply than the other country. Assume, to begin with, that both countries produce and consume one unit of both commodities – that is, a situation of autarchy prevails. Obviously, if country a has an absolute advantage in commodity x and country b has a similar advantage in commodity y there will always be an economic incentive for a to specialize in x and b to specialize in y and for both countries to exchange their surplus product with one another. However, even if one country has an absolute advantage in both commodities, there are still gains to be earned from specialization and trade, providing that each country concentrates on its *comparative* advantage. This result is demonstrated in more detail in the appendix to this chapter. In the simple example of two countries and two commodities outlined here, we can simply aver that out of the two possible configurations of specialization and trade (country a specializes in commodity x and country b in commodity y, or vice versa), there is always one that yields a lower aggregate cost than pure autarchy, and this solution means that each country is now specializing in its comparative advantage. In this manner, we maintain the same levels of production and consumption that prevailed before specialization, but at a lower overall cost. The burning question that remains, and that the theory of comparative advantage as such does not address, is who appropriates the gains from trade – that is, the surplus that is generated by the lowering of overall cost?

Ricardo's theory of comparative advantage was amended in the early 20th century by Heckscher and Ohlin (1991), who suggested that the commodities in world trade can in the end be equated with the bundles of natural endowments or factors of production that went into their production. Let us again restrict attention to two countries and two commodities and add the assumption that we only need to deal in this exemplary situation with two factors of production. The Heckscher–Ohlin theory then states that the law of comparative advantage will lead to a situation where each country exports the commodity that uses its relatively abundant factor and imports the commodity that uses its relatively scarce factor. For example, Australia has abundant and relatively cheap land that can be used for producing wool; China has abundant and relatively cheap labor that can be employed in making shoes. All else being equal, it should therefore be to the mutual benefit of Australia and China to exchange wool from the former country for shoes made in the latter. Stolper and Samuelson (1941), in turn, elaborate on the Heckscher–Ohlin theory by formulating the so-called factor-price equalization theorem which predicts that, after trade, the price of the abundant factor in each country will rise, while the price of its scarce factor will fall. These adjustments will continue until the prices of equivalent factors in each country are equalized.

In so far as it goes, the simple Ricardian theory of comparative advantage is a useful first approximation to the conditions that foster specialization and trade, and its later theoretical elaborations by Heckscher–Ohlin and Stolper–Samuelson offer further serviceable insights, even if the underlying assumptions of constant returns to scale and perfect competition – not to mention instantaneous adjustment and factor immobility – are highly restrictive. In contrast to these ideas, both the new trade theory and the new economic geography that were developed by scholars after the 1980s recognize that today's economic order is more typically characterized by increasing returns to scale (both internal and external to individual units of production) in a world of imperfect competition, including monopolistic competition à la Chamberlin (cf. Krugman 1991; Scott 2008b; Storper 1997). In these circumstances, and notably where agglomeration economies exist, any systematic drive toward a market-driven *optimum optimorum* will tend to break down. Moreover, systems of production and trade do not generally move instantaneously from one static equilibrium to another, but are almost always subject to path-dependent evolutionary processes over time. This means that any specific outcome occurring at time t is dependent on the outcome that prevailed at time $t–1$, as the model developed by Krugman (1991) so clearly demonstrates. A further troubling issue is the neglect by much international trade theory with regard to any wider framework of social and political relations (Sheppard 2012). We must bear in mind that the gains from trade are always a contentious issue between trading partners, and that behind any given "factor of production" there lies a set of specific human interests focused on the income from that factor. Accordingly, the economic logic of trade is always interwoven with a complementary political logic, as exemplified by the classic case of the opposition of early 19th century British landlords to any lowering of the tariffs on imported wheat,[1] and the hostility of American, Canadian, and Mexican labor unions today to different provisions of the North American Free Trade Agreement.

These comments explain why policy-makers are invariably and necessarily involved in trade relations, in part because they have a strategic role to play in pushing toward economically efficient outcomes, and in part because these outcomes must also be sustainable in the wider political arena. Additionally, where path dependency is present, collective action is required to guide production and trade into superior pathways of develop-ment and to avert lock-in to adverse pathways. This point is dramatically illustrated by the infant industry argument originally proposed by List (1841 [1977]). The argument focuses on the fragility of developing econo-mies in relation to competition from more robust producers, and claims that policy measures are imperative in the former situation to protect budding entrepreneurial ventures. List justifies his argument by reference not to comparative advantage but to the positive externalities that can be obtained by establishing defensive tariff barriers. Above all, he points to the need to foster industrialization in 19th century Germany, not only as a goal in its own right, but even more importantly, as a necessary prerequi-site for building skills, know-how, technological competencies, and other accoutrements of modernization that would otherwise lie dormant if the German economy continued to be dominated by agriculture. It was in the light of this sort of reasoning that the German states, led by Prussia, established the *Zollverein*, or customs union, in the early 1830s. Once the *Zollverein* was in place, British manufactures could no longer freely enter into German territory, making it possible for German industry to develop and for German society to modernize. Strict Ricardian doctrine, based on the theory of comparative advantage, would categorically proclaim the inefficiency and undesirability of this measure, leaving Germany to remain predominantly a land of farmers constantly lagging behind Britain in terms of social and economic progress.

The case of 19th century Germany demonstrates that comparative advantage is not, as Ricardo thought, rooted eternally in pre-given natural endowments, but can be constructed and reconstructed through concerted action. A further striking example of this same point is provided by the efforts on the part of the Japanese government after the Second World War to promote a successful domestic car industry, despite arguments from opponents that Japan's comparative advantages did not warrant such a policy (Cusumano 1985). Later in the 20th century, other Asian countries, including Hong Kong, South Korea, Singapore, and Taiwan also escaped from their supposed destiny (written into their natural endowments) as peripheral backwaters of the world system. Economies, in other words, can be shifted in whole or in part from one developmental pathway to another by means of conscious social and political choice. The pure concept of comparative advantage has thus mostly had its day, and is now subservient to more powerful theories based on notions of *competitive advantage* and *strategic trade,* even if echoes of comparative advantage are still to be found in these more recent formulations. These theories recognize, on the one side, the importance of socially-constructed enhancements to competitive prowess (for example, via technological innovation or investment in education), and on the other side, the developmental benefits that can be obtained by selected governmental shaping of external trade relations, especially where production is characterized by increasing returns effects (Porter 1985; Borrus et al. 1986). In the emerging system of cognitive–cultural capitalism, the notions of competitive advantage and strategic trade have come into their own as analytical tools and keys to policy-making, for they offer important ways of understanding the complex patterns of development and international commerce in a world where natural endowments can no longer be automatically equated with fate. They also function as robust conceptual arms against neoliberal rhetoric to the effect that policy must always fail in comparison with the alleged universal superiority of markets in coordinating trade relationships.

In the light of these remarks, the notions of competitive advantage and strategic trade are of special interest in local economic systems where agglomeration economies prevail. The collectively-produced benefits of agglomeration enhance each individual producer's competitive capacities. Therefore, strategic trade initiatives (such as trade fairs or export-promotion delegations) that boost local exports will by the same token further increase agglomeration economies, and, in turn, competitiveness. At this stage, we must also consider the impact of a third important variable on location and trade, namely chamberlinian competition or product differentiation. If competition were based purely on price, as in classical *laisser-faire*, then presumably, to the degree that the production of any given good or service is intrinsically embedded in place-bound agglomerations, just one geographic center would eventually come to function as the sole world-wide supplier of that good or service. Of course, this remark presumes that transport costs continue to fall in the long term and that agglomeration diseconomies can be kept at bay. However, where chamberlinian competition prevails, as in much of today's cognitive–cultural economy, agglomerations producing similar types of outputs but with locally-specific variations can often thrive in stable co-existence. Variations like these derive from many different factors, including traditions, skills, cultural features, stylistic norms, special kinds of product performance criteria, and so on, namely, unique geographically-specific resources that can be embodied in final products and that bestow a competitive edge on them over and above the element of price. By the same token, today's polymorphous cognitive–cultural economy, with its insistent product differentiation, is far from leading in the direction of a world geography where each individual good or service originates from a monocentric supply center. On the contrary, current evolutionary tendencies point increasingly to a multicentric world in which many different agglomerations produce not only many different types of outputs but also many different varieties of each type.

A WORLD BEYOND CORE AND PERIPHERY

Over much of its history, capitalism has been characterized by the persistence of core–periphery spatial structures, both at the national level and at the world level. The advent of fordism in the 20th century consolidated and sharpened these structures, particularly at the world scale, and over much of the second half of the century it was commonplace to refer to this situation in terms of a "dialectic of development and underdevelopment" (Blaut 1976). Even as fordism was in its heyday, however, parts of the periphery were already evincing signs of breaking out of the vicious circle of underdevelopment. As fordism began to wane, this trend continued to assert itself, and has accelerated to the present day, though clearly not yet to the degree that severe underdevelopment has been eliminated from the face of the earth. We might ask, how has this trend expressed itself over the last half century, and what does it presage with regard to the world that is currently in emergence?

Peripheral Development in Fordist Capitalism

As early as the 1950s, Singer (1950) and Prebisch (1959) independently postulated, in opposition to the Stolper–Samuelson model, that international trade was not always "efficient" in the Ricardian (or Pareto-optimal) sense of unfailingly bringing benefits to at least one party in any given exchange relationship and, at worst, never being deleterious to the other party, but that it was demonstrably unfair or unequal.[2] The then prevailing ("old") international division of labor presented a crucial test-bed for their ideas. This was a system in which the core capitalist countries exported manufactures to peripheral countries, which in turn exported raw materials and agricultural products to the core. This is not the place to go into the detailed analytics of the Singer–Prebisch hypothesis, except to say that it was based on the notion that the superior organizational and political power of the core countries enabled them consistently to appropriate the lion's share of productivity gains in manufacturing. One important source of this power can be traced back to the ability of trades unions in core countries to push workers' wages periodically upward. By contrast, the producers of raw materials in less developed countries had much less discretionary power, and were in any case caught up in self-defeating cut-throat competition with one another centered on standardized basic commodities. Thus, the terms of trade between economically developed and underdeveloped countries were more or less permanently subject to deterioration from the point of view of the latter, thereby condemning them to continuing underdevelopment. The evident policy deduction from this analysis was that countries on the world periphery should free themselves from dependency on raw materials production and embark on independent industrialization programs that would allow them to achieve a significant degree of national economic autarchy.

This deduction from the Singer–Prebisch hypothesis was highly per-suasive in the post-War decades to many political groups, from the center to the far left, in different parts of the periphery, and especially in Latin America. One major consequence was that significant numbers of Third World countries now set about attempts to promote economic develop-ment by means of intensified investment in manufacturing, above all in mass production industry. This development strategy reposed on two main pillars. First, investment (both domestic and foreign) in large mass produc-tion units – that is, lead plants – was actively encouraged, and these plants in turn were intended to function as the drivers of associated multitiered input–output systems or "growth poles." Second, import-substitution policies were pursued by means of protective tariffs designed to encour-age the emergence of local producers (both domestic and foreign-owned) able to supply alternatives to the imports that were otherwise needed both directly and indirectly to feed the lead plants. Brazil, Chile, and Mexico in Latin America, together with South Korea, Taiwan, Indonesia, and Malaysia in Asia were early exponents of this developmental model, fol-lowed by other peripheral countries over the 1960s and 1970s. Much of the productive activity in these growth poles was concentrated in manufac-turing zones located around the edges of large overgrown urban centers. São Paulo in Brazil was undoubtedly the most advanced expression of this phenomenon in the world periphery. By the 1950s and 1960s, Ford, GM, Volkswagen, and Mercedes had all established lead plants in the so-called ABCD municipalities[3] in the southeast portion of the São Paulo metropolis where dense arrays of local and foreign-owned input suppliers were also concentrated (Klink 2001; Rodríguez-Pose and Tomaney 1999; Scott 2001).

Large multinational corporations headquartered in the core actively participated in these growth-pole ventures in the Third World, partly because they were attracted by the availability of cheap labor and partly because locations in this part of the world gave them entry to foreign markets that were otherwise protected by high tariff barriers. Still, cheap labor and market access alone were not enough to entice foreign direct investment to peripheral countries. In addition, multinationals based in the core sought out locations where some degree of political stability could be relied upon, and where favorable fiscal advantages such as tax breaks, subsidies, permissive regulations regarding the repatriation of profits, and so on, were available. Many countries in Latin America and Asia also set up export-processing zones, often with special tax and employment regulations, in efforts to enhance the attractiveness of their territories to foreign-owned branch plants. Early examples of such zones include Kaohsiung Export Processing Zone in Taiwan (established in 1966), Bayan Lepas Free Trade Zone in Penang, Malaysia (established in 1969), and Masan Free Trade Zone near Busan in South Korea (established in 1970), all of them located in areas adjacent to global gateway cities. In subsequent years, right to the present, hundreds of other special economic zones – including the maquiladoras of Mexico – have been established all over the world.

By the middle of the 1970s, at the time when the crisis of fordism in the core capitalist countries was reaching a peak, Third World development policies based on the search for national economic autarchy via growth poles and import substitution were starting to run out of steam. The limited size of domestic markets in the periphery was partly responsible for this state of affairs, particularly as the efficiency of mass production enterprise is dependent on the achievement of high levels of scale. Import substitution policies, with their huge demands for continual capital invest-ment, also contributed strongly to the debt crisis that now hung so heavily over much of the Third World and that was inducing wholesale retrench-ment leading to the so-called "lost decade" of the 1980s in Latin America. These events cast a pall over the import-substitution model. As it happens, and just as import-substitution was encountering severe limits to its further progress, an alternative approach to economic development based on export-oriented industrialization was starting to forge ahead, especially in selected parts of Asia. This new model dispensed with the search for national autarchy in favor of strategies focused on finding viable export niches in the international division of labor, and as it went from success to success it diffused rapidly across a wide spectrum of low- and middle-income countries. The old import-substitution policies were steadily thrown to the winds in many less-developed countries that had previously seen them as the best way forward. In this economic climate, and given the low wages in these countries, various kinds of labor-intensive and often quite fragmented industrial sectors were able to establish a strong footing. Export-oriented industrialization did not involve the complete abandonment of mass production in less developed parts of the world, but it did mean that mass production enterprise now had to steer a course through the new, more open and competitive economic environment that was coming to prevail. These developments coincided with the early years of postfordism in the advanced capitalist countries, and they helped to mark the start of a new relationship between the core and periphery of the emerging global system.

The New Industrial Spaces of Postfordist Capitalism

The collapsing foci of fordist production in the advanced capitalist countries over the 1970s brought forth a series of deeply pessimistic accounts of economic decay and disaster in North America and Western Europe. A spate of papers and books were published at this time on topics of regional crisis, decline, job loss, regional inequalities, poverty, and so on (for example, Blackaby 1978; Bluestone and Harrison 1982; Carney et al. 1980; Massey and Meegan 1982). This was also the moment when Fröbel et al. (1980) declared that a new international division of labor was coming into being under the aegis of the multinational corporation. In contrast to the old international division of labor, this new arrangement, they thought, would eventually take the form of a split represented by the specialization of the periphery in blue-collar manual work, and the specialization of the core in the basic white-collar managerial, technical and professional tasks needed to keep multinational enterprises running on an even keel. Had fordism regained the onward momentum that had typified it over the period of the long post-War boom, it is not inconceivable that something like this may actually have come to pass.

In practice, many elements of the postfordist economy were actually in place even as fordism was approaching its climacteric in the late 1960s and early 1970s. While these were not thought of at the time as pioneering edges of a new capitalism, many of them were primed to burst into full bloom once the fordist wave had receded and the new technological–organizational models of postfordism had appeared. The industries of the Third Italy are the outstanding example of this phenomenon. We might also illustrate the point by reference to the media and fashion industries of the world's great cosmopolitan centers like New York, Los Angeles, London, Paris, and Tokyo. The banking and financial services sectors of many of the same centers were also about to take off into a new era of growth. Instances of similar outcomes were observable in parts of southern Germany, particularly in Baden-Württemburg and Bavaria with their traditional mechanical engineering industries, and in Denmark with its many small-scale but high-performance industries, from food processing to furniture. And in what were shortly to become the "Four Little Tigers" of East and Southeast Asia (that is, Hong Kong, Singapore, South Korea, and Taiwan), there were, in the 1960s, burgeoning labor-intensive industries like wig-making, artificial flowers, furniture, toys, clothing, and electronic gadgets with widening international markets. In addition, the technopoles of the US Sunbelt (Silicon Valley, Orange County, Phoenix, Research Triangle Park, the Denver–Boulder Corridor, and numerous others) were beginning their rise to prominence at this time. Significantly, all of these places lie well outside the spatial orbit of the old fordist model.

Over the late 1970s and early 1980s, as postfordism came into ever greater prominence, these premonitory cases flourished apace, and their growth was accompanied by further spatial extension of the postfordist model into the wider world. We might say that a window of locational opportunity opened up as the new technologies, new labor processes, new organizational structures, and new products of this alternative model induced producers to abandon the spaces that had been made in the image of fordism and to seek out new locations, where, in addition, they could avoid the workerist culture of fordist communities and the power of the unions to organize the labor force. The end result was the consolidation of a series of dynamic new industrial spaces located not only in the old national peripheries of the advanced capitalist countries but in many different parts of the wider world periphery too (Scott and Angel 1987). From the 1980s onward, these new industrial spaces have been well in the vanguard of capitalist development. In favored parts of the old international periphery, moreover, their rise has been accompanied by accelerated escape from the condition of underdevelopment, and, in many instances, accession to levels of income and human capital development on a par with levels obtaining in some of the countries that had participated in earlier historical rounds of capitalist development. The countries of East and Southeast Asia, above all, displayed remarkable prowess in exploiting the economic opportunities that opened up so widely after the 1980s, and, as the flying geese metaphor suggests, they have been equally proficient in moving rapidly from one developmental level to the next.

THE GLOBALIZATION OF PRODUCTION

The global system today is made up of a palimpsest of the old and the new, or better yet, a collage of geographic spaces incorporating regions at many different levels of development and marked by many different models of economic activity and social life. A few of these spaces are given over to traditional ways of life and remain largely outside the logic of capitalism; some, especially the urban slums and the rural backwaters of the global South, are mired in poverty and desperation; some, like a few remaining areas of the old US Manufacturing Belt, have still not recovered from the crisis of fordism; while others, like parts of Malaysia, the Philippines, Thailand, and Vietnam are heavily colonized by foreign branch plants in search of cheap labor; and yet others, such as the burgeoning industrial districts of central Mexico or the Pearl River Delta in China, are marked by high levels of local entrepreneurship and subcontract production for firms located in more prosperous countries. Others, again, have moved decisively forward on the basis of core cognitive and cultural sectors in advanced technology production, financial and business services, and the cultural industries; and while these latter spaces coincide mainly with major city-regions in the global North, selected city-regions in the global South are also starting to participate in the same trend. It is the world-wide system of city-regions above all that is the focus of the remaining chapters of this book, but as the above remarks suggest, we must not lose sight of the economic and spatial diversity of the world in the 21st century. We must acknowledge, too, the continued significance of the multinational corporation, though in contrast to the fordist firm with its hierarchical model of top-down managerial control, the large corporation today has largely given way to a much flatter heterarchical form of organization where each individual unit operates as a profit center in its own right. As Sassen (2001) has pointed out, the city-regions of the Global North, but also and increasingly of the Global South, function as major centers of command and control over the far-flung constituents of the multinational enterprise.

If agglomeration and urban resurgence are hallmarks of the economic geography of the 21st century, another and complementary feature is the networks that increasingly tie these clusters together in relations of competition and collaboration. From some points of view, indeed, the world map of production and trade should really be redrafted as a map of cities and their interlinkages. In line with this proposition, Jacobs (1969) observed some time ago that cities were in some respects a more appropriate unit for organizing ideas about world trade than countries, and her point has more recently been taken up by a number of world systems theorists with their critique of state-centric analyses of global economic interactions (cf. Brown et al. 2010). This concept of global economic space as being partially composed out of agglomerations and their functional interlinkages is expressed in the world-wide ramification of *global production networks.* This is a term that updates an older vocabulary revolving around *global commodity chains* and *global value chains* and appropriately brings the ideas associated with this vocabulary into closer alignment with the theory of production in general (cf. Coe et al. 2004; Gereffi and Korzeniewicz 1994; Gereffi et al. 2005). Thus, a global production network can be represented as a collection of processing centers or agglomerations scattered across the world and tied together through input output connections in a resolutely roundabout division of labor. The transactional relationships within these networks are mediated via a great variety of institutional structures ranging from simple arm's length exchange, through various types of subcontracting activity, to intra-firm trade. They are, in a nutshell, marked by an enormous diversity of organizational and transactional practices. The subcontracting of work from firms in high-wage countries to firms in low-wage countries is especially important in today's global economy and has been expanding at a rapid rate in step with the growth of global production networks at large (Andreff 2009; Feenstra 1998; Schmitz 2007; Sturgeon 2002).

The early waves of international subcontracting that occurred in the 1980s were for the most part restricted to forms of work that could easily be disarticulated or vertically-disintegrated from operations in the home country (Henderson and Scott 1987). In the terms established by Williamson (1975), this type of work is low in asset specificity and easily codifiable. The first stages of global production network development, therefore, concerned relatively standardized, low-skill work such as apparel sewing functions and simple electronics assembly (Herrigel and Zeitlin 2010). The batches of work involved also tended to be relatively large in order to achieve economies of scale in transport and transacting. With growing levels of experience and proficiency, firms in low-wage countries have in many instances been able continually to upgrade their operations. In particular, firms taking on subcontract orders frequently acquire know-how from order givers, and with the establishment of trust between subcontracting partners, the stage is set for the products at issue to become increasingly complex and information-intensive (Kaplinsky et al. 2003; Salomon and Shaver 2005; Schmitz and Knorringa 2000). Through this kind of collaborative interaction, firms in numerous low-wage countries are finding it ever more possible to improve their process and product configurations. Thus, much clothing subcontracting from the Global North to the Global South has nowadays gone far beyond simple sewing operations and consists in large measure of "full package" operations in which the product is designed and marketed in the North while the physical output itself is made from beginning to end in the South. In some cases even design operations are handed off to foreign subcontractors.

Today, an enormous diversity of products at different levels of design and performance complexity, including furniture, shoes, pharmaceuticals, machinery, electronic equipment, aerospace parts, and so on, move through subcontracting relations embedded in global production networks. Even service firms in the Global North increasingly subcontract-out batches of work, including software programming, to firms in the

Global South (Saxenian 2005; Scott and Zuliani 2007). Perhaps the most celebrated instance of this type of subcontracting is the putting-out of software programming from Silicon Valley to Bangalore in India. Other examples are the subcontracting of business services from Western Europe to producers in Eastern and Central Europe (Stare and Rubalcaba 2009) and (at the lower end of the skills spectrum) call center operations to the Caribbean, India, the Philippines, and other parts of the world periphery (Srivastava and Theodore 2006). Similar phenomena can be observed in cultural products industries. This aspect is dramatically exemplified by the operations of Hollywood production companies with offshoots in Vancouver, and, to a rising degree, in other satellite centers in Mexico, Australia, New Zealand, and Eastern Europe (Scott and Pope 2007). In a further illustration of the same point, Fuerst (2010) describes a case involving the putting-out of three-dimensional computer animation tasks to firms in Bogotá. As these global production networks have formed, moreover, the wider developmental effects have often been remarkable, and have helped to plant the seeds of cognitive–cultural agglomerations in several parts of the former periphery. As both Saxenian (2002) and Yu (2009) have indicated, foreign direct investments and subcontracting orders originating from Silicon Valley and directed to Hsinchu Science Park and the Kaohsiung Export Processing Zone during the 1980s did much to encourage the growth of an indigenous high-technology industry in Taiwan. As the firms in this industry expanded over the 1990s and 2000s, so they in turn started to outsource production to electronics agglomerations in the Pearl River Delta and the Shanghai–Jiangsu–Zhejiang region. Indeed, probably no other low-wage country has benefited more from the development of global production systems than modern China with its burgeoning industrial districts and its aggressive export-oriented industrialization programs. All of this activity is manifest in the deepening functional and spatial integration of different economic spaces within global production networks, and is intimately dependent on the increasing sophistication of logistics capabilities and supply chain management, together with the electronic communications systems that enable these activities to operate at high levels of efficiency (Loo 2012).

CITY-REGIONS: THE GLOBAL MOSAIC

The discussion in this chapter has sought to describe some of the historical and geographical dynamics that underpinned the rise and fall of one major pathway of world development (via internationalism), and that are now ushering in another (via an assertive globalization). Something of the diversity and complexity of the emerging world system has also been examined, and this serves to contextualize the more focused discussion in other parts of this book on the cognitive–cultural economy and its spatial underpinnings. To be sure, the new cognitive–cultural economy still accounts for only a small proportion of total world production, though it is of greatly increasing importance in the Global North and it is now diffusing rapidly into many different parts of the Global South, especially in the large cities of East and Southeast Asia.

Both of these realms of the new global system contain increasing numbers of mega city-regions, and among other functions, these city-regions serve in different ways as the main locations of the cognitive–cultural economy. At the same time, however, virtually all of these city-regions, especially in the South, are marked by enormous economic and social contrasts that also reflect a number of trends in the new capitalism (see Chapter 7). Thus, even as the old peripheral spaces of fordist capitalism recede, new lines of separation between the wealthy and the poor continue to be drawn, and nowhere more so than through the internal spaces of today's emerging city-regions. There is no agreement as to a definitive list of city-regions in the world today, but the United Nations has identified 443 urban agglomerations or city-regions with populations of one million or more, and we can at least provisionally accept most of these centers as a rough approximation to such a list, even if there are vast differences of wealth and developmental prospects between them. These 443 city-regions contain 38.3 percent of the world's urbanized population, which in turn accounts for just over half of world population as a whole, both rural and urban. Half a century ago, over two-thirds of all cities in the world with populations of a million or more were in the Global North. Today, two-thirds are in the Global South. Indeed, among the top ten city-regions in the world today, in addition to Tokyo and New York, we find eight, namely, Delhi, São Paulo, Mumbai, Mexico City, Shanghai, Kolkata, Dhaka, Karachi, and Buenos Aires that are located in countries of the periphery. The significant point for present purposes is that the cartography of the world system is undergoing major transformation in the 21st century. The former core–periphery model of world development, which, according to Wallerstein (1979), has been one the most enduring geographic features of international capitalism over the last couple of centuries, is now, it seems, fading into the background, to be superseded by a new model in the shape of the new global mosaic. The city-regions that anchor this still-emerging mosaic, moreover, function to ever-increasing degree as the basic engines of the global economy.

Something of this new geography is captured schematically in Figure 4.1. Individual city-regions are represented in the figure by a central met-

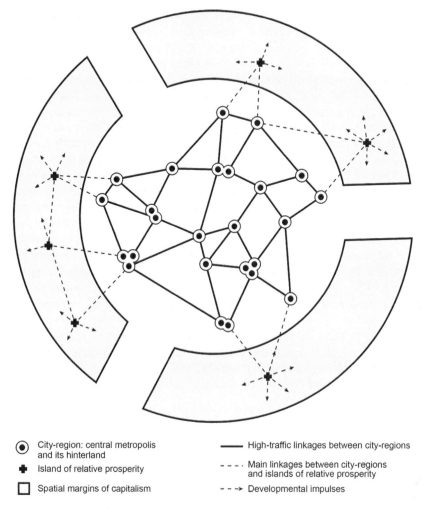

⊙	City-region: central metropolis and its hinterland	—— High-traffic linkages between city-regions
✚	Island of relative prosperity	– – – · Main linkages between city-regions and islands of relative prosperity
☐	Spatial margins of capitalism	– – ➤ Developmental impulses

Figure 4.1   A schematic representation of the emerging mosaic of global city-regions

ropolitan area, or a group of spatially-overlapping metropolitan areas, together with a surrounding hinterland of varying size. Any given hinterland encompasses a wide stretch of territory, often with smaller urban settlements dispersed over its entire extent. High-traffic linkages representing global value-added networks are shown, and these integrate the world-wide collection of city-regions into a composite functional system. Beyond this mosaic lie the spatial margins of capitalism – that is, the retreating remnants of the old periphery. These margins harbor cities that we might designate as islands of relative prosperity, though they are almost always marked internally by great contrasts of wealth and poverty. They are linked in various ways to major city-regions of the mosaic, but have not yet themselves attained full global city-region status. In some cases, such as the Kinashasa described by De Boeck et al. (2005) and De Boek (2012) their evolution far outside of any capitalist mainstream means that they are stamped with unique developmental features that – even more than the city-regions of the mosaic – dramatically express the specificities of their local social and cultural contexts. Many of these cities in the remnants of the periphery also function as foci of growth for the territories in which they are located, and developmental impulses flow outward from them into their surrounding territorial dependencies. Eventually, with the continued advance of global capitalism, some of these islands of relative prosperity attain to global city-region status, and as they do so, the areas around them prosper accordingly, and the periphery shrinks yet further. In recent decades, cities like Seoul, Hong Kong, Singapore, Shanghai, Mexico City, and São Paulo have rather clearly acceded to the global mosaic, and many cities in the remaining segments of the periphery are likely soon to follow in their footsteps. One probable candidate for rapid accession is Accra in Ghana, which as Grant and Nijman (2004) suggest, is now developing apace on the basis of its dynamic manufacturing, producer services and financial sectors; and other African cities such as Dakar, Ibadan, and Nairobi are poised to follow suit.

APPENDIX

The theory of comparative advantage can be set forth on the basis of the example that Ricardo himself used in his original exposition. Consider the case of trade between England and Portugal in cloth and wine. If both countries produce and consume one unit of each commodity (that is, a state of autarchy prevails), then the total cost of cloth and wine production in England will be $k_{ec} + k_{ew}$, and Portugal's total cost will be $k_{pc} + k_{pw}$, where k represents unit cost, and the subscripts e, p, c, and w represent England, Portugal, cloth and wine, respectively. Total costs of this autarchic system will thus be $K = k_{ec} + k_{ew} + k_{pc} + k_{pw}$. Obviously if one country has an *absolute* advantage in one of these commodities (that is, it can produce that commodity more cheaply than the other country) and the other country has an absolute advantage in the other commodity, then there will always be an economic incentive for the two countries to specialize in their respective absolute advantages and exchange their surplus product with one another. However, even if we admit that one country has an absolute advantage in both commodities, there will still be gains from specialization and trade. This outcome is based on the logic of *comparative* advantage in production and trade. Comparative advantage is assessed by examining the production costs for each commodity in each country. Let us now define the cost difference between England and Portugal in regard to cloth production as $d_c = k_{ec} - k_{pc}$; similarly, the difference between the two countries with regard to the cost of wine can be written as $d_w = k_{ew} - k_{pw}$. If we find that $d_c < d_w$ then England will specialize in cloth and Portugal in wine; in the converse case, England will specialize in wine and Portugal in cloth. Once the two countries have adjusted their economies so that each is specialized in its comparative advantage, then each will produce two units of its specialty. Accordingly, each country will consume one unit of its domestic output and will exchange the remaining unit for the other country's surplus unit of the other commodity. The critical point of all of this is that aggregate production and consumption remain the same as before, but total costs of production will now be $K' < K$.

NOTES

1. In the early part of the 19th century, British landowners – a group that was strongly represented in the House of Lords – fought vociferously to maintain the Corn Laws (that is, a system of tariffs on imported wheat), thus keeping the rent of land in Britain high. Against them were arrayed the rising class of manufacturers, represented above all by the House of Commons, together with the working class. The abolition of the Corn Laws was eventually achieved in 1846, and this meant that cheap imported wheat could now enter the country, thus lowering the price of bread. The abolition brought about an increase in workers' standards of living according to Cobden (cf. Schonhardt-Bailey 1996), or a reduction of workers' wages according to Marx (1856 [1935]), or probably a bit of both.
2. This claim gave rise to the later theories of unequal exchange and unequal development as proposed by analysts like Amin (1973), Emmanuel (1969), and Frank (1978).
3. Santo André, São Bernardo do Campo, São Caetano do Sul, Diadema.

5.   Emerging cities of the third wave

COGNITIVE–CULTURAL CAPITALISM AND THE CITY

Earlier chapters of the book have laid out an argument to the effect that a very special episode of capitalist development and urbanization started to emerge some time in the early 1980s. This episode can be described in terms of an initial postfordist phase that subsequently evolved into a more expansive system of cognitive–cultural capitalism representing a major developmental edge in the contemporary world economy. The still-unfolding spatial system that is coming into being as all of this occurs can in large part be described in terms of an assertive mosaic of great city-regions that have made their appearance, unequally but definitely, in countries at many different levels of average income. These city-regions are intrinsically intertwined with complex globalization processes that bind them ever more tightly together as mutually-dependent nodes in an international network of social and economic relationships. As this global amalgam of city-regions comes to the fore, so a reorganization of older national urban hierarchies into a more integrated international system is steadily coming about. A selected set of these city-regions forms the vanguard of what I call here the "third wave" of urbanization.

One of the analytical devices underlying the present discussion is the idea that the peculiar urbanization processes that accompany any given major historical episode of capitalist development can be schematized in terms of an abstract or ideal-type description. I realize that this proposition flies in the face of much current scholarly work that insists emphatically on the empirical specificity of individual cities. As Massey (1984, p. 8) puts it, "each place is unique," which is a perfectly reasonable statement in so far as it goes, but leaves open the broader question about the degree to which at least some places (or cities) can be meaningfully compared with one another. This question is particularly difficult in the present instance because cities exhibit such enormous variation from one to another in terms of their historical trajectories and their complex internal geographies. My line of attack here is not to assert that the theoretical ideas I put forward describe the empirical totality of this or that city, much less to claim that they describe all cities; but rather to acknowledge that the new capitalism penetrates (and is penetrating) into different cities at different rates and in different substantive forms, and to see what, if any, generalizations can be made about processes and outcomes, however mediated they may be in practice by local circumstances. An ideal type approach is a convenient way of synthesizing ideas while recognizing that detailed concrete outcomes on the ground are not necessarily or even usually invariant. In the present context, this approach is based on an attempt to lay out a notional description of intra-urban space as structured by a specific system of capitalist social and property relations. As the argument unfolds in subsequent chapters, then, frequent reference is made to a generalized abstraction (though one that is constantly exemplified by reference to empirical cases) comprising a particular kind of economic base and employment system, specific forms of human and social capital, a complex local labor market, and a generalized pattern of residential activity reflecting prevailing socio-economic relations. All of these disparate elements of the urban amalgam are caught up in an overall process of spatial integration in which a synthetic urban land nexus, or intra-urban locational system, makes its appearance. A set of governance relationships is typically grafted onto this synthetic structure in order to work out and implement policy agendas focused in part on the problems and predicaments that are inherent to its operation. Of course, no precisely corresponding city will ever be found in empirical reality, even if we have correctly identified all the relevant variables. In this regard, the best we can do, no doubt, is to pick illustrative but invariably debatable cases, such as, say, Manchester in 19th century factory and workshop capitalism, or Chicago and Detroit in the era of high fordism, or London and Seoul today. The so-called LA School of urban analysis that briefly flourished in the 1980s and 1990s (Cenzatti 1993; Scott and Soja 1996; Soja and Scott 1986) proclaimed Los Angeles as *the* paradigmatic city of post-fordism, though the idea encountered considerable opposition at the time and still does today (Judd and Simpson 2011). Even so, and despite its flaws and reticences, the work of the LA School represents a sort of premonition of the kinds of theoretical research and ideological critique that, as I shall argue here, are called for as the third wave of urbanization begins to move beyond its incipient stages of formation.

With the wisdom of hindsight it is now clear that Los Angeles – and Southern California more generally – is only one of a number of city-regions that shifted at an early stage beyond the wave of urbanization coinciding with fordism and that are now in the forefront of a global trend. Again, there can be no unambiguous statement about which cities constitute the essential core of this new wave, and there is certainly no single city whose inner constitution is an expression of the new cognitive–cultural order alone. Different cities participate to different degrees in this new order, and even those that are most advanced in this respect are also characterized by other registers of development. Perhaps the most effective way of identifying at least some of the participants in this third urban wave is to refer to the 75 cities listed in the MasterCard Worldwide Centers of Commerce Index for 2008 (MasterCard Worldwide 2008). The Index evaluates these cities across seven dimensions, covering not only quality of life and legal/political issues, but also financial and business conditions, knowledge creation, and flows of information. These dimensions are in turn broken down into 43 indicators and 74 sub-indicators. Like any of the competing city rankings currently available, this one has its deficiencies, but it has the peculiar merit for present purposes of seeking to replicate the everyday opinions of global business elites about what constitutes a successful metropolis in the early 21st century, not because these are necessarily disciplined opinions, but because they reflect relevant preconceptions about what is most cutting-edge in world city development at the present time. The variables that make up the Index do not completely capture the full scope of cognitive–cultural urbanism in the early 21st century, but they do provide some diagnostic elements that take us part of the way toward what is at stake, and this particular ranking is probably about as good a representation of a first-cut geography of third wave urbanization as we are likely to get at the present time. Note that the number of cities listed in the MasterCard Index is considerably less than the 443 cities worldwide that have populations over one million as recorded by the United Nations, and this remark already points to the status of the emerging third wave as a still quite nascent phenomenon in much of the world today.

The full set of 75 cities is mapped out in Figure 5.1, where each city is represented by a circle whose size corresponds to its score on the MasterCard Index. What stands out above all from a first glance at this figure is the dominance of three major geographic realms containing important hubs of cognitive–cultural economic development, namely North America, Western Europe, and the Asia-Pacific region. The three highest-scoring cities or city-regions on the Index are London, New York, and Tokyo, in that order, each of them occupying a core position in one of the three realms mentioned. The Asia-Pacific region has emerged with enormous insistence in recent decades, and a number of former entrepôt cities located there, like Singapore, Hong Kong, Seoul, Taipei, and Shanghai, are now all ranked in the top half of the Index. As we scan through the bottom half of the rankings a certain number of cities from other parts of Asia also make their appearance, together with selected cities in the Middle East and Latin America. With the exception of Cairo and

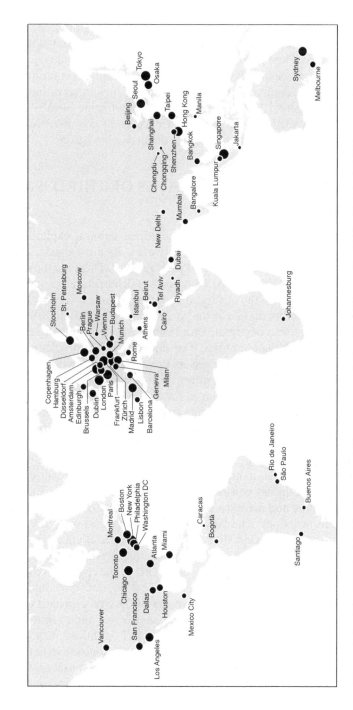

Figure 5.1   The 75 Worldwide Centers of Commerce as defined by MasterCard Worldwide (2008)

Johannesburg, cities in Africa are notably absent. Some of the cities in the bottom half of the rankings (especially those located in the Global South) are at best only marginal participants in the third wave, and many of these cities also contain large impoverished populations that remain far outside any wider capitalist reality (Roy 2011). In spite of these reservations, the cities shown in Figure 5.1 offer an initial glimpse of some of the critical places around the world where important clusters of cognitive–cultural activity are crystallizing out on sections of the urban landscape.

INTERNAL PRODUCTION SPACES OF THIRD WAVE CITIES

Notwithstanding the circumstance that cognitive–cultural capitalism is typically embedded in extended global networks, its most dynamic segments are overwhelmingly concentrated in large cities. These are the places *par excellence* that sustain the massive cohorts of disintegrated production activities characteristic of the advanced technical, business service, financial, and cultural sectors that lie at the core of this type of capitalism, and where the requisite forms of cognitive and cultural human capital are to be found in sufficiently large quantities. The same places are privileged sites of important adjunct operations such as upscale retail functions, entertainment services, and cultural facilities. Within these places, moreover, much of the productive employment in the new economy is concentrated within specialized marshallian districts or clusters, which, by reason of their agglomeration economies, serve as dense and relatively durable poles that anchor the internal space of the city.

Recall that agglomerated production systems typically emerge out of three main lines of force, namely: (a) dense networks of specialized but complementary producers constituting functional complexes of interrelated firms; (b) large and many-sided local labor markets; and (c) learning and innovation processes. The latter processes are based on dense grids of socio-economic interaction that function with special effectiveness in situations where tacit knowledge is being exchanged (Asheim and Coenen 2005; Gertler 2003). Virtually all major segments of the cognitive–cultural economy today embody different aspects of these lines of force, thus generating the tightly-wrought production spaces of the city, or what I earlier referred to as proto-urban forms. The city as a whole comes into being around these production spaces as contingent socio-political phenomena unfold and act reflexively back upon the local production system to create intra-urban space in its full sweep. The resulting space of the city assumes the appearance of a highly variegated patchwork of interlocking land uses, especially where multiple industrial clusters or districts make their appearance and where individuals with widely varying social backgrounds and skills are drawn into the corresponding employment opportunities of the city and then condense out in a system of socially differentiated neighborhoods.

Figure 5.2 offers an ideal-type representation of production space and some of its principal appendages in the context of the capitalist city. This representation is particularly relevant to the case of the cognitive–cultural economy with its strong proclivities to agglomeration, but it is by no means uniquely specific to this case. The figure emphasizes the central importance of the production system as a city-building mechanism, and this is shown here as a set of dominant intra-urban agglomerations complemented by a first tier of agglomeration-specific suppliers and a second tier of generic input providers such as banking facilities, office supplies, or delivery services. All of these production arrangements are articulated with a local labor market, and hence, by implication, with a set of multifaceted residential functions where subtle and detailed forms of social reproduction occur. In turn, this composite body of economic and social activities is enmeshed in a general geographical milieu that typically incorporates place-specific assets and resources, such as the research-drenched atmosphere of Silicon Valley, or the cultural traditions of Paris, or the political stability of Singapore. In addition, the market failures, developmental blockages, and social conflicts that are inherently accessory to urbanization in capitalist society and that constantly threaten intra-urban stability mean that instruments of remedial collective action and authority must always be present if eventual collapse is to be avoided. These instruments assume many different institutional guises, ranging from formal agencies of local government, through private–public partnerships, to civil organizations of many different kinds. In today's world, with its intensifying global economic threats and opportunities, the instruments of collective intra-urban order are frequently oriented – in addition to all the other tasks they face – to the fostering of agglomeration economies in support of local economic development. This entire system of localized and mutually sustaining relationships is complemented by various kinds of external economic relations, two of which are of major significance. One important set of relations revolves around distribution and marketing channels that secure effective dissemination of local products to distant consumers. The other set consists of satellite locales offering advantages (for example, relatively cheap labor or fiscal subsidies) that can be tapped into by firms in major production centers via subcontracting or direct investment. These satellite production locales sometimes develop into self-sustaining clusters in their own right, as illustrated by the growth of the

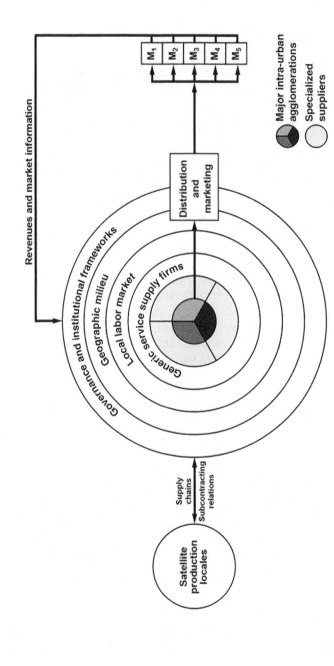

Figure 5.2   Schematic representation of an urban production system with connections to satellite production locations and five external markets, M1, M2, ..., M5

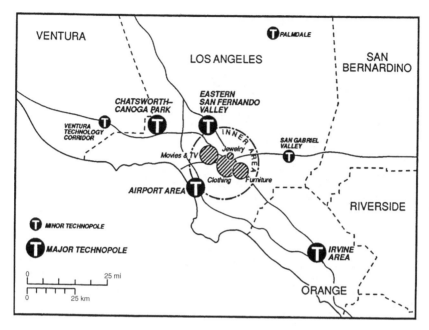

Source: Scott (2008b).

Figure 5.3 *Major industrial districts in the Greater Los Angeles Area*

Vancouver film industry after the 1980s on the basis of runaway production from Hollywood (Scott and Pope 2007).

A brief examination of the case of Los Angeles helps to ground some
of these general propositions about the geography of the cognitive–
cultural economy inside the large metropolis. Given the notable diversity
of its high-technology and cultural industries, Los Angeles is actually an
advanced empirical instance of this sort of geography. The city's industries generate a twofold system of industrial districts, comprising on the
one side a group of technopoles encircling the fringes of the entire urban
area, and on the other side a group of media, entertainment, and fashion-
oriented clusters concentrated in and around the inner area of the city
(see Figure 5.3). This bipartite locational pattern, which appears to be
replicated in a number of other major cities, can presumably be explained
in terms of some sort of Von Thünen model, though to my knowledge, no
actual analysis of this sort has ever been undertaken. The geography of the
industrial districts as shown in Figure 5.3 is evidently highly schematized,
and in practice none of these districts is as tightly configured in spatial
terms as the figure suggests. Thus, the district labeled "movies and TV"

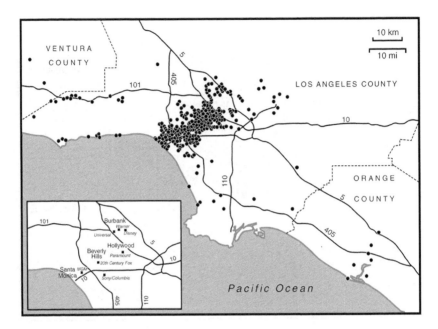

Note: The inset shows locations of the majors and selected place-names.

Source: Scott (2005).

Figure 5.4   Motion-picture production companies in Southern California

consists of multiple specialized subdistricts that cover a wide swath of the metropolitan area. For example, film production companies, as shown in Figure 5.4, spill over from the central nucleus of Hollywood proper into Santa Monica in the west and the San Fernando Valley in the northwest. Also, a number of the industrial districts shown in Figure 5.3 are linked to facilities offshore in a system of spatially disarticulated production such that firms in Los Angeles are tending more and more to concentrate on high-level front-end and back-end functions like design, financing, and marketing while the processing of relatively routinized or self-enclosed batches of work is put out to satellite centers in other parts of the world. The point is exemplified by the rising incidence of both offshore film shoot-ing in the motion-picture industry and the subcontracting out of sewing and other manual tasks in the clothing industry to facilities in Mexico, China, and other low-wage countries (Kessler 1999; Scott 2002).

As we have seen, much economic development policy-making in large cities at the present time is focused precisely on industrial clusters of the sort we have examined in the case of Los Angeles. The goal of this kind of intervention is not only to seek economic growth and employment expansion but in many cases also to revitalize the physical fabric of the city. With respect to the latter goal, the specifically cultural segment of the cognitive–cultural economy has been the object of much attention in recent years and all the more so because this segment – as in the case of Los Angeles – almost always adopts locational niches in inner city areas (see, for example, Hutton 2008; McRobbie 2004; Pollard 2004; Rantisi 2004). This tendency offers many opportunities to policy-makers to revitalize deteriorated sections of the city where abandoned manufacturing and warehousing buildings can be converted into spaces for cultural producers. In Manchester, for example, an area of recycled factories and warehouses known as the Northern Quarter has come to function as a magnet for diverse types of cultural production. This area, lying on the northern fringe of the central business district, is now one of the main foci of Manchester's new cultural economy, with its lively club scene, a music industry, and a nascent group of web designers (de Berranger and Meldrum 2000). Sheffield, a similar case, is endowed with a Cultural Industries Quarter forming a central city enclave, and a burgeoning array of clubs, restaurants, theaters, educational institutions, and other cultural activities have developed in and around this location (Brown et al. 2000). In the same way, San Francisco's South of Market neighborhood, formerly an area of industrial and wholesaling activity, is now the site of a dense cluster of multimedia and web design industries. Analogous experiments in urban revitalization by upgrading relics of the industrial past for cultural purposes are occurring in scores of cities all over the world today. In many instances, these experiments are making very significant contributions to the reprogramming of urban landscapes of production and consumption in the new capitalism (see Chapter 8).

CREATIVE MILIEU AND COMPETITIVE ADVANTAGE IN THE THIRD WAVE CITY

As third wave cities take shape on the global landscape, their often hyper-innovative propensities become increasingly evident. These propensities can in significant ways be ascribed to the formation of synergistic creative fields within these cities. More generally, clusters of cognitive–cultural producers and their attendant relational extensions typically function as active ingredients in processes of learning, creativity and innovation, and this propensity in turn continually enhances the competitive advantages of the city. Learning, creativity and innovation are, of course, overlapping and mutually sustaining phenomena, and the lines of separation between them can never be drawn with any degree of sharpness. We may proceed on the basis of the provisional understanding that *learning* provides important informational and procedural foundations for creative and innovative activity; that *creativity* is concerned with thought and action (at the level of both the individual and the group) directed to the production of novel insights and perceptions that may or may not eventually have tangible significance; and that *innovation* derives from these insights and perceptions but is more specifically focused on their implementation in various domains of practical application.

Hall (1998) has argued in great detail that cities are places in which learning, creativity, and innovation have always flourished, though the shape and substantive content of these phenomena differ greatly from time to time and from place to place depending on prevailing social and economic circumstances. In 19th century Lancashire, learning, creativity, and innovation revolved insistently around the cotton textile industry, and were directed most especially to improvements in spinning and weaving technologies; in Detroit in the period of fordism they were heavily concentrated on the car industry; in today's cognitive–cultural economy they are above all rooted in technology-, service-, information-, and culture-intensive sectors – that is, sectors in which processes of creativity often seem to take on a rather more abstract, numinous quality than in previous rounds of capitalist development. Small wonder, then, that as postfordism came along concepts like the "innovative milieu" and the "learning region" should figure so strongly on the agendas of urban scholars and policy-makers, and that as the cognitive–cultural economy became more clearly delineated in empirical terms, the notion of the "creative city" should also rise to prominence. At the outset, this conceptual shift was notably conspicuous in research on high-technology industrial regions, and above all in studies of burgeoning technopoles where round after round of endogenous innovative impulses were widely observed (Camagni 1995; Maillat and Vasserot 1986). This line of work was later complemented and confirmed by research on patenting activity which showed that streams of ideas can frequently be traced out in genealogies of patent citations concentrated in a particular region (Jaffe et al. 1993). In more recent years, questions about the creative class and the creative city have become matters of some urgency (Cooke and Lazzeretti 2007; Currid 2007; Florida 2002; Landry and Bianchini 1995). The shift of register from "innovation" to "creativity" is nowadays most apparent in the literature that specifically addresses the cultural economy, no doubt because so many of its component activities, such as film or music production, evoke notions of creativity in some of its most exalted forms.

In practice, however, learning, creativity, and innovation are all deeply embedded in the concrete economic and social constitution of the city. As opposed to the formal top-down R&D model that was so characteristic of fordism (and that has still by no means disappeared), economically useful modes of learning, creativity, and innovation today operate increasingly on the basis of a bottom-up process that is inextricably implanted in the many small-scale informal exchanges of information built into so much of the cognitive–cultural economy, especially in regional contexts. The principal vehicles of these exchanges are the constant interactions that occur in the dense, transactions-intensive milieux that typify vertically-disintegrated but agglomerated groups of producers. In particular, interdependent producers with rapidly changing process and product configurations are apt to engage with one another at frequent intervals in continual attempts to align their production capacities (on the supply side) and their needs (on the demand side) with one another. As they proceed in this manner, bits of information are passed backward and forward, often resulting in a degree of learning on one or the other side of the transactional relation, leading to new creative insights that sometimes give rise to practical innovations – however small – such as the modification of a machine or the redesign of a product component (Russo 1985). These innovations may be almost imperceptible on an individual basis, but they sometimes result cumulatively in enduring system-wide advances and hence in continually intensifying competitive advantages. In the light of the creative potentials that so often accompany transactional interchange, there is a growing tendency in many segments of the new economy to organize employees specifically in work-groups that seek to capture and concretize these potentials. Grabher (2001a) has shown that this method of proceeding is especially evident in the case of the advertising industry where project-oriented teams composed of selected individuals are brought together for a period of time in order to work on a given assignment. The objective of these teams is to pool the know-how of their members and to encourage the cross-fertilization of individuals' ideas in a context of close collaboration directed to problem-solving exercises.

These ideas feed directly into the proposition that whatever forms of creativity (and innovation) may be operative in the economic system of cities today, they reside in important ways, though certainly not exclusively, in the organizational peculiarities of the local production milieu and its social appendages, and in the specific challenges and opportunities that these phenomena throw out to individuals positioned within and around them. In other words, the endemic inventiveness that is observable in many cities emerges in the context of a creative field that continually throws out particular kinds of questions, generates information that can be combined and recombined in ways that shape creative thinking, and offers concrete frames of reference that color possible innovative solutions. By the same token, cities in which the cognitive–cultural economy is highly developed are often unusually "creative" in the sense that the complex webs of work, life, and landscape all combine to sustain the technical and affective aptitudes that help constantly to renew localized competitive advantages. One major implication of these propositions is that policies in support of urban development and growth can never be viable so long as they rely unilaterally on efforts to attract creative talent from outside the city while neglecting to pay attention to the conditions under which locally relevant forms of talent can be socially reproduced inside the city over the longer term (see Chapter 2).

To be sure, the peculiar stocks of knowledge and the cultural traditions that accumulate in given cities also play an important role in defining the creative field, and in establishing definite patterns of learning, creativity and innovation. The point, again, however, is that the individuals who compose any particular community typically internalize elements of their daily environment and reflect these back in more or less socially conditioned creative efforts. Moreover, the terrain of creativity, comprising as it does strong contextual and relational components with varying degrees of inertia suggests that creative activities are prone to be marked by path-dependency. Where path-dependency prevails, the creative powers of the labor force will be all the more likely to move in channels that are closely regulated by wider social conditions. An important manifestation of this phenomenon is apparent in the emergence of what Dosi (1982) has called "technological paradigms" or integrated structures of knowledge and practice in industrial systems. Prevailing paradigms facilitate certain kinds of (intra-paradigmatic) innovation yet simultaneously put obstructions in the way of extra-paradigmatic exploration. In the same manner, we might refer to aesthetic and semiotic genres or archetypes as establishing relatively durable frames of reference for creativity in the cultural economy. Long-term lock-in to given archetypes is not uncommon, leading to stability and conservatism with positive or negative results depending on the precise nature of local production activities. Communities of harpsichord makers, for example, are doubtless apt to be rather conservative in their practices given the weight of tradition that overlies this particular craft, whereas communities of digital-effects workers are presumably under much greater pressure to strive for more radical innovations in their particular domain of activity (Amin and Roberts 2008; Brown and Duguid 1991). At the same time, underlying shifts in prevailing technological paradigms may well have dramatic effects on aesthetic and semiotic archetypes – and hence on creative expression – as illustrated by the impact of sound recording on the Hollywood motion-picture industry in the 1930s, or the transformative influence of digital visual effects on the making of films today (Scott 2005). I should add that while all of these creative field effects are strongly evident within individual cities, they are also increasingly taking on a multiscalar complexion as cities and their creative fields function more and more in the context of a deepening constellation of extra-urban connections, extending in the final analysis to the global level (Sunley et al. 2008). In short, while the creative field of the individual city remains a critical source of learning, creativity and innovation effects, and is typically imbued with locally idiosyncratic features, it is also stretched out at varying distances across geographic space as a function of steadily diminishing impediments to inter-city contact.

These arguments help us understand something of how complex process and product innovations come about in cities where the cognitive–cultural economy is highly developed, and how the bases of place-based chamberlinian competition are maintained and renewed. In recent years, it has become evident that cities as a whole are also caught up in a sort of chamberlinian competition with one another via attempts to re-brand themselves and to establish unique images that appeal especially to the transnational capitalist class, and in this way to attract inflows of capital and skilled workers. Re-branding, too, is often a reflection of a municipal will to consolidate or to readjust local patterns of path-dependent evolution. One expression of this phenomenon can be found in the diverse Silicon Alleys, Gulches, Glens, Casbahs, and Wadis that have sprung up over the last few decades. Place branding in these cases seems largely intended to function as a flag that will attract investors and skilled migrants, though with what effectiveness remains an open question. An allied form of branding springs from the aspirations of some cities to advertise or confirm their ambitions to function as centers of cultural significance, and above all as producers of culture with some sort of global appeal. Some of the most assertive versions of this sort of cultural re-branding are to be found in Asia, where Singapore – once the electronics subcontracting capital of the world – now refers to itself as the "global city of the arts," where Bangkok is actively formulating policies that will turn it into a "global creative city," and where Seoul has recently branded itself as the "city of design."

ENVOI

The third wave of urbanization and the cognitive–cultural economy that is in large degree thrusting it forward have developed as important facets of the global landscape, but they are still very far indeed from being ubiquitous. Even so, these phenomena have deepened their hold over particular places and spread geographically by leaps and bounds over the last few decades, and there is every reason to suppose that their importance will continue to grow as the technologies, organizational structures, and labor processes of the new capitalism invade more and more economic and geographic space. In spite of the fact that numerous scholars have referred to these trends as ushering in a new era of creativity, we need to exercise caution in how we utilize this idea, both as an indicator of ongoing events and as a normative reference for policy-making, for there are serious problems with regard to the overall macro-stability of this form of capitalism, as well as a number of important demurrers that need to be advanced about some of its social consequences, as we shall learn in the next few chapters. The notion of the "creative city," in particular, is deeply suspect given its quasi-utopian resonances. All that being said, the third wave of urbanization is now clearly on the march, and this raises many new questions not only about the shape and form of urban theory in the 21st century but also about the policy responses that must be constructed in order to deal with its more wayward effects.

6. Human capital and the urban hierarchy

In previous chapters, I have alluded to the increasing imbrication of national urban hierarchies within a composite global system. This does not mean that national urban hierarchies no longer have any significance or interest, or that the dynamics shaping the hierarchical order of cities in individual countries have ceased to operate. In fact, significant economic variations across the urban hierarchies of different countries can almost always be observed, and urban systems in the 21st century are no exception to this. Systematic variations between cities at different levels of the urban hierarchy are notably observable in the United States, and the present chapter is focused on this particular case, which presents a rich and subtly modulated illustration of how diverse categories of human capital vary as a function of city size. More specifically, we inquire in this chapter into the ways in which different types of cognitive, cultural, and practical human capital interact with one another across the US urban hierarchy, and how this helps us understand certain aspects of the dynamics of urbanization in the 21st century. We want to know, in particular, how the transition in US metropolitan areas from a more traditional 20th century manufacturing base to an expanding 21st century cognitive–cultural economy is reflected in and associated with changes in their human capital endowments. All of this feeds into a broader theoretical question, namely: what is the relationship between the production system and forms of human capital in any given city, and what kinds of causal relationships between these two sets of phenomena might be invoked in order to understand general processes of urban growth and development?

PRELIMINARY OBSERVATIONS

Considerable evidence has accumulated in recent years to show that cities in general tend to exhibit relatively high levels of productivity and skill development. There is also a strong finding in the literature to the effect that these variables bear a strong positive relationship to urban size. In particular, previous research has shown that general measures of human

Table 6.1   Labor force participation in selected industries in US metropolitan areas (2000)

Two-digit industrial sector	Total employees: metropolitan areas	Correlation coefficients	Percent of employees with bachelor's degree
Professional, scientific, management, administrative etc. services	11 082 975	0.63**	26.1
Information and communications	3 590 691	0.50**	30.3
FIRE (finance, insurance, real estate and rental and leasing)	7 819 667	0.39**	28.6
Wholesale trade	3 945 128	0.25**	19.4
Transport and warehousing	4 604 488	0.24**	12.5
Other services	5 170 721	0.04	12.3
Public administration	4 822 579	−0.02	24.6
Arts, entertainment, recreation, accommodations, and food services	8 756 629	−0.06	10.3
Manufacturing	13 666 329	−0.13*	15.9
Educational, health and social services	20 345 347	−0.24**	23.2
Retail trade	12 453 168	−0.27**	12.8

Notes: Correlation coefficients show the relationship between the percentage of the metropolitan labor force employed in a given sector and the logarithm of total metropolitan employment for all 283 metropolitan areas. ** Significant at the 0.01 level; * significant at the 0.05 level.

Source: Calculated from census data via IPUMS (http://usa.ipums.org/usa/).

capital – expressed primarily in terms of average years of education – tend to attain significantly higher levels in large cities than in small (Berry and Glaeser 2005; Glaeser and Maré 2001; Rauch 1993; Simon and Nardinelli 2002; Wheeler 2007). A growing body of evidence suggests that different types of human capital also vary significantly depending on city size (Duranton and Puga 2004; Markusen et al. 2008; Scott 2008b), and the present chapter is focused on further exploration of this matter.

As a first step in this direction, it is of some interest to consider a few broad trends in employment by sector in American metropolitan areas. Here, we focus on employment in two-digit sectors in 283 metropolitan areas in the United States in the year 2000, as given by the census. Table 6.1 shows three main bodies of data, namely: (a) the total number of employees, aggregated over the 283 metropolitan areas, in each two-digit sector; (b) the correlations between the percentage of the labor force in a given sector and the logarithm of the total labor force, where the units of observation are metropolitan areas;[1] and (c) the percentage of employees in each sector (again aggregated over metropolitan areas) with a bachelor's degree. One of the striking general features of table 6.1 is the correspondence between the designated correlation coefficients and the percentages of employees with a bachelor's degree. The rank correlation between the two latter variables is 0.61 (significant at the 0.05 level), and if we eliminate two sectors with a strong focus on government-funded public service (that is, public administration; and educational, health, and social services), the rank correlation rises to 0.85 (significant at the 0.01 level). These results are fully consistent with the proposition that cognitive–cultural forms of work tend to gravitate to larger as opposed to smaller cities. Further evidence in favor of this idea is provided by the observation that the top three correlation coefficients shown in Table 6.1 correspond to the following sectors: (a) professional, scientific, management, etc. services; (b) information and communications; and (c) finance, insurance, and real estate. These sectors are major components of the cognitive–cultural economy. By contrast, and as is to be expected, the correlation coefficients associated with manufacturing and retail trade are notably low, though we should not overlook the fact that pockets of low-wage manufacturing employment continue to subsist in even the very largest metropolitan areas of the United States. Retail trade is at the very bottom of the rankings, no doubt reflecting its relatively low levels of human capital, but also, in part, its wide geographic distribution as a function of the dispersion of demand. Between these two extremes (and again eliminating the public-service sectors) come: (a) wholesale trade; (b) transport and warehousing; (c) other services; and (d) arts and entertainment etc. The relatively high positive correlation of the first two sectors of this group with city size presumably reflects the continued role of cities as important nodal centers within the national system of transportation and distribution. The negative (but non-significant) correlation attached to the arts and entertainment etc. sector is possibly surprising at first sight, but on closer examination we find that the sector comprises a great diversity of subsectors like bowling alleys, recreational vehicle parks, motels, and drinking establishments that, like retail trade, are not especially associated with high levels of human capital and are apt to be widely dispersed in geographic terms.

These comments provide a very preliminary sense of the changing pattern of human capital across the US metropolitan hierarchy, and they roughly indicate that human capital tends to be disproportionately concentrated in large cities. They do not, however, tell us anything about temporal trends in this regard or about the different forms of human capital that are to be found in cities of different sizes. In the next section,

therefore, we probe more deeply into these questions, with a special focus
on three different types of human capital that capture something of the
cerebral, relational, and practical capacities of workers for the years 1980,
1990, and 2000.

DIMENSIONS OF HUMAN CAPITAL IN US CITIES, 1980–2000

The *Dictionary of Occupational Titles* (DOT) published by the US
Department of Labor provides data on three main types of human
capital defined by reference to workers' abilities and aptitudes vis-à-vis
data (that is, calculation and quantitative evaluation), people (that is,
communication and personal interaction) and things (that is, practical
and physical work). The DOT provides scores for each of these types of
human capital on occupational categories as defined by the US Standard
Occupational Classification System. By themselves, the DOT data refer
only to occupations, and are entirely devoid of geographical coordinates
(see Table A6.1 in the appendix to this chapter). In order to translate the
data into terms relevant for urban analysis we must therefore obtain sup-
plementary information that connects them to some sort of spatial grid.
Accordingly, an additional body of data was obtained on employment
by occupation and metropolitan area from the 5 percent sample of the
2000 Census via the Integrated Public Use Microdata Series (IPUMS)
at the Minnesota Population Center.[2] The information from the DOT
is then combined with the employment data to generate three indexes of
human capital by metropolitan area and year. The indexes are designated
here as DATA, PEOPLE and THINGS, in line with the DOT variables
from which they are derived. The nature of these operations and the data
on which they are based are described in detail in the appendix to this
chapter. Unfortunately, publication of the DOT was suspended in the late
1990s, and this circumstance, together with frequent revisions of official
US occupational codes, means that consistent data panels for this exercise
can only be constructed for the three census years, 1980, 1990, and 2000.
The analysis is carried out over 219 metropolitan areas, representing the
maximum number of observations for which comparable census data are
available for 1980, 1990, and 2000. As it happens, the DOT was succeeded
by an online information system known as the Occupational Information
Network (O*Net), and data from this system will be put to use in the next
section of the present chapter as a way of gleaning deeper insight into
some basic cross-section trends in human capital formation in US cities
for the year 2000.

It should be noted that we cannot make direct quantitative comparisons between the DATA, PEOPLE, and THINGS indexes since the DOT data on which they are partly based are purely ordinal, though it is entirely legitimate to compare scores within any one index across time. Metropolitan areas with high scores on the DATA index have a relatively large proportion of their labor force concentrated in occupations that demand advanced levels of mental activity like synthesizing and coordinating, whereas those with low scores are more likely to be characterized by occupations that rely on more simple mental operations like copying and comparing. Metropolitan areas with high scores on the PEOPLE index are marked by a labor force that is relatively skilled in mentoring and negotiating activities (which call for subtle human interactions), whereas low values signify that the labor force is more involved in activities such as serving and taking instructions (which are much less challenging in terms of interpersonal capabilities). The THINGS index provides a measure of workers' capacities in any given metropolitan area with respect to physical tasks, ranging from highly skilled setting up and precision working operations to relatively unskilled feeding–offbearing and handling work. In view of these definitions, we might say that the DATA index is a proxy for levels of cognitive expertise in the labor force. The PEOPLE index is explicitly focused on interpersonal skills, but overlaps to some extent with various cultural capacities of workers. The THINGS index refers to purely practical or applied forms of work. The three indexes thus offer a fairly broad range of human capital measures, though they certainly do not capture the full extent of cognitive–cultural aptitudes and sensibilities in the 21st century. They are especially deficient in regard to the cultural dimension, but it is probably fairly plausible to expect that metropolitan areas with high levels of employment in cultural work will tend to score relatively highly on the DATA and especially the PEOPLE indexes, whereas metropolitan areas with low levels of cultural work will tend to have relatively high scores on the THINGS index. A fourth human capital variable, labeled EDUC, is also brought into play in this analysis. EDUC is defined as the proportion of individuals in the labor force of any metropolitan area who have attained a level of education equivalent to four years of college or more. This variable helps to sharpen our focus on cognitive–cultural issues.

Average values of these four human capital variables across all 219 metropolitan areas are shown in Table 6.2 for 1980, 1990, and 2000. The time-invariant and ordinal character of the original DOT data on which the DATA, PEOPLE and THINGS indexes are partly based means that the variance across time (and space) of these measures is low in comparison with the EDUC variable. The information in Table 6.2 reveals that

*Table 6.2   Average values of human capital variables across all
metropolitan areas (1980–2000)*

	1980	1990	2000	Percentage change, 1980–2000
DATA	3.63	3.77	3.83	5.45%
PEOPLE	2.90	2.99	3.08	6.42%
THINGS	3.24	3.14	3.06	−5.64%
EDUC	0.17	0.21	0.25	47.06%

the DATA and PEOPLE indexes increase regularly in value from 1980 to 2000 whereas the THINGS index declines. EDUC also increases significantly over the specified time period. These observations are consistent with a situation of increasing cognitive and cultural human capital assets in the labor force of US metropolitan areas over the last couple of decades, while they also point to a definite reduction in overall levels of physical and practical human capital. The latter point can no doubt be accounted for by the significant decline of manufacturing in US metropolitan areas as a result of decentralization to off-shore locations as well as by the elimination of many kinds of blue-collar craft skills by automation.

Our next task is to inquire as to how these temporal shifts relate to one another across the urban hierarchy. To this end, correlation coefficients are computed between all four human capital measures identified here, for 1980, 1990, and 2000, using the standard 219 metropolitan areas as observations. The results of this exercise are laid out in Table 6.3. In all three time periods, the DATA, PEOPLE, and EDUC measures are significantly and positively correlated with one another, while they are all also significantly and negatively correlated with the THINGS index. In all of these cases, significance levels far surpass the 0.01 level. These results inform us that since at least 1980, metropolitan areas with high levels of human capital that correspond approximately to cognitive–cultural endowments have been associated with low levels of practical/physical human capital, and vice versa, and the distinction has become somewhat more marked over time. We may ask in relation to these findings, which individual metropolitan areas specialize in which specific kind of human capital? And do forms of specialization have some systematic relation to variations across the metropolitan hierarchy?

To answer these questions we first of all aggregate US metropolitan areas into five different population size categories defined on the basis of population data for 2000; the cut-points are: (a) less than 250 thousand; (b) 250 thousand to 500 thousand; (c) 500 thousand to 1 million; (d) 1

Table 6.3   *Simple correlation coefficients between human capital measures (1980, 1990, and 2000)*

Human capital variables	DATA	PEOPLE	THINGS	EDUC
1980				
DATA	1.000			
PEOPLE	0.934	1.000		
THINGS	−0.340	−0.519	1.000	
EDUC	0.791	0.822	−0.421	1.000
1990				
DATA	1.000			
PEOPLE	0.933	1.000		
THINGS	−0.563	−0.669	1.000	
EDUC	0.859	0.817	−0.525	1.000
2000				
DATA	1.000			
PEOPLE	0.949	1.000		
THINGS	−0.577	−0.660	1.000	
EDUC	0.899	0.717	−0.519	1.000

Notes: Cases are represented by the standard set of metropolitan areas (n=219). All correlations are significant at the 0.01 level.

million to 5 million; and (e) more than 5 million. Table 6.4 sets forth average values of the four human capital measures in each of the five different metropolitan size categories in 1980, 1990, and 2000. For comparative purposes, data for nonmetropolitan America are also presented in the table. In parallel with the information given in Table 6.2, the values of DATA, PEOPLE, and EDUC arrayed in Table 6.4 increase systematically (in each time period) with increasing size of metropolitan area. They also increase steadily from 1980 to 2000 for all metropolitan size categories as well as for the case of nonmetropolitan. It is evident, then, that there has been a relative concentration of human capital assets focused on mental and interpersonal capabilities at the upper end of the metropolitan hierarchy, together with a broad overall intensification of these assets in American metropolitan areas over the last few decades. By contrast, in all three time periods, the THINGS index declines steadily as metropolitan size increases. Moreover, the values of the THINGS index decrease systematically from 1980 to 2000 across the entire hierarchy. It follows from

Table 6.4 Average values of human capital variables by metropolitan size category

		Metropolitan size categories				
	Non-metropolitan areas	Less than 250 000	250 000 to 500 000	500 000 to 1 000 000	1 000 000 to 5 000 000	More than 5 000 000
DATA 1980	3.54	3.54	3.61	3.64	3.78	3.79
DATA 1990	3.65	3.67	3.76	3.81	3.96	3.96
DATA 2000	3.67	3.73	3.82	3.83	4.02	4.01
Percentage change 1980–2000	3.67%	5.36%	5.74%	5.32%	6.52%	5.88%
PEOPLE 1980	2.82	2.83	2.89	2.92	2.99	3.00
PEOPLE 1990	2.88	2.93	2.99	3.01	3.10	3.11
PEOPLE 2000	2.95	3.02	3.08	3.09	3.20	3.23
Percentage change 1980–2000	4.61%	6.82%	6.55%	6.49%	6.94%	7.65%
THINGS 1980	3.52	3.29	3.23	3.24	3.21	3.18
THINGS 1990	3.40	3.19	3.15	3.13	3.09	3.06
THINGS 2000	3.32	3.10	3.06	3.04	3.01	2.98
Percentage change 1980–2000	-5.68	-5.86%	-5.26%	-5.93%	-6.25%	-6.38%
EDUC 1980	0.07	0.15	0.16	0.17	0.19	0.20
EDUC 1990	0.10	0.18	0.20	0.21	0.25	0.26
EDUC 2000	0.11	0.21	0.23	0.23	0.29	0.30
Percentage change 1980-2000	57.14%	37.95%	43.75%	41.15%	46.60%	50.00%
Number of metropolitan areas	–	69	64	38	43	5

these statements that whereas things-oriented forms of human capital are declining overall in the American economy, they tend nowadays to be rather more highly developed (in relative terms) in smaller metropolitan areas than in larger, and they are even more highly developed in non-metropolitan areas.

These results are in harmony, at least for the case of the United States, with the claim that has been advanced in earlier chapters of this book to the effect that the cognitive–cultural economy has a special tendency to form large agglomerations in very large cities. However, the nature of the data underlying these results leaves much to be desired, and a number of ambiguities remain. In the next section, therefore, I attempt to close part of this gap by examining a more informative body of data that has recently become available on human capital in American metropolitan areas.

A CROSS-SECTION ANALYSIS

The US Department of Labor has now replaced the old *Dictionary of Occupational Titles* with a much more comprehensive database, known as O*Net.[3] The information available in this database makes it possible to construct more multidimensional measures of human capital in American metropolitan areas than those represented by the DATA, PEOPLE and THINGS indexes as defined above. Since O*Net has become available only in the very recent past, it cannot be used for in-depth time-series work, though in combination with employment data from the census it does give us the opportunity to examine some critical variations in human capital over the metropolitan hierarchy for the year 2000. In fact, the data extracted from the O*Net database for the purposes of the present analysis are such that we should more properly refer to the computed indexes as providing information not only on human capital but also on work content. The computed indexes provide much information on the cognitive, relational and physical dimensions of human capital and work, but again are rather deficient in regard to the cultural dimension.

O*Net provides data on literally hundreds of different human capital and work content measures for all of the occupations within the official US Standard Occupational Classification System. Reduction of this information to meaningful and reasonably parsimonious indexes by metropolitan area requires a number of complex operations involving both factor analysis and additional procedures analogous to those set forth in the Appendix for combining DOT data with census data. Because of the complexity of these matters, I refrain from describing the details here, but the interested reader can find them laid out in full in Scott and Mantegna

(2009). In practice, 26 different human capital and work content indexes were derived by combining selected O*Net data with census data. For the sake of simplicity, these indexes are not computed for each individual metropolitan area, but are defined only with respect to three different levels of the US metropolitan hierarchy. The top level incorporates all metropolitan areas with populations of a million or more; the middle level incorporates metropolitan areas from 250 000 to one million people; and the bottom level incorporates metropolitan areas with populations of less than 250 000. Out of the total of 283 metropolitan areas for which the census provides data in 2000, 49 are in in the top level of the hierarchy, 109 in the middle, and 125 in the bottom.

A composite view of all this information is shown graphically in Figure 6.1. Here, for comparative purposes, each index is normalized by setting the value for the smallest metropolitan size category equal to zero and then adjusting values for the middle and largest size categories accordingly. Scrutiny of the figure reveals conspicuously regular patterns in the relationships between the different indexes and the metropolitan size categories. Thus, measures of human capital and work content that are predominantly focused on the cognitive and relational (for example, self-motivation versus direction from others; communication and information knowledge; relational skills) vary systematically and positively with metropolitan size. By contrast, measures that revolve around physical labor and practical know-how (for example, body strength and stamina; physical versus mental work contexts; equipment and materials handling) vary inversely with metropolitan size. A number of additional regularities should also be noted. Thus, on the cognitive and relational side, values of indexes representing analytical and independent work styles, administrative and business interests, and concern for job stability, are much higher in large metropolitan areas than in small. On the more things-oriented side, practical skills, physically hazardous work, and strong perceptual capacities are more important in small metropolitan areas than in large. Between these two polarities lies a cluster of indexes that are much more evenly distributed across metropolitan size classes. Among these, three are of special interest in the present context, namely cooperative and relational work styles; leadership; and team tasks versus individual tasks. A broad deduction that we might draw from the latter information is that irrespective of the different economic vocations of US metropolitan areas as a function of size, labor processes right across the hierarchy seem to require distinctly more collaborative interactions and less authoritarian control than was the case in classical fordism.

Thus, the empirical evidence mustered here demonstrates with some force that varieties of human capital diverge markedly as we move from

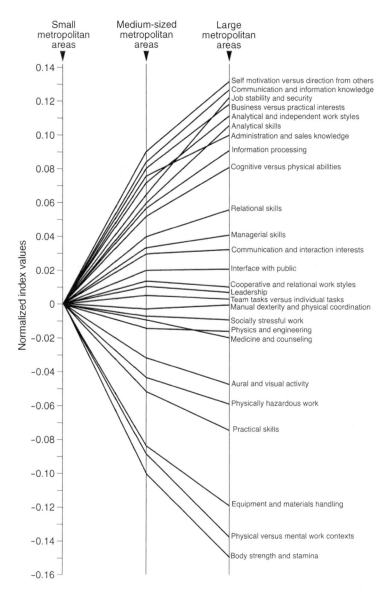

Notes: For comparative purposes, each index is set equal to zero for the smallest metropolitan size category, and all other values are normalized relative to this base. Small metropolitan areas have populations less than 250 000, medium-sized metropolitan areas have 250 000 to one million, and large metropolitan areas have more than one million.

Figure 6.1   Human capital and work content indexes by metropolitan size class (2000)

level to level in the urban hierarchy. Large metropolitan areas are relatively specialized in types of human capital directed to high-level cognitive and relational (and presumably cultural) tasks, whereas small metropolitan areas are not only more specialized in physical and practical types of human capital, but on average have higher endowments of these assets than large metropolitan areas. Even so, while these broad patterns are certainly dominant, they are by no means without exceptions. Above all, there are numerous small cities in the United States where abundant stocks of cognitive–cultural human capital can be found. These are represented by college towns like Gainesville, Florida; artists' colonies like Taos, New Mexico; tourist centers like Savannah, Georgia; small but dynamic foci of high-technology production like Austin, Texas; and so on. These exceptions do not negate the broad trends observed here, but they do indicate that elements of the cognitive–cultural economy are also selectively colonizing certain lower-order cities in the United States, and we might add for that matter in many other parts of the world too (see Chapter 9).

Obviously, there is a critical sense in which human capital is the lifeblood of any city, and an essential condition of continued urban growth and development. In line with the discussion already put forward in Chapter 2, however, there can be no argument to the effect that human capital functions as an independent variable and that the urban economy then expands as a simple dependent outcome. Rather, the forms of human capital that we find in different cities are themselves dependent effects of the concrete varieties of productive activity that occur in those cities. Better yet, the development of local production systems and the accumulation of specific forms of human capital are typically caught up in path-dependent and recursive relationships over time, but in ways that are almost always subject to the dominance of the former. There is, however, one notable exception that we must make to this generalization, and this concerns the formation of communities whose incomes are not directly dependent on local employment opportunities. The outstanding instance of this phenomenon is urban growth that derives from the in-migration of retirees. As I have shown elsewhere (Scott 2010a), migrant engineers in the United States are drawn above all to employment opportunities that match their specialized competences, but as engineers approach retirement age, this relationship fades away in favor of the search for warm winter climates.

APPENDIX

The main sources of data for this study are the *Dictionary of Occupational Titles* (DOT), published by the US Department of Labor, and the national census accessed through the Integrated Public Use Microdata Series (IPUMS). The former source provides diverse measures of human capital; the latter provides abundant demographic and population data and, most importantly, employment by occupation.

The DOT data offer a unique set of insights into the attributes of different occupations by means of three critical measures of the human capital assets that workers variously bring to their jobs, namely their functional capacities for: (a) calculation and evaluation; (b) communication and personal interaction; and (c) practical/physical work. These sets of measures are designated by the DOT as DATA, PEOPLE, and THINGS, respectively. The three measures are quantified by the DOT in terms of ranked component elements as shown in Table A6.1. Note that in order to ease statistical interpretations, the original DOT rankings have here been reversed and a value of one added.[4] The designated rankings represent a rough ordinal grading of different tasks for any given variable, going from the more complex and demanding (high values) to the less complex and demanding (low values).

The *Dictionary of Occupational Titles* covers a total of 12 741 occupations and provides scores for each of them on the PEOPLE, DATA, and THINGS rankings. A first task in preparing the data for analysis was to transfer the rankings from the DOT occupational categories to the much smaller number of census occupational categories. Unfortunately, the occupational categories used by the DOT differ in a number of important ways from those identified in the census and so it is not possible to accomplish this task of transference without the aid of some mechanism for reconciling the two sets of occupational listings. The crosswalk provided by the National Crosswalk Center linking DOT and census occupational categories provides just such a mechanism.[5] In the present instance, the specific matching to be accomplished is between the DOT categories and the census categories as recorded in the IPUMS variable OCC1990 (see next paragraph). The crosswalk matches varying numbers of DOT categories to any one OCC1990 category. Accordingly, the numerical values of the PEOPLE, DATA, and THINGS variables used here are computed for each OCC1990 category as simple averages of the corresponding values for the relevant DOT occupations identified by the crosswalk.

The OCC1990 variable given by IPUMS provides a uniform inter-temporal classification of occupations based on the basic schema used in the 1990 census. By means of this variable, we can achieve data comparability

Table A6.1   *Rankings of occupational tasks in relation to DATA,*
              PEOPLE, and THINGS

DATA	PEOPLE	THINGS
7 Synthesizing	9 Mentoring	8 Setting up
6 Coordinating	8 Negotiating	7 Precision working
5 Analysing	7 Instructing	6 Operating–controlling
4 Compiling	6 Supervising	5 Driving–operating
3 Computing	5 Diverting	4 Manipulating
2 Copying	4 Persuading	3 Tending
1 Comparing	3 Speaking–signalling	2 Feeding–offbearing
	2 Serving	1 Handling
	1 Taking instructions	

Source: US Department of Labor, *Dictionary of Occupational Titles* (4th edn), 1991, accessed at http://www.oalj.dol.gov/libdot.htm#appendices.

for all occupations across the years 1980, 1990, and 2000, though at a definite cost to the analysis because the OCC1990 variable excludes a number of occupations (such as advertising and promotions managers, meeting and convention planners, computer hardware engineers, or database administrators) that appear in the more recent IPUMS occupational classification. It also excludes other occupations that figure in earlier classifications but have subsequently been abandoned. The data presented by the DOT were collected by the US Department of Labor over an extended period stretching through the 1970s and 1980s, which means that they are reasonably well matched to census data for 1980, and probably even to 1990, but that some further and unknown degree of distortion almost certainly creeps in as we extend the match to 2000. Despite these problems, employment and human capital data by occupation were assembled for 1980, 1990, and 2000 from the DOT and IPUMS sources. Further standardization of the data for each of these years was also required in order to achieve inter-temporal comparability. The OCC1990 classification comprises 389 different occupations, though the number of cases for which data are reported varies from one census year to another. It was therefore necessary to eliminate from further consideration all occupations that are not recorded consistently by IPUMS for 1980, 1990, and 2000. All military occupations were also eliminated. These procedures reduce the final set of occupations to a total of 334. Similarly, the set of metropolitan areas used in the analysis was standardized by only referring to those areas that appear consistently in all three IPUMS data sets. Accordingly, there are 219 metropolitan areas in the final data set deployed here.

Given these preliminary operations, three specific human capital variables were computed for 1980, 1990 and 2000, with US metropolitan areas representing the observations. In line with the terminology of the DOT, these variables are labelled DATA, PEOPLE, and THINGS. The method for calculating the indexes is outlined as follows. For the United States as a whole (more accurately, for the 219 metropolitan areas on which the present study is founded) the value of the variable for the kth category of human capital at time t is defined as $I_k^t = \Sigma_i e_i^t s_{ik}/E^t$ where $E^t = \Sigma_i e_i^t$. Here, e_{it} represents total employment in occupation i at time t in the 219 metropolitan areas, and s_{ik} is the score of occupation i on human capital measure k as given in Table A6.1. The quantity E^t represents aggregate employment in the standard 334 occupations in the standard 219 metropolitan areas, and it thus ensures that the values of the I_k^t are independent of any temporal fluctuations in the size of the total labor force. Recall that the scores, s_{ik}, apply only to occupations and not to individuals, which means that the same broad human-capital scores as derived from the DOT are being imputed to all individuals in any given occupation. Since the fit between the capacities of individuals and the requirements of their jobs is rarely perfect this suggests that there is likely to be some derivative unknown margin of error in the calculations, though in view of the systematically meaningful character of the statistical calculations presented in this chapter, this margin would not appear to be so wide as to invalidate the main results. In addition, the time-invariant character of the DOT data means that examination of intensive variations in the strict sense as identified by Autor et al. (2003) – that is, changes in task content within occupations (see also Attewell 1987) – is beyond the scope of the present analysis. Rather, the index I_k^t is an extensive measure of human capital in that it varies only as occupational employment levels vary. In other words, each individual human capital measure (s_{ik}) for the ith occupation is constant over time and space so that variations in values of I_k^t are driven solely by differential shifts in employment across occupations. Any I_k^t can be seen, then, as an index expressing the kth human capital endowment of the (weighted) "average" worker at time t across all 219 metropolitan areas.

NOTES

1. The logarithmic transformation is designed to mitigate the very high level of heteroskedasticity in the metropolitan population variable.
2. http://usa.ipums.org/usa/
3. The O*Net information system is available at http://online.onetcenter.org/
4. The original rankings are deployed in the official code for every occupation as laid out

in the *Dictionary of Occupational Titles*. The fourth digit of each occupational code identifies its specific relation to DATA, the fifth its relation to PEOPLE, and the sixth to THINGS.

5. See ftp://ftp.xwalkcenter.org/download/xwalks

7. Symbolic analysts and the service underclass

INTRODUCTION

I have argued that the emergence of the new economy in American cities over the last three or four decades is bringing in its train a radically new division of labor and, as a consequence, a significant recomposition of urban society. I have already made reference to this recomposition in Chapter 3, where the bipartite division of the labor force in advanced capitalist societies was briefly discussed. In the present chapter, I shall deal further and at length with this matter using detailed data available from official American sources. One side of this changing division of labor is captured in the work of scholars like Reich (1992) and Florida (2002) who write about the recent rise of an upper fraction of the labor force marked by high levels of education, formal qualifications, and distinctive cognitive–cultural skills. Another side is reflected in the large body of research that has been published in recent years by urban geographers, labor sociologists, feminist scholars, and others on the chronic degradation of work that is observable at the lower end of labor markets in advanced capitalist societies (see, for example, Appelbaum and Schmitt 2009; McDowell 2009; Peck and Theodore 2001). This degradation is evident in both manufacturing and service sectors, but is most especially manifest in the recent proliferation of a service underclass in large cities (DeFilippis et al. 2009), and the relative expansion of low-wage service work is all the more emphatic in view of the rapidly falling levels of manufacturing employment in the same cities.

In what follows, I engage in a statistical exploration of these issues by means of a highly focused analysis of two groups of selected occupations. Following Reich (1992), I refer to the first of these groups as "symbolic analysts" (that is, highly qualified cognitive and cultural workers). The second group is designated the "service underclass." Official sources do not lend themselves readily to any precise statistical demarcation of either of these two groups, especially as the individual occupations that make them up are almost always quite heterogeneous in terms of the levels of skill and qualification that they encompass. For these reasons, any attempt to provide a meaningful statistical account of symbolic analysts and the service underclass is apt to be fraught with difficulties. My own way of approaching this definitional issue is to combine occupational data with other criteria from the US Census and the American Community Survey (accessed through the University of Minnesota's Integrated Public Use Microdata Series (IPUMS-USA))[1] in an attempt to isolate groups of occupations that can plausibly be taken as representative (but not exhaustive) of symbolic analysts on the one side and the service underclass on the other. More particularly, specific occupations characterizing symbolic analysts are selected on the basis of educational criteria, and occupations characterizing the service underclass are selected on the basis of educational and income criteria together with a judgmental element based on occupational description. Thus the symbolic analyst and the service underclass categories as codified for this chapter are symptomatic of, but much more narrowly defined than, the "selected professional occupations" and the "low-wage service occupations," respectively, identified in Chapter 3. With the aid of these two groups of occupations we are able all the more effectively to isolate some of the core characteristics of the upper and lower tiers of the labor force in American cities today.

OCCUPATIONAL DEMARCATION OF SYMBOLIC ANALYSTS AND THE SERVICE UNDERCLASS

The changes that are made in the US occupational classification from time to time add further to the problems enumerated above. Because of these changes, detailed and consistent occupational analysis of US cities for any reasonably recent time period is restricted to the years 2000 and 2010. This time period is not ideal in view of the severe financial crisis that occurred in the second half of the 2000–2010 decade, but in the end, the results do not appear to be unduly distorted by this circumstance. Even though there are high levels of comparability between the official occupational classifications for 2000 and 2010, a number of adjustments need to be made in order to achieve definitional consistency, and any occupations that cannot be fully matched across both years are excluded from the following analyses.

In the first place, then, the symbolic analyst group is taken to comprise all those detailed census occupational categories in which the median worker had an educational level equal to four years of college or more in the year 2000. This definition runs parallel to the way in which Florida (2002) identifies his "creative class," although I prefer the term "symbolic analysts" that was coined by Reich (1992) as being somewhat less tendentious. Income plays no role in this particular definition because there are many occupations where workers have high quotients of human capital (for example, writers and authors, archivists, social workers, teachers, and so on) but are relatively poorly paid. A total of 92 occupations were selected in this way. These occupations are shown in Table 7.1, together with their employment levels in 2000 and 2010. Symbolic analysts work in a great diversity of occupations, but especially in activities like finance, advanced business services, science and technology, engineering, education and social services, media and culture, and medicine.

In the second place, identification of the occupations representing the service underclass depends in part on education (that is, a median educational level of grade 12 or lower in the year 2000), but this criterion alone is not sufficiently discriminating for present purposes because it does not exclude occupations where educational levels are relatively low but where income levels are relatively high. Nor does it exclude obviously non-service occupations with low median educational levels like agriculture, mining, production work, and so on. In addition, then, two other selection criteria are applied. One is that only occupations with a median annual salary and wage level less than or equal to US $11 239 in 2000 are included, where the figure of US $11 239 represents the official 2000 poverty threshold for a nonfarm family of two (that is, two adults or one adult and one child) as defined by the Social Security Administration. The other is that the official description of the occupation must indicate that it involves some sort of "service-oriented" activity, and here there is admittedly room for a degree of arbitrariness. I have incorporated into the analysis not only what the standard occupational classification designates explicitly as "services" (for example, waiters and waitresses, janitors and building cleaners, and child care workers), but also a number of service-like occupations in construction trades (for example, paperhangers), installation, maintenance and repair (for example, helpers), and transportation and material-moving occupations (for example, taxi drivers and packers and packagers). By contrast, I have excluded all office and administrative-support occupations on the grounds that workers in these occupations are somewhat more likely to participate in the formal labor market than workers in the occupations that I have already designated as the service underclass. Accordingly, a total of 45 occupations were chosen as primary representatives of the service underclass, and these are listed in Table 7.2, where employment levels in 2000 and 2010 are also shown. We might quibble at a few of the occupations included in Table 7.2, as in the case, perhaps, of library technicians and teacher assistants, though upon further scrutiny it is evident that these particular occupations entail very low levels of qualification and very low wages. By and large there can be little question but that all the selected occupations involve low-level service functions

*Table 7.1   Selected symbolic analyst occupations – employment for 283
US metropolitan areas*

Census occupational code	Description	2000	2010	Percent change
4	Advertising and Promotions Managers	80 542	54 137	−32.8
5	Marketing and Sales Managers	1 064 130	846 395	−20.5
6	Public Relations Managers	63 775	50 244	−21.2
11	Computer and Information Systems Managers	316 967	498 674	57.3
12	Financial Managers	917 125	1 015 528	10.7
15	Purchasing Managers	186 625	182 872	−2.0
23	Education Administrator	625 110	787 655	26.0
35	Medical and Health Services Managers	361 301	499 920	38.4
36	Natural Sciences Managers	18 934	22 875	20.8
42	Social and Community Service Managers	224 673	288 093	28.2
50	Agents and Business Managers of Artists, Performers, and Athletes	39 555	48 576	22.8
71	Management Analysts	573 354	721 629	25.9
80	Accountants and Auditors	1 713 925	1 973 967	15.2
81	Appraisers and Assessors of Real Estate	82 070	75 322	−8.2
82	Budget Analysts	45 872	50 574	10.3
83	Credit Analysts	32 249	25 903	−19.7
84	Financial Analysts	66 769	87 883	31.6
85	Personal Financial Advisors	248 051	334 006	34.7
90	Financial Examiners	11 400	14 629	28.3
100	Computer Scientists and Systems Analysts	689 028	546 749	−20.6
101	Computer Programmers	665 677	468 538	−29.6
102	Computer Software Engineers	710 270	868 753	22.3
106	Database Administrators	77 360	102 223	32.1
120	Actuaries	21 699	24 758	14.1
122	Operations Research Analysts	108 639	124 864	14.9
124	Miscellaneous Mathematical Science Occupations	30 125	43 327	43.8
130	Architects, except Naval	195 902	180 220	−8.0
131	Surveyors, Cartographers, and Photogrammetrists	29 930	31 288	4.5
132	Aerospace Engineers	118 984	136 031	14.3
135	Chemical Engineers	63 087	58 659	−7.0
136	Civil Engineers	260 965	286 610	9.8
140	Computer Hardware Engineers	67 048	62 530	−6.7
141	Electrical and Electronics Engineers	305 027	229 542	−24.7

Table 7.1 (continued)

Census occupational code	Description	2000	2010	Percent change
142	Environmental Engineers	32 470	26 983	−16.9
143	Industrial Engineers, Including Health and Safety	173 273	162 684	−6.1
144	Marine Engineers	9 695	8 954	−7.6
145	Materials Engineers	33 256	31 986	−3.8
146	Mechanical Engineers	259 262	198 705	−23.4
152	Petroleum, Mining and Geological Engineers	19 077	28 812	51.0
153	Miscellaneous Engineers, including Agricultural and Biomedical	316 101	410 193	29.8
160	Agricultural and Food Scientists	22 475	23 828	6.0
161	Biological Scientists	73 886	70 263	−4.9
164	Conservation Scientists and Foresters	12 269	12 818	4.5
170	Astronomers and Physicists	20 385	13 604	−33.3
171	Atmospheric and Space Scientists	10 256	8 426	−17.7
172	Chemists and Materials Scientists	103 961	84 084	−19.1
174	Environmental Scientists and Geoscientists	76 784	64 366	−16.2
176	Physical Scientists, all other	150 109	184 764	23.1
180	Economists	28 047	25 167	−10.3
182	Psychologists	160 791	180 347	12.2
184	Urban and Regional Planners	20 967	18 535	−11.6
186	Miscellaneous Social Scientists, including Sociologists	37 088	56 287	51.8
191	Biological Technicians	17 847	19 807	11.0
200	Counselors	526 032	659 224	25.3
201	Social Workers	573 878	715 312	24.6
202	Miscellaneous Community and Social Service Specialists	238 760	318 643	33.5
204	Clergy	320 429	351 095	9.6
205	Directors, Religious Activities and Education	50 622	46 123	−8.9
220	Postsecondary Teachers	1 082 544	1 331 148	23.0
231	Elementary and Middle School Teachers	2 728 504	3 197 965	17.2
232	Secondary School Teachers	655 343	743 842	13.5
233	Special Education Teachers	148 855	216 802	45.6
240	Archivists, Curators, and Museum Technicians	33 872	44 463	31.3
243	Librarians	176 357	153 305	−13.1
255	Other Education, Training, and Library Workers	50 695	102 134	101.5

Table 7.1   (continued)

Census occupational code	Description	2000	2010	Percent change
271	Producers and Directors	144 429	153 705	6.4
281	News Analysts, Reporters, and Correspondents	88 225	80 922	−8.3
282	Public Relations Specialists	149 845	147 749	−1.4
283	Editors	180 926	173 674	−4.0
284	Technical Writers	75 729	68 436	−9.6
285	Writers and Authors	171 526	213 979	24.8
300	Chiropractors	43 742	43 346	−0.9
301	Dentists	143 764	151 860	5.6
303	Dietitians and Nutritionists	76 350	83 423	9.3
304	Optometrists	26 166	27 836	6.4
305	Pharmacists	186 055	233 703	25.6
306	Physicians and Surgeons	688 815	797 145	15.7
311	Physician Assistants	54 777	99 994	82.5
312	Podiatrists	10 750	7 629	−29.0
313	Registered Nurses	2 066 250	2 304 470	11.5
314	Audiologists	11 476	12 775	11.3
315	Occupational Therapists	60 821	75 307	23.8
316	Physical Therapists	122 265	166 223	36.0
321	Recreational Therapists	15 417	12 640	−18.0
323	Speech-Language Pathologists	83 632	106 772	27.7
325	Veterinarians	45 277	58 874	30.0
326	Health Diagnosing and Treating Practitioners, all other	10 047	20 194	101.0
330	Clinical Laboratory Technologists and Technicians	291 102	328 907	13.0
354	Other Healthcare Practitioners and Technical Occupations	60 450	70 175	16.1
482	Securities, Commodities, and Financial Services Sales Agents	391 385	318 731	−18.6
493	Sales Engineers	32 643	32 064	−1.8
903	Aircraft Pilots and Flight Engineers	138 183	133 768	−3.2
	Total	23 550 105	26 177 032	11.2

Source: United States Census, via IPUMS-USA.

marked not only by minimal wage and educational levels but also by inferior working conditions including much part-time and temporary labor
contracting (Peck 1996; Peck and Theodore 2001). Thus, according to
2000 census data, individuals in service underclass occupations worked on
average a total of 38.0 weeks in 1999 as against 47.1 weeks for symbolic

analysts; and equivalent figures for the usual hours of work per week were 33.2 versus 41.4, respectively. Even more significantly, the standard deviations around these means are proportionately very much greater for the service underclass than they are for symbolic analysts.[2] Workers in service underclass occupations contribute, on the one side, to sustaining the amenities and facilities of the urban system (for example, waiters and waitresses, janitors, ushers, painters, and taxi drivers), and on other side, to supporting the domestic and personal needs of the citizenry at large and above all the upper tier of the labor force (for example, child-care workers, personal aides, hairdressers, and nonfarm animal caretakers).

All the information offered in Tables 7.1 and 7.2 refers exclusively to the 283 metropolitan areas in the United States for which data are reported in both 2000 and 2010. The 26.2 million individuals employed in the symbolic analyst occupations given in Table 7.1 represent 18.5 percent of all individuals with designated occupations in US metropolitan areas in 2010. The 30.8 million individuals employed in service underclass occupations as given in Table 7.2 constitute 21.7 percent of the same total. Hence, the overall number of workers involved represents more than 40 percent of the relevant total labor force, though in view of the tight restraints on the definitions used here, the actual percentage should unquestionably be very much greater than this. In passing, we may note that Standing (2011) and others refer to a "precariat" that has many of the features of the service underclass as identified in this book. However, the analysis here is focused strictly on labor market issues whereas the notion of the precariat usually includes social fractions such as the dangerous classes, the homeless, and the unemployable, which, important as they may be, lie outside the scope of the present investigation.

EMPLOYMENT TRENDS BY METROPOLITAN AREA AND HIERARCHICAL LEVEL

As Tables 7.1 and 7.2 indicate, employment of symbolic analysts in the 283 metropolitan areas of the United States grew by 11.2 percent from 2000 to 2010, and employment of the service underclass grew by as much as 20.0 percent. In comparison, employment in the selected professional occupations discussed in Chapter 3 grew by 7.9 percent and the low-wage service occupations discussed in the same chapter grew by 2.1 percent; while, over the same period, the labor force as a whole in the United States *declined* by 2.0 percent. It is apparent, then, that relative growth rates for the symbolic analyst group and the service underclass, as defined, are unusually high (especially if we take into account the difficult economic circumstances

Table 7.2   Selected service underclass occupations – employment for 283 US metropolitan areas

Census occupational code	Description	2000	2010	Percent change
244	Library Technicians	53 085	58 044	9.3
254	Teacher Assistants	841 523	1 015 249	20.6
395	Lifeguards and other Protective Service Workers	151 008	292 995	94.0
402	Cooks	1 786 957	2 197 901	23.0
403	Food Preparation Workers	579 934	905 031	56.1
405	Combined Food Preparation and Serving Workers	368 483	361 718	−1.8
406	Counter Attendants	236 564	288 510	22.0
411	Waiters and Waitresses	1 845 959	2 277 578	23.4
412	Food Servers, Nonrestaurant	165 760	208 006	25.5
413	Dining Room and Cafeteria Attendants, etc.	360 650	416 036	15.4
414	Dishwashers	289 757	334 725	15.5
415	Hosts and Hostesses, Restaurant, Lounge, and Coffee Shop	240 809	339 879	41.1
422	Janitors and Building Cleaners	2 018 760	2 485 959	23.1
423	Maids and Housekeeping Cleaners	1 308 670	1 591 293	21.6
425	Grounds Maintenance Workers	1 021 993	1 394 413	36.4
434	Animal Trainers	29 380	38 204	30.0
435	Nonfarm Animal Caretakers	111 153	191 325	72.1
441	Motion Picture Projectionists	9 765	10 459	7.1
442	Ushers, Lobby Attendants, and Ticket-Takers	74 467	58 137	−21.9
443	Miscellaneous Entertainment Attendants and Related Workers	176 976	240 737	36.0
450	Barbers	83 548	90 786	8.7
451	Hairdressers, Hairstylists, and Cosmetologists	615 252	701 283	14.0
452	Miscellaneous Personal Appearance Workers	148 341	280 666	89.2
460	Child-Care Workers	1 421 640	1 534 004	7.9
461	Personal and Home-Care Aides	293 690	1 004 335	242.0
465	Personal Care and Service Workers, all other	47 013	117 609	150.2

Table 7.2   (continued)

Census occupational code	Description	2000	2010	Percent change
472	Cashiers	3 248 487	3 872 292	19.2
474	Counter and Rental Clerks	172 841	133 668	−22.7
476	Retail Salespersons	3 772 202	3 817 241	1.2
490	Models, Demonstrators, and Product Promoters	74 594	98 851	32.5
494	Telemarketers	334 475	193 497	−42.1
495	Door-to-Door Sales Workers, etc.	195 075	193 635	−0.7
526	File Clerks	389 614	432 953	11.1
530	Hotel, Motel, and Resort Desk Clerks	108 361	134 272	23.9
540	Receptionists and Information Clerks	1 234 059	1 330 517	7.7
642	Painters, Construction and Maintenance	571 819	637 772	11.5
643	Paperhangers	17 679	6 228	−64.8
660	Helpers, Construction Trades	73 668	76 236	3.5
761	Helpers – Installation, Maintenance, and Repair Workers	19 653	24 896	26.7
785	Food Cooking Machine Operators and Tenders	7 167	9 880	37.9
914	Taxi Drivers and Chauffeurs	267 831	373 648	39.5
915	Miscellaneous Motor Vehicle Operators	27 094	70 580	160.5
935	Parking Lot Attendants	73 875	97 004	31.3
961	Cleaners of Vehicles and Equipment	365 346	386 073	5.7
964	Packers and Packagers, Hand	446 499	504 499	13.0
	Total	25 681 476	30 828 624	20.0

Source: United States Census, via IPUMS-USA.

of the 2000–2010 decade), and, as I shall argue, these outcomes can be ascribed primarily to continued shifts in the American economy at large toward a more cognitive–cultural configuration, and away from traditional manufacturing.

Table 7.3   Employment in symbolic analyst and service underclass occupations in the US metropolitan hierarchy (2000 and 2010)

Hierarchical level	Metropolitan size class	Number of metropolitan areas in size class	Employment in symbolic analyst occupations (000s)		Employment in service underclass occupations (000s)		Symbolic analyst occupations as a percentage of total population		Service underclass occupations as a percentage of total population		Ratio of symbolic analysts to service underclass employment	
			2000	2010	2000	2010	2000	2010	2000	2010	2000	2010
1	>5 000 000	5	5 482	5 876	5 577	6 500	11.34	11.45	11.49	12.66	0.98	0.91
2	1 000 000–5 000 000	44	10 889	12 289	11 038	13 497	11.71	11.65	11.87	12.8	0.99	0.91
3	500 000–1 000 000	38	2 689	3 002	3 275	3 922	9.95	9.97	12.12	13.03	0.81	0.76
4	250 000–500 000	71	2 561	2 849	3 170	3 769	9.9	10.03	12.44	13.27	0.81	0.76
5	<250 000	125	1 929	2 161	2 622	3 141	9.65	9.71	13.11	14.12	0.74	0.69
	Non-metropolitan areas	–	5 098	5 720	8 054	9 147	7.57	7.97	11.96	12.74	0.63	0.63
	Total, USA	283	28 648	31 897	33 736	39 976	10.18	10.31	11.99	12.92	0.85	0.8

Source: United States Census, via IPUMS-USA.

Important additional insights into these employment data can be obtained by breaking them down according to levels of the metropolitan hierarchy. The same five hierarchical levels as were defined in Chapter 6 are used here. The incidence of employment for the 92 symbolic analyst occupations and the 45 service underclass occupations was then calculated for each hierarchical level for the years 2000 and 2010 as displayed in Table 7.3. The objective is now to examine the variations in the distribution of symbolic analysts and the service underclass across the metropolitan hierarchy. As the data in Table 7.3 clearly show, the ratio of symbolic analysts to both the population as a whole and to the service underclass declines significantly as we move from the upper to the lower levels of the hierarchy (Glaeser and Maré 2001; Scott 2010b). Correspondingly, the incidence of service underclass workers increases fairly systematically as we descend the hierarchy, indicating that in relative terms the economies of smaller cities tend to be somewhat more service-oriented in general than those of larger cities (though, as we shall see, there are significant differences between the specific types of service underclass jobs that prevail in large and small cities). Furthermore, evidence published by Bacolod et al. (2009) and Scott (2009) suggests that the skills of service underclass workers tend to *increase* with decreasing city size. Bacolod et al. (p. 229) enlarge on this latter remark when they write that "Low skill workers in large cities are . . . even less skilled than the low skill workers in small cities." The precise reasons for this gradation remain unclear. They may be related to the dominant types of jobs that service underclass workers perform in cities of different sizes, or they may be due to the fact that service underclass workers in large cities are much more likely to be immigrants from poor countries where education is relatively less accessible than in the United States, or they may reflect some combination of these factors. The evident implication of these data is that labor market polarization is greater (and increasing more rapidly) in larger than in smaller cities of the United States. The hierarchical differences in terms of percentages and ratios that are shown in Table 7.3 are relatively subdued but very consistent, and perhaps more importantly, as will be revealed, they are overlain by a number of important qualitative variations as a function of urban size.

DETAILED OCCUPATIONAL VARIATIONS ACROSS THE METROPOLITAN HIERARCHY

We have seen that symbolic analysts and the service-oriented underclass are not spread haphazardly across the metropolitan hierarchy but are distributed in relative terms as a function of urban size. We now need to nuance this finding in order to ascertain its detailed relationships to the locational characteristics of the cognitive–cultural economy. Hence, in this section and the next, we examine how the observed hierarchical variations of symbolic analysts and the service underclass are further modulated in relation to occupational specialization and the demographic features of the labor force.

We begin by computing indices of representation (or equivalently, location coefficients) expressing the relative incidence of each of the 92 symbolic analyst and 45 service underclass occupations in each of the five designated tiers of the metropolitan hierarchy. The index of representation is defined as the ratio of (a) the proportion of workers in a given occupation in a given tier of the hierarchy relative to all workers in that tier, to (b) the proportion of workers in the same occupation in the United States as a whole relative to all workers in the United States.[3] Therefore, a value of the index greater than one tells us that the proportion of workers in the given occupation and the given hierarchical level is unusually high by comparison with the national average; conversely, a value less than one tells us that the proportion is unusually low by comparison with the national average. These operations provide us with two matrices of indices, one of dimensions 92×5 for symbolic analysts, the other of dimensions 45×5 for the service underclass. From these matrices we extract two 5×5 matrices of correlation coefficients, one expressing levels of correlation between the different tiers of the metropolitan hierarchy for symbolic analyst occupations, the other expressing analogous correlations for service underclass occupations.

Figures 7.1 and 7.2 present correlograms derived from these correlation coefficients for symbolic analysts and the service underclass, respectively. In both figures, only the correlations between (a) level 1 of the hierarchy and all other levels, and (b) level 5 and all other levels are shown. An explicit accounting of all the remaining evidence contributes little in the way of additional information. What is particularly striking about both figures is that the greater the (ordinal) distance between any two levels of the hierarchy, the lower the level of correlation, a finding that indicates in turn that levels of occupational specialization differ significantly from one another depending on hierarchical tier. In addition, for both symbolic analysts and the service underclass, the top tier of the hierarchy is the one that is most noticeably different from the others in terms of occupational specialization.

Consider, now, the detailed occupational categories that characterize these different levels of the metropolitan hierarchy, though actually, again for ease of exposition, only tiers 1 and 5 are treated here in depth. Tables 7.4 and 7.5 lay out the essential information for this exercise. These two

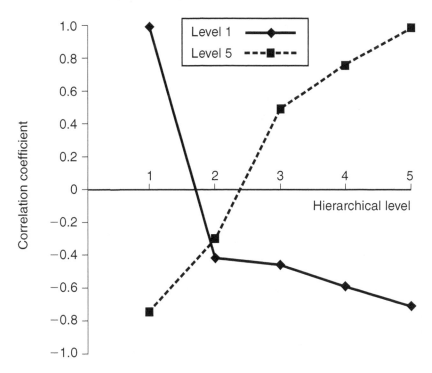

Notes: The diagram shows: (a) correlations between the indexes of representation for all symbolic analyst occupations in the top level (level 1) of the metropolitan hierarchy and equivalent indexes for all other levels of the hierarchy; and (b) correlations between the indexes of representation for all symbolic analyst occupations in the bottom level (level 5) of the metropolitan hierarchy and equivalent indexes for all other levels of the hierarchy.

Figure 7.1   Symbolic analysts: correlogram for indexes of representation

tables show, respectively, detailed symbolic analyst and service underclass occupations together with their scores on the index of representation for tiers 1 and 5 of the hierarchy. Only occupations with large indices of representation are of interest here, and thus the information displayed in Tables 7.4 and 7.5 is restricted to those ten occupations with the highest scores for tiers 1 and 5 of the hierarchy.

As indicated in Table 7.4, the top scoring symbolic analyst occupations on the index of representation in tier 1 of the hierarchy involve activities like arts and entertainment (producers and directors; agents and business managers of artists; etc.), publishing (editors; writers and authors), business services and finance (securities, commodities, and financial service sales agents; actuaries; advertising and promotions managers; financial analysts), and health-related occupations (podiatrists; psychologists).

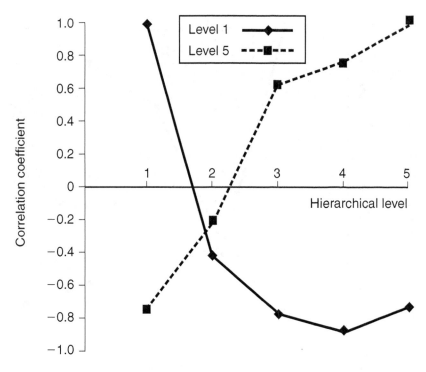

Notes: The diagram shows: (a) correlations between the indexes of representation for all service underclass occupations in the top level (level 1) of the metropolitan hierarchy and equivalent indexes for all other levels of the hierarchy; and (b) correlations between the indexes of representation for all service underclass occupations in the bottom level (level 5) of the metropolitan hierarchy and equivalent indexes for all other levels of the hierarchy.

Figure 7.2   Service underclass occupations: correlogram for indexes of representation

These occupations correspond to the main forms of cognitive–cultural economy that occur in large US cities. Top scoring symbolic analyst occupations in tier 5 of the hierarchy are much more focused on the specific needs of smaller communities and surrounding rural areas. Here, there is a preponderance of scientific and technical professions reflecting the focus of the local economic activity on the land and its resources. These include conservation scientists and foresters; petroleum, mining and geological engineers; surveyors, cartographers, and photogrammetrists; biological technicians; and veterinarians. Postsecondary teachers and physical scientists (for example, agricultural and food scientists; atmospheric and space scientists; and biological scientists) are also an important fraction of the symbolic-analyst stratum in cities that lie at the bottom of the met-

Table 7.4   *Symbolic analysts: ten top-scoring occupations on indexes of representation for levels 1 and 5 of the US metropolitan hierarchy (2000)*

Hierar-chical level	Census occupa-tional code	Description	Index of represen-tation
1	271	Producers and Directors	1.83
1	50	Agents and Business Managers of Artists, etc.	1.75
1	482	Securities, Commodities, and Financial Services Sales Agents	1.66
1	120	Actuaries	1.59
1	4	Advertising and Promotions Managers	1.58
1	283	Editors	1.56
1	84	Financial Analysts	1.54
1	285	Writers and Authors	1.47
1	312	Podiatrists	1.40
1	182	Psychologists	1.20
5	164	Conservation Scientists and Foresters	2.47
5	152	Petroleum, Mining, and Geological Engineers	1.72
5	160	Agricultural and Food Scientists	1.72
5	171	Atmospheric and Space Scientists	1.53
5	220	Postsecondary Teachers	1.47
5	131	Surveyors, Cartographers, and Photogrammetrists	1.36
5	354	Other Healthcare Practitioners and Technical Occupations	1.34
5	191	Biological Technicians	1.34
5	161	Biological Scientists	1.34
5	325	Veterinarians	1.33

Notes: Level 1 of the hierarchy is defined as all metropolitan areas with populations greater than 5 000 000; level 5 comprises all metropolitan areas with populations less than 250 000 (see Table 7.3). See text for the definition of the index of representation.

Source: United States Census (2000), via IPUMS-USA.

ropolitan hierarchy, and this state of affairs is undoubtedly related to the relatively high incidence of colleges and universities at lower levels of the hierarchy where programs of research and teaching are frequently geared to local conditions.

Table 7.5 displays similar information for the service underclass. Service underclass occupations with top scores on the index of representation in

Table 7.5   *Service underclass occupations: ten top-scoring occupations on indexes of representation for levels 1 and 5 of the US metropolitan hierarchy (2000)*

Hierar-chical level	Census occupa-tional code	Description	Index of represen-tation
1	914	Taxi Drivers and Chauffeurs	1.76
1	442	Ushers, Lobby Attendants, and Ticket-Takers	1.55
1	964	Packers and Packagers, Hand	1.39
1	935	Parking Lot Attendants	1.38
1	452	Miscellaneous Personal Appearance Workers	1.34
1	254	Teacher Assistants	1.17
1	422	Janitors and Building Cleaners	1.09
1	915	Miscellaneous Motor Vehicle Operators, including Ambulance Drivers and Attendants	1.06
1	423	Maids and Housekeeping Cleaners	1.04
1	540	Receptionists and Information Clerks	1.04
5	785	Food Cooking Machine Operators and Tenders	1.46
5	414	Dishwashers	1.46
5	530	Hotel, Motel, and Resort Desk Clerks	1.39
5	441	Motion Picture Projectionists	1.36
5	395	Lifeguards and other Protective Service Workers	1.32
5	405	Combined Food Preparation and Serving Workers, including Fast Food	1.29
5	402	Cooks	1.25
5	461	Personal and Home-Care Aides	1.22
5	411	Waiters and Waitresses	1.21
5	435	Nonfarm Animal Caretakers	1.20

Notes: Level 1 of the hierarchy is defined as all metropolitan areas with populations greater than 5 000 000; level 5 comprises all metropolitan areas with populations less than 250 000 (see Table 7.3). See text for the definition of the index of representation.

Source: United States Census (2000), via IPUMS-USA.

tier 1 of the metropolitan hierarchy can be generally divided into two main sub-groups, though with some overlap between them. On the one hand, a distinctive sub-group of workers can be discerned on the basis of the roles they play in the physical maintenance of urban functions (taxi drivers and chauffeurs; packers and packagers; parking lot attendants; janitors and building cleaners). On the other hand, we can distinguish another sub-group of occupations whose functions are mainly oriented to personal services of various kinds (ushers, lobby attendants, and ticket takers; miscellaneous personal appearance workers;[4] teacher assistants; maids; and receptionists). These two sub-groups represent an echo of the bipartite division of service underclass workers that was proposed earlier in this chapter. In tier 5 of the metropolitan hierarchy, the main service underclass occupations revolve in significant degree around restaurant and hospitality functions (food cooking machine operators; dishwashers; hotel, motel, and resort desk clerks; combined food preparation and serving workers; cooks; and waiters and waitresses). These occupations are typical of small-town economies where much service activity is dedicated to providing for the needs of transitory visitors as well as the population of surrounding rural areas. Other service underclass occupations with a relatively high incidence in tier 5 of the hierarchy are motion picture projectionists; lifeguards; personal and home-care aides; and nonfarm animal caretakers.

Two main points of summary follow from all of this. First, from an occupational point of view, the very largest metropolitan areas of the United States are markedly distinctive in comparison with the other metropolitan areas in the country. These are not only the places where the cognitive–cultural economy, as such, has insistently taken root and generated a wide variety of symbolic analyst occupations, but also where a large cohort of service underclass workers can be found with a central focus on urban maintenance and personal support. Second, as we move down the tiers of the hierarchy, the nature of symbolic analyst occupations changes dramatically. They become less and less involved in sectors like software, financial services, or cultural production and increasingly concerned with technical expertise in support of more traditional local industries, though exceptions to this generalization no doubt occur in small towns that have important educational, touristic, and cultural functions. In addition, the service underclass in smaller metropolitan areas seems to be more related to the role these places play as way-stations and to a lesser extent as centers of demand for basic restaurant and cafeteria services.

GENDER, RACE, ETHNICITY, AND NATIVITY DIFFERENTIALS

Demographic Differentials by Occupation

One of the common elements of employment systems in all varieties of capitalism is the way in which divisions of labor can be identified not only

Table 7.6 Symbolic analysts: highly represented demographic groups, by occupation (2000)

Females	Percent	African-Americans	Percent	Hispanics	Percent	Asians	Percent	Foreign-born	Percent
323. Speech–Language Pathologists	94.8	202. Miscellaneous Community and Social Service Specialists	24.9	202. Miscellaneous Community and Social Service Specialists	12.9	326. Health Diagnosing and Treating Practitioners, all other	32.5	176. Physical Scientists, all other	40.1
313. Registered Nurses	92.6	201. Social Workers	23.2	201. Social Workers	10.1	176. Physical Scientists, all other	24.4	326. Health Diagnosing and Treating Practitioners, all other	39.6
315. Occupational Therapists	91.0	200. Counselors	21.0	311. Physician Assistants	9.5	102. Computer Software Engineers	21.3	180. Economists	30.7

303. Dietitians and Nutritionists	90.0	303. Dietitians and Nutritionists	17.6	200. Counselors	9.4	140. Computer Hardware Engineers	19.1	102. Computer Software Engineers	30.3
233. Special Education Teachers	87.1	42. Social and Community Service Managers	14.9	303. Dietitians and Nutritionists	8.0	191. Biological Technicians	16.4	306. Physicians and Surgeons	28.4

Notes: The table shows the five occupations in which females, African-Americans, Hispanics, Asians and the foreign-born, respectively, are most highly represented in terms of their percentage incidence. All data refer to the standard set of 283 metropolitan areas.

Source: United States Census (2000), via IPUMS-USA.

in terms of occupation, sector, and skill, but also by the demographic characteristics of the labor-force. Thus, it has long been recognized that women, both highly qualified and less highly qualified, are apt to be stereotyped by concentration in services that entail emotional work such as health support and child care occupations (Hochschild 1989). Many kinds of occupations that involve a human interface are also highly feminized, like personnel officers, hotel clerks, restaurant servers, retail sales workers, and manicurists (Dyer, McDowell, and Barnitzky 2008; Kang 2003; McDowell 2009). Highly qualified male workers are apt to be dominant in occupations like management, finance, science, and engineering. By contrast, males in service underclass occupations, are typically concentrated in jobs that entail mechanical equipment operation, dirty and noisy environments, muscular exertion, and the like. Illustrative jobs in this category include building maintenance, gardening, painting, and service station activities (Cranford 2005; Ramirez and Hondagneu-Sotelo 2009). When women are a majority in physically challenging service occupations, these usually concern domestic or care-giving activities like housecleaning, bedmaking, and caring for the sick and the infirm.

Tables 7.6 and 7.7 help to underline these remarks about the division of labor in the new American economy by revealing not only how gender, but also race, ethnicity, and nativity are articulated with symbolic analyst and service underclass occupations. Table 7.6 shows how a number of significant demographic groups in American society (that is, females, African-Americans, Hispanics, Asians, and the foreign-born) are distributed over symbolic analyst occupations; and Table 7.7 lays out analogous data for service underclass occupations. Observe that with the exception of African-Americans and Asians these groups are not necessarily mutually exclusive. The five top-scoring occupations (in terms of their percentage incidence in the United States as a whole) are shown for each group.

Among symbolic analysts (Table 7.6), female workers clearly dominate in health and education-related work involving occupations such as registered nurses, occupational therapists, dieticians, and special education teachers. African-Americans are well represented in symbolic analyst occupations related to employment in public institutions. The occupations at issue in this instance are, for example, community and social service specialists, social workers, and counselors, no doubt reflecting the circumstance that the relevant institutional employers are strongly oriented to serving the African-American community. Hispanics are poorly represented throughout the spectrum of symbolic analysts, even when we look only at the five top-scoring occupations for this ethnic group; but they are deployed in occupational categories that run more or less parallel to those characteristic of African-Americans. The top-scoring occupations for

Asian symbolic analysts are all in the fields of medicine, physical science, and engineering, an observation that testifies to the generally high level of formal qualification of this fraction of the labor force in American cities. Top-scoring foreign-born symbolic analysts are similarly concentrated in medicine, physical science, and engineering.

Among service underclass workers (Table 7.7) females are in an overwhelming majority in occupations like child-care workers, receptionists, teacher assistants, and personal appearance workers. African-Americans are well represented as barbers, telemarketers, food-servers, maids, and personal/home-care aides. Hispanics in service underclass work are conspicuously present as hand-packers and packagers, maids and housekeeping cleaners, helpers in maintenance and construction trades, and grounds and maintenance workers – that is, in occupations that are for the most part not only low prestige but that also often entail physical and practical work of a rather arduous and disagreeable kind. Asians have an exceptionally strong incidence in miscellaneous personal appearance occupations where they represent 35.1 percent of all workers. The latter kind of activity represents a niche in which Asians seem to have established a definite presence as small entrepreneurs (that is, in beauty salons, nail parlors, hairdressing establishments, and so on). Service underclass Asians, too, are relatively well represented as taxi drivers, food-cooking machine operators, hotel and motel desk clerks, and library technicians. The most highly represented occupations among foreign-born service underclass workers constitute an amalgam that, as we might expect, is quite characteristic of Hispanics and Asians.

These brief comments indicate that both symbolic analyst and service underclass occupations are significantly differentiated according to the demographic characteristics of the individuals who comprise them. The male/female occupational divide is especially prominent in the cases of both symbolic analysts and the service underclass, and, of course, the same divide also finds echoes in occupations in which African-Americans, Hispanics, Asians, and the foreign-born are prominently represented. For symbolic analysts, the other noteworthy demographic feature is the high concentration of well-qualified immigrants (especially Asians) in technically-oriented occupations. For the service underclass, racial and ethnic differentiation of occupations is quite pronounced, and in all probability, community-based job recruitment networks, as well as social discrimination, account in large degree for the observed occupational differences between African-Americans, Hispanics, and Asians (with the latter two groups making up much of the foreign-born category) (Anderson 1974; Fernandez and Fernandez-Mateo 2006; Sanders, Nee, and Sernau 2002). What these different demographic groups within the

Table 7.7 Service underclass: highly represented demographic groups, by occupation (2000)

Females	Percent	African-Americans	Percent	Hispanics	Percent	Asians	Percent	Foreign-born	Percent
460. Child Care Workers	94.3	450. Barbers	28.9	964. Packers and Packagers, Hand	39.8	452. Miscellaneous Personal Appearance Workers	35.1	452. Miscellaneous Personal Appearance Workers	46.5
540. Receptionists and Information Clerks	92.5	494. Telemarketers	26.2	423. Maids and Housekeeping Cleaners	34.9	914. Taxi Drivers and Chauffeurs	9.4	914. Taxi Drivers and Chauffeurs	41.2
254. Teacher Assistants	90.8	412. Food Servers, Nonrestaurant	25.6	761. Helpers –Installation, Maintenance, and Repair Workers	34.0	785. Food Cooking Machine Operators and Tenders	8.9	423. Maids and Housekeeping Cleaners	40.3

451. Hairdressers, Hairstylists, and Cosmetologists	89.3	423. Maids and Housekeeping Cleaners	23.7	660. Helpers, Construction Trades	34.0	530. Hotel, Motel, and Resort Desk Clerks	7.5	964. Packers and Packagers, Hand	38.6
452. Miscellaneous Personal Appearance Workers	89.1	461. Personal and Home Care Aides	23.6	425. Grounds Maintenance Workers	33.8	244. Library Technicians	6.5	785. Food Cooking Machine Operators and Tenders	32.9

Notes: The table shows the five occupations in which females, African-Americans, Hispanics, Asians and the foreign-born, respectively, are most highly represented in terms of their percentage incidence. All data refer to the standard set of 283 metropolitan areas.

Source: United States Census (2000), via IPUMS-USA.

Table 7.8   Symbolic analysts in the American metropolitan hierarchy:
*   percentage incidence of workers by gender, race, ethnicity, and*
*   nativity (2000)*

Metropolitan size class	Female percent	African-American percent	Hispanic percent	Asian percent	Foreign-born percent
1	52.7	10.8	7.4	11.0	22.3
2	52.5	8.9	5.3	7.0	14.5
3	54.8	7.4	5.6	4.9	8.3
4	54.5	6.7	3.7	3.3	8.4
5	55.4	5.3	3.9	2.9	7.2
All metropolitan areas	53.3	8.6	5.5	6.9	14.3

Source: United States Census, via IPUMS-USA.

service underclass in American cities have in common is that they all contain significant complements of politically-marginal individuals who are thus susceptible to various forms of exploitation in the workplace, including their subjection to inferior working conditions and low levels of remuneration.

Demographic Differentials by Hierarchical Level

As revealing as the information presented in Tables 7.6 and 7.7 may be, we can extract yet further insights into the data by now recoding our main demographic variables according to their incidence in different tiers of the metropolitan hierarchy. The results of this exercise are laid out in Tables 7.8 and 7.9 for symbolic analysts and the service underclass, respectively.

Table 7.8 indicates that in the case of symbolic analysts, the incidence of female workers increases as we move from larger to smaller metropolitan areas, which reflects the traditional dominance of males in the high-order cognitive and cultural occupations that prevail in large cities. However, the incidence of African-American, Hispanic, Asian and foreign-born symbolic analysts is positively related to urban size, for these kinds of workers presumably face a number of barriers (for example, diminished job-recruitment networks, the absence of relevant social communities, a higher degree of discrimination) in small town labor markets.

Table 7.9 shows that in each of the five tiers of the hierarchy, all of our demographic categories (with the exception of Asians) are much

Table 7.9   *The service underclass in the American metropolitan hierarchy: percentage incidence of workers by gender, race, ethnicity, and nativity (2000)*

Metropolitan size class	Female percent	African-American percent	Hispanic percent	Asian percent	Foreign-born percent
1	57.6	16.5	32.7	7.0	37.6
2	60.5	16.4	18.3	4.8	20.7
3	62.4	14.8	14.9	4.7	12.0
4	62.3	13.9	11.3	2.3	10.7
5	63.2	12.4	10.6	1.9	8.2
All metropolitan areas	60.7	15.5	19.3	4.7	20.8

Source: United States Census, via IPUMS-USA.

more highly represented in the service underclass than they are in the symbolic analyst category. This state of affairs is suggestive once more of the intimate connection that exists between low-wage, relatively casual forms of employment and marginalized minorities in American labor markets, above all in the largest metropolitan areas where many undocumented immigrants are concentrated (Fortuny et al. 2007). Once more, the incidence of female service underclass workers is inversely related to metropolitan size, and the incidence of African-Americans, Hispanics, Asians and the foreign-born declines as we move down the metropolitan hierarchy.

FROM THE DIVISION OF LABOR TO SOCIAL STRATIFICATION

In both this and the previous chapter, I have shown that the two major groups of occupations designated here as symbolic analysts and the service underclass have grown strongly, relative to overall population growth in American metropolitan areas over the last decade. The many changes in the standard occupational classification prohibit the compilation of a consistent statistical record for these two groups for years prior to 2000, but rough approximations indicate that the types of work entailed by these occupations have been growing significantly, both in absolute and relative terms for a number of decades (see also Autor et al. 2006; Autor et al. 2003;

Levy and Murnane 2004). As the numbers of symbolic analysts and service underclass workers in American metropolitan areas have expanded, corresponding changes in the main outlines of urban social stratification have occurred, and these changes have been reinforced by the decline of manufacturing employment in large cities and the consequent elimination of many traditional white-collar and blue-collar jobs. Symbolic analysts and service underclass workers are to be found all across the urban hierarchy of the United States, but there are significant quantitative and qualitative variations in their occurrence as a function of city size. In particular, the largest metropolitan areas of the United States have the highest incidence of symbolic analysts, but are at the same time marked by large complements of service underclass workers with very low levels of formal skills, and hence these cities are notably segmented in their socio-economic structure. In large cities, workers in service underclass occupations are especially marginal with respect to American society as a whole, as indicated not only by their poverty-level incomes but also by the high representation of subaltern social groups among them. The jobs performed by these service underclass workers are strongly oriented to the functions of sustaining the facilities and infrastructure of the urban system, and to supporting the domestic and personal needs of the urban citizenry at large. In the end, this remark implies that service underclass work is especially (though by no means exclusively) geared to serving the direct and indirect demands of the upper echelon of workers in the cognitive–cultural economy. Crucially, in view of the important but deeply disadvantaged position of service underclass workers in the modern American economy and their entrapment in deteriorated labor market conditions where in general wages are low, work conditions inferior, benefits non-existent, job security minimal, hours irregular, and future prospects strictly limited, we need clearly to identify them as a significant and distinctive fraction of urban society. Their social situation and growing numbers suggest (with apologies to Hayek 1944) that a new road to serfdom has opened up in American cities. Accordingly, an alternative and perhaps even more descriptive term for the service underclass is the *new servile class*.

The origins of this class, like the origins of symbolic analysts, can best be understood in relation to the new division of labor that has come into being over these last few decades as the cognitive–cultural economy has risen to the fore and taken root above all in major metropolitan areas. In contrast to the elite labor-force of contemporary America whose work is posited on its command of technical knowledge, analytical prowess, and cultural sophistication, the assets of service underclass workers reside largely in their muscles and sinews and their capacities for everyday empathy and contact in dealing with others. It would be a grave mistake, however, to suppose that the work of this class is devoid of cognitive–cultural skills. On the contrary, consider the kinds of discretionary decisions that must be made continually by janitors, motor-vehicle operators, and crossing guards; or the communicative capacities that must be mobilized by child-care workers, home-health aides, beauty salon personnel, and so on. Even though they occupy subordinate positions in urban labor markets, these workers habitually face real challenges as they go about their daily tasks. In spite of this subordination, there is evidence of rising political militancy among certain fractions of the service underclass, as exemplified in dramatic terms by the Bus Riders Union and the Janitors for Justice campaign in Los Angeles (Milkman 2006; Soja 2010). Yet another example can be found in the recent rapid growth of community-based workers' centers across the United States, offering help to low-wage and especially immigrant workers in their quest for improved wages and working conditions (Fine 2005). These are hopeful signs, though the dynamics that I have tried to capture in this discussion suggest that even more massive and organized political forces will be necessary if significant incursions on the status quo are to be made. Moreover, analogous and even more extreme situations of the sort described here are now clearly proliferating in large metropolitan areas in many less economically advanced areas of the world.

NOTES

1. http://usa.ipums.org/usa/
2. That is, 49.6 percent greater in the case of weeks worked, and 12.6 percent greater in the case of usual hours of work per week. For the record, the annual median wage and salary level for the symbolic analyst group was US \$37 800 and for the service underclass it was US \$6100 according to the 2000 US census.
3. More formally, the index of representation for occupation j in level k of the metropolitan hierarchy is given by the expression $I_{jk} = (e_{jk}/\Sigma_j e_{jk})/(\Sigma_k e_{jk}/\Sigma_j \Sigma_k e_{jk})$, where e_{jk} is employment in occupation j in level k of the hierarchy.
4. Personal appearance workers are mainly composed of manicurists, shampooers, and skincare specialists.

8. Social milieu and built form of the city

Over the course of the 20th century and into the first decade of the 21st, capitalism has evolved from a plurinational base, coinciding principally with the country-based economies of North America and Western Europe, into a steadily integrating, if still quite unfinished, global system. Over this same extended period of time, increasing numbers of cities around the world have been brought within the ambit of the capitalist system and hence have been at least partially remade in its image. To be sure, as Kloosterman (2010) and others have suggested, individual cities are always unique in certain ways, and we should resist the temptation to describe them as though everything about them was cloned from a standard set of genetic instructions. This remark applies with special force, no doubt, to the social geography of the city where particular kinds of cultural logics with strong local-cum-national inflections are almost always in play at different times in different parts of the world. Even so, we can certainly talk in meaningful general terms about certain forms of intra-urban space specific to the fordist capitalism of North America and Western Europe in the 20th century, and I shall argue that we can talk in equally meaningful terms about intra-urban space in a widening circle of cities that lie under the sway of a globalizing cognitive–cultural capitalism in the 21st century. In what follows, I seek to identify some of these terms in an argument that lays particular stress on the dynamics of residential space and built form, starting with a brief scene-setting view of how these aspects of city life were resolved in the era of fordist capitalism.

INTERNAL STRUCTURE OF THE FORDIST CITY

By the early part of the 20th century, American industrialists were starting to adopt the large-scale mass production methods and the associated labor relations systems that Gramsci in the prison notebooks of the 1930s dubbed "fordism" (Gramsci 1975), a term later enthusiastically appropriated by French regulationist economists like Aglietta (1976), Boyer (1986) and Lipietz (1986) as a general descriptor of the regime of accumulation that prevailed over the greater part of the century. Fordist capitalism and its various appendages were, in turn, the driving force behind the growth of the great metropolitan areas of the US Manufacturing Belt and corresponding regions of Western Europe from the 1910s to the mid-1970s.

Among the many urban areas that flourished in America's Manufacturing Belt in the early 20th century, Chicago – at that time the second-largest city in the United States – was certainly one of the most advanced in terms of its embrace of the new economic ethos and its expressions in the social space and built form of the city. Chicago's economic base revolved around large-scale manufacturing sectors like iron and steel, electrical machinery, agricultural equipment, and meat-packing. In 1900, its population was already 1.7 million, and by 1930, this had grown remarkably to as many as 3.4 million. The rapid social change and associated turbulence that accompanied this period of Chicago's growth sparked the interest of a number of scholars at the University of Chicago who constituted the so-called Chicago School of Urban Sociology. Among the many statements published by these scholars, one of the most influential was the generalized description of Chicago – "The City" – by Park, Burgess and McKenzie (1925). The schematized map of Chicago drawn up by these scholars represents the first attempt to provide an overall codification of the social space of the capitalist city, notwithstanding various anticipations of this accomplishment, such as the study of Manchester by Engels (1845 [1950]) or the strictures of Simmel (1903 [1950]) on European city life. Curiously, the Chicago School theorists refrained from any attempt to relate social patterns in Chicago to the underlying dynamic of industrialization. Instead, they sought to explain intra-urban spatial patterns by invoking a now discredited social Darwinism, in which the geographic location and character of residential neighborhoods were seen as resulting from struggles among differentially endowed social groups for living space in the wider milieu of the city, which, in its turn, was conceived as an essentially biotic organism. In spite of its questionable theoretical underpinnings, the descriptive model of urban social space delineated by Park, Burgess and McKenzie provides important and useful insights about the internal structure of the then emerging fordist metropolis. The interest of this model for our purposes is in its depiction of the internal space of the city as comprising a series of concentric zones successively comprising (from the center outward) a central business district, a factory zone, a zone of working class residential areas (partly broken up into ethnically- and racially-distinctive neighborhoods), and an outer zone of suburban development. There is more to the model than is suggested by this bare summary, but it nonetheless represents a broadly plausible diagram of the social space of the North American fordist city, at least in its earlier stages; and it provides a descriptive baseline from which we can begin to trace out a subsequent evolutionary trajectory.

Various attempts were made by other researchers in the 1930s and 1940s to improve on the Chicago School model by offering alternative formal diagrams but little in the way of further conceptual elaboration or correction (see, for example, Harris and Ullman 1945; Hoyt 1939). In terms of the theoretical ideas presented in this book, we might say that the internal space of Chicago in the 1920s was actually a reflection of the social dynamics of the early fordist metropolis. Thus, the residences of blue-collar workers were concentrated around the city center where accessibility to appropriate employment centers was high, and where, despite the elevated price of land, the high density of settlement resulted in relatively low per-capita rent payments. White-collar workers lived further out from the city center and at correspondingly lower density where they could achieve forms of family life to which they were normatively attuned, and large segments of this social fraction commuted to jobs located in the inner city. These jobs included not only managerial, technical, and clerical work in manufacturing plants but also work in the corporate headquarters, financial institutions, and adjunct office functions of fordist capitalism. This, at least, was the dominant pattern in the large industrial cities of the United States and Britain. In France and other parts of Europe, where industrial growth often occurred in a series of locational accretions around the edges of old historic centers, the spatial pattern typical of the American fordist metropolis was significantly inverted. Thus, despite the existence of persistent blue-collar neighborhoods in the central areas of European cities throughout the 20th century, much of this segment of the labor force was, from the start, pushed out into suburban enclaves, while white-collar segments tended to dominate in more prestigious central areas.

After the Second World War, blue-collar suburban communities began to make a more forceful appearance in American cities too. By the late 1940s, manufacturing plants were moving in increasing numbers away from the central areas of large industrial cities and relocating in the urban fringe so as to take advantage of cheaper land and less congested surface traffic. This trend accelerated greatly over the 1950s and 1960s, though with the continued passage of time industrial decentralization steadily bypassed the suburbs in favor of more distant locations in national and international peripheries. At the outset, the shift of blue-collar employment from central to suburban locations was accompanied by so-called "reverse commuting," as workers living in central city neighborhoods now travelled from the center to suburban employment places. Subsequently, as central cities lost more and more manufacturing jobs to urban fringe areas, blue-collar workers increasingly set up residence in suburban neighborhoods, a process that was much intensified by the displacement caused by the urban renewal programs of the 1950s and 1960s (Kain 1968). African-Americans represented a notable exception to this general trend for they remained largely concentrated in the central ghettoes of large cities, and, as a result of various discriminatory practices in housing and employment markets, were in significant ways hampered from moving into suburban areas (Holzer 1994; Kain 1992; Stoll 1999).

Among the more vibrant elements of large American cities were the central business districts that were growing apace by the early decades of the 20th century, partly as a consequence of the increasing physical detachment of high-level corporate functions from actual manufacturing operations and their reconstitution – along with allied business and financial activities – at the urban core. The accelerating growth of these areas was manifest in the recurrent intensification of central land uses and continually rising skylines expressing in part an evolving modernist aesthetic of urban space. Land use intensification itself can be ascribed in general to the search for augmented Ricardian rent by means of an increase in floor space (and/or gross product per unit of land area) (Nowlan 1977; Scott 1980). Any such increase will exert a multiplier effect on existing levels of rent, which means in turn that the most insistent forms of land use intensification will occur at sites where rent is already high (see the appendix to this chapter for elucidation of these points). Accordingly, unusually dense concentrations of floor space are always to be found at central city locations and at other points where local peaks of land rent occur. Properties at these sites are subject to periodic reconstruction as latent increments to land rent start to outweigh the costs of redevelopment. The same properties are frequently decked out in avant-garde architectural gestures both because design elaboration is cost-effective in these circumstances and because it yields valuable symbolic capital to the owners and users of specific buildings. At the end of the 19th century and the beginning of the 20th, Chicago and New York were in the vanguard of this type of development, notably in the case of Chicago's Loop where the pioneering functionalist architecture of Burnham, Richardson, Sullivan, and others, was achieving iconic status (Condit 1964). Eventually, this proto-modernism gave way to the full-blown modernist architecture – whose spirit is captured in the idea that less is always more – that came to dominate the central business districts of large American metropolitan areas in the 20th century (Cuthbert 2006).

The internal spaces of these metropolitan areas were thus in many different ways subject to a powerful socio-economic logic whose underlying character can best be grasped in the wider context of fordist capitalism and its diverse implications for the organization of productive labor and patterns of daily life. As the discussion now moves forward to embrace the 21st century, we shall observe a replay of many broadly similar kinds of outcomes, but in a key that is more attuned to the pressures and demands of urban life in cognitive–cultural capitalism.

SOCIO-SPATIAL DYNAMICS IN THE CITY AFTER FORDISM

A Brief Excursion around Los Angeles

A distinctive LA School of urban studies, explicitly in opposition to the Chicago School, took wing in the early 1980s. Much of the early work – or what we might refer to as phase 1 – of the LA School was focused on the *post*fordist elements of the urban economy, and unlike the Chicago School, was concerned to show that the social space of the city was not an outcome of a darwinian struggle for survival in a system of biotic forces but was at least in part related to underlying workplace and local labor market dynamics in an increasingly flexibilizing, re-agglomerating and re-urbanizing production system (Soja and Scott 1986; Scott and Soja 1996). The work of the LA School was also deeply concerned with rising levels of inequality and social marginalization in the city, and in this regard it drew heavily on work by earlier radical urban theorists like Castells (1972), Harvey (1973) and Lefebvre (1970). The writings of Mike Davis, who hovered around the margins of the LA School, added a certain aura of quixotic pessimism to the School's vision of urban life (see, in particular, Davis 1990). At the same time, the seminal ideas of Jameson (1984), with their ironic promotion of the Bonaventure Hotel as an architectural icon helped to foster an emerging view of Los Angeles as a focus of new postmodern cultural sensibilities.[1] Jameson's reflections encouraged further rounds of research on postmodern urbanism (Soja 1989), leading eventually to phase 2 of the School's work. This second phase is represented partly by the continued ruminations of Soja (1996; 2000), but above all by the publications of Dear, who pushed the theoretical advocacies of the School away from their earlier *marxisant* tendencies and into directions that seemed increasingly to dissolve the city into a kaleidoscope of purely idiosyncratic visions (see, for example, Dear 2000 and Dear and Flusty 1998).

   Much of the notoriety of the LA School revolved around its claim that Los Angeles was an anticipatory and paradigmatic instance of a new model of urban development. This claim was certainly an exaggeration, but it can perhaps be understood in the light of the intellectual climate of the late 1970s and early 1980s, and the failures of Chicago School theory in the

Table 8.1   Los Angeles–Long Beach Metropolitan Area, employment in selected occupational categories (2000–2010)

	2000	2010	Percent change
Symbolic analysts	1 440 413	1 636 752	13.6
Low-wage service-oriented workers	1 491 598	1 711 190	14.7
Production workers	706 354	490 311	−30.6
All other occupations	3 475 298	3 674 035	5.7
Total	7 113 663	7 512 288	5.6

Note: Symbolic analysts and low-wage service-oriented workers are defined as in Chapter 7.

Source: United States Census, via IPUMS-USA.

face of the changing realities of the city in North America and Western Europe at that time. These failures became increasingly obvious as a new urbanism started to appear in response to the decisive turn to postfordism in advanced capitalist societies within a globalizing neoliberal political environment. Along with this turn came important transformations of the occupational structure of many different metropolitan areas, as marked above all by the rising importance of symbolic analysts and low-wage service-oriented workers in the urban economy. To come back to the specific case of the Los Angeles–Long Beach metropolitan area these two fractions, as identified in Chapter 7, now constitute 44.6 percent of the local labor force. We must bear in mind that the detailed occupational definitions of symbolic analysts and low-wage service-oriented workers used here are very tightly circumscribed, so that the 44.6 percent statistic assuredly understates the actual incidence of these broad types of employment in the Los Angeles economy. Employment of symbolic analysts and low-wage service-oriented workers continues to grow in the Los Angeles–Long Beach metropolitan area. As shown in Table 8.1, the number of workers in these two occupational groupings expanded significantly between 2000 and 2010, while production worker employment declined by as much as 30.6 percent.

We now need to examine how these changes manifest themselves in the social space of the contemporary city, and we continue again with examples drawn from the case of Los Angeles. An obvious first approach in this regard is simply to map out the residential locations of symbolic analysts and low-wage service-oriented workers. Unfortunately, this task is vitiated to some degree by the very limited availability of published statistics on numbers of individuals in detailed occupational categories for small

geographic areas, and so it is not possible to examine the residential locations of symbolic analysts and low-wage service-oriented workers on the
basis of the precisely defined categories given earlier. That said, broadly
relevant data can be assembled for this purpose by means of two proxy
variables. We will approximate the symbolic analyst fraction by combining eight two-digit occupations in the standard occupational classification – that is, management occupations; business and financial operations
occupations; computer and mathematical occupations; architecture and
engineering occupations; life, physical, and social science occupations;
legal occupations; arts, design, entertainment, sports, and media occupations; and healthcare practitioner and technical occupations. In the
Los Angeles–Long Beach metropolitan area in the year 2000, there were
2.2 million workers in these occupations (compared with the 1.4 million
symbolic analysts noted in Table 8.1). The low-wage service-oriented fraction is approximated by combining three two-digit occupations – that is,
food preparation and serving related occupations; building and grounds
cleaning and maintenance occupations; and personal care and service
occupations. In the Los Angeles–Long Beach metropolitan area in 2000
there were 0.9 million workers in these occupations (compared with the
1.5 million low-wage service-oriented workers noted in Table 8.1). Maps
of the relative incidence of these occupational groupings in Los Angeles
are presented in Figures 8.1 and 8.2. For comparative purposes, a map
of the relative incidence of production workers in the residential space of
Los Angeles is also given in Figure 8.3. At first glance, the socio-spatial
patterns portrayed in Figures 8.1, 8.2, and 8.3 do not seem to differ unduly
from those that we might expect to observe in the typical late fordist city,
though as the discussion proceeds, we will note a number of significant
divergences. Three immediate descriptive comments can be offered.

First, and unsurprisingly, the proxy variable for symbolic analysts traces
out a pattern of residential activity coinciding with the most environmen-
tally-favored parts of the metropolitan area (Figure 8.1). A major axis of
settlement of this group of workers stretches from northwest to southeast
along the Pacific coast through a series of affluent beach communities.
A second axis can be detected running from Santa Monica and Beverly
Hills in the west through the Hollywood Hills to Pasadena in the east.
Extensions of the central part of this second axis into areas around downtown Los Angeles represent a widening front of gentrification in the city.

Second, the proxy for low-wage service-oriented workers reveals a
pattern of settlement that is relatively spread out, but with notable concentrations surrounding major business and commercial locations in Los
Angeles, Burbank–Glendale, Long Beach and Orange County (Figure
8.2). These concentrations contain large ethnic immigrant communities

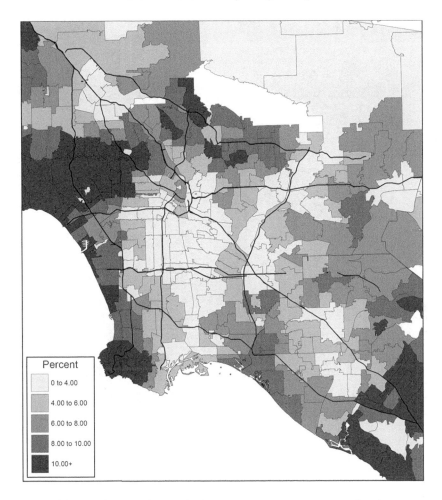

Notes: The map shows employment in these occupations as a percentage of total population by zip code in the year 2000. Main freeways are shown. Data are missing for land areas left blank.

Source: US Census (2000).

Figure 8.1 *Los Angeles and Orange Counties: residential distribution of workers in management occupations; business and financial operations occupations; computer and mathematical occupations; architecture and engineering occupations; life, physical, and social science occupations; legal occupations; arts, design, entertainment, sports, and media occupations; and healthcare practitioner and technical occupations*

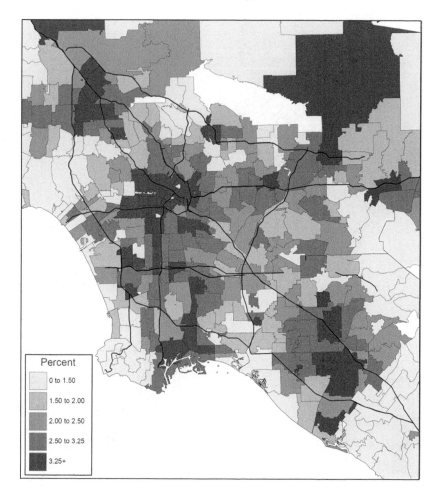

Notes: The map shows employment in these occupations as a percentage of total
population by zip code in the year 2000. Main freeways are shown. Data are missing for
land areas left blank.

Source: US Census (2000).

*Figure 8.2   Los Angeles and Orange Counties: residential distribution of
              workers in food preparation and serving related occupations;
              building and grounds cleaning and maintenance occupations;
              and personal care and service occupations*

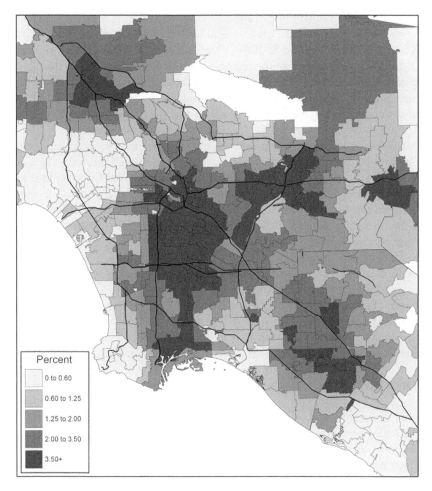

Notes: The map shows production workers as a percentage of total population by zip code in the year 2000. Main freeways are shown. Data are missing for land areas left blank.

Source: US Census (2000).

Figure 8.3   Los Angeles and Orange Counties: residential distribution of workers in production worker occupations

(especially Asians and Hispanics) together with a number of African-American neighborhoods. Residents of these areas have relatively ready access to downtown locations where many of them are employed, as well as access to affluent neighborhoods providing work in domestic and maintenance activities.

Third, despite continuing declines in manufacturing in the Los Angeles–Long Beach metropolitan area, a significant concentration of production workers is to be found in South-Central Los Angeles (Figure 8.3), an area that overlaps with some of the region's main remaining industrial districts, many of which are dominated by sweatshop activities in clothing, furniture, jewelry, and allied industries. Secondary concentrations of production workers also occur in fringe areas of the metropolis especially in and around the technopoles whose locations are shown in Figure 5.3.

As we might expect – since low-wage service-oriented workers and production workers share many common socio-economic features – there is a degree of overlap in the residential patterns of these two groups, but far from an unqualified correspondence. The simple correlation coefficient between the two patterns (using zip code areas as observational units) is in fact a rather modest 0.26 (with $n = 670$). Residential patterns of low-wage service-oriented workers and production workers are negatively and significantly correlated with those of symbolic analysts. These observed patterns are consistent with the idea that residential neighborhoods in the city are differentiated not only by social identity, as in Chicago School theory, but also, and certainly in the case of low-wage workers, by access to relevant workplaces. Obviously, the discussion above is far from being conclusive on this point, but it is in line with other and more rigorous analyses presented by Ellis et al. (2007) and Wright et al. (2010).

The Widening Social Divide and its Urban Expressions

This discussion of Los Angeles helps to identify some of the features of the social space of the city in 21st century capitalism, but it does not yet pinpoint all of the major mechanisms underlying the observed trends. One such mechanism has already been alluded to at frequent intervals, namely the steady drain of manufacturing jobs from metropolitan areas in the advanced capitalist societies to cheap labor countries in the world periphery, leading to the concomitant shrinkage of production work in the former areas. In spite of these declines, the creation of low-wage service jobs more than keeps pace with losses in manufacturing, and this in turn helps to maintain a steady stream of immigrants from less developed countries into the large metropolitan areas in the United States and other advanced capitalist countries. Of course, the Chicago School of Urbanism was already strongly focused on the question of immigration and its effects on the social space of the city. In the first half of the 20th century, immigrants into the large cities of the United States consisted principally of people from Southern and Eastern Europe together with a large number of African-Americans moving from agricultural occupations in the Old South to jobs in the Manufacturing Belt. Nowadays, low-income immigrants into American cities originate from a far greater diversity of locations than was the case a century ago, for they come from virtually everywhere in the Global South, above all from countries in East and Southeast Asia, Central and South America, and the Caribbean. Even many large metropolitan areas outside the traditional core capitalist countries are now subject to massive flows of immigrants from places with yet lower average wage levels. These trends are leading to new and intensified political predicaments in many different cities, as discussed later in Chapter 10. At the same time, the upward spiral of low-wage immigration into American metropolitan areas is intertwined with the deeply-seated technological and political changes that have occurred since the demise of fordism, and has almost certainly helped to intensify concomitant polarization of intra-urban income levels. This kind of polarization is well illustrated again by the case of the Los Angeles–Long Beach metropolitan area, where in the year 2000, the median wage and salary income of symbolic analysts was almost six times greater than the median wage and salary income of low-wage service-oriented workers (both groups defined as in Chapter 7), and by 2010 the ratio had increased to a value of almost seven. Observe that these ratios – large as they may be – are computed with respect to median values only and thus do not reflect the extreme differences that occur if we look only at the tails of the relevant income distributions.

One of the most pronounced shifts in the character of intra-metropolitan social space over the last few decades has been the steadily mounting movement of members of the upper tier of the labor force into residential areas in the inner city that were formerly given over to blue-collar housing and workplaces. The term "gentrification," now widely used to describe this process, was originally coined in the 1960s by Glass (1964) who had observed significant social transformation of a number of poor neighborhoods in central London (for example, Islington, Paddington, North Kensington) as a result of upper middle-class individuals moving in and upgrading the local housing stock. In the fordist era, much of the white-collar fraction was concentrated in suburban neighborhoods (though durable high-income residential enclaves could always be found in major metropolitan areas like New York or London), but already in the later years of fordism gentrification was starting to occur in many large cities. Today, gentrification is pervasive in much of North America and Western Europe and has spread to numerous other parts of the globe as well. The term is often used in a broadened sense to designate not only upgrading of former working-class neighborhoods in central city areas, but also the regeneration of industrial and commercial land uses. For the purposes of clarity, I shall restrict my use of the term here to mean specifically the conversion of low income housing in order to provide housing for upper-tier workers, and I will deal with the regeneration of industrial and commercial land uses in the city under another rubric (see next section of this chapter). I shall argue that the wider unfolding of these trends is fundamentally linked to growing pressures emanating from the expansion of the cognitive–cultural economy in large urban areas.

There is currently much debate about whether gentrification entails direct displacement of the original low-income residents of central city areas or merely succession on the part of more privileged groups as the original residents start to moved away (for example, Freeman 2005; McKinnish et al. 2010; Wyly et al. 2010). In all likelihood different combinations of displacement and succession are at work in different cities depending on local circumstances. Certainly, one of the mechanisms underlying this kind of neighborhood change has been the steady decline of inner city manufacturing jobs and the concomitant outmigration of working-class residents from adjoining neighborhoods. The early stages of gentrification are often signaled by a phase in which abandoned working-class housing and nearby empty warehouses and factory buildings start to be colonized by artists and bohemians, and where a corresponding expansion of local services (such as bars and music venues) catering to the needs and tastes of this demi-monde occurs (Lloyd 2002; Zukin 1982). Eventually, these neighborhoods also become attractive to high-level cognitive–cultural workers, especially as employment opportunities in financial, business-service, and cultural industries in and around central business districts continue to grow. Thus, many of these workers now start to colonize these neighborhoods and to upgrade local property, thereby causing rental rates to rise to levels that remaining low-income residents can no longer afford. The pace of change in this phase is no doubt often boosted by unscrupulous landlords and over-eager city councils anxious to reap the benefits of upgraded land use and to enhance the image of the city (Lees, Slater, and Wyly 2008; Slater 2006; Wacquant 2008). As these trends proceed, further inward movement by members of the upper tier of the labor force occurs, especially by individuals with demographic profiles like young professionals and executives, cohabiting couples, people in same-sex unions, apartment sharers, and so on (Haase et al. 2010; Hamnett and Whitelegg 2007; Harris 2008; Islam 2005; Rubino 2005). In some cases, too, expensive high-rise apartment buildings are erected on abandoned industrial sites, as illustrated by Concord Pacific Place, Vancouver, where a major prestige residential redevelopment scheme has risen on land that was formerly dominated by the lumber industry (Lowry and McCann 2011). Gentrification is also starting to reach into many of the older neighborhoods of suburban areas. Even as these processes move forward, however, employment opportunities for low-wage workers in central city areas continue to grow (especially for ethnic immigrants engaged in the low-grade service segment of the urban economy) and despite the pace of gentrification, many of these workers manage to maintain a residential foothold in the inner city (Salway 2008; Sassen 2001; Sassen-Koob 1982).

The broad dynamic of gentrification was first examined in theoretical terms by Smith (1982; 1986) who put forward the concept of the so-called "rent gap" as the main explanatory mechanism of this process. According to Smith, the origins of the rent gap lie in the difference between the low local property values (sustained by neighborhood effects) that prevail in inner city areas when working-class families dominate, as compared with the higher values that are obtainable once gentrification paves the way for "better and higher" use of the land. As plausible as it certainly is as a starting point (though see the appendix to this chapter for an equivalent formulation based on the notion of land use intensification), the rent gap theory nevertheless fails to provide all the elements of a coherent explanation. More specifically, we need some further account of the historical timing of gentrification in relation to a wider view of changing urban structures over time as fordism gives way to postfordism and then to cognitive–cultural capitalism. I have already indicated that one of the reasons for working class abandonment of inner city areas in the post-War decades was local deindustrialization and the concomitant shift of workers to suburban neighborhoods with ready access to employment opportunities in manufacturing facilities in the urban fringe. In addition, and notably after the 1970s, the remarkable growth of the cognitive–cultural economy was accompanied by an enormous expansion of employment demands in central business districts and surrounding areas of the city for highly qualified workers in business services, finance, media, advertising, fashion industries, cultural production, and so on. This expansion created, and still creates, a major incentive for well-paid upper tier workers to move into residential locations nearby (Hutton 2008; Ley 1996). A simple illustration of the forcefulness of these developments is offered by the fact that in the 1980s the population of the center of Manchester had declined to only a few hundred, whereas today, after gentrification, the population is over 20 000 (Ward et al. 2010).

These shifts have accelerated greatly in American metropolitan areas since the early 1980s. Consider the data set forth in Table 8.2, which shows percentage changes in aggregate residential population by occupational group inside and outside the central cities of US metropolitan areas from 2000 to 2010. The first two columns of Table 8.2 indicate that the number

Table 8.2 *Percentage change in the number of individuals living in central cities or outside central cities by occupational category, US metropolitan areas (2000–2010)[a]*

	All metropolitan areas		Selected metropolitan areas in the Northeast[b]	
	Living in central cities	Living outside central cities	Living in central cities	Living outside central cities
Symbolic analysts	14.7	14.8	19.2	8.2
Low-wage service-oriented workers	12.8	20.8	11.4	14.9
Production workers	−30.0	−20.0	−34.8	−23.9
Total population	4.6	10.7	2.6	5.1

Notes: [a]Symbolic analysts and low-wage service-oriented workers are defined as in Chapter 7. [b]Selected metropolitan areas are Baltimore, Boston, Buffalo–Niagara Falls, Chicago, Cincinnati–Hamilton, Cleveland, Detroit, Milwaukee, Minneapolis–St. Paul, New York–Northeastern NJ, Philadelphia, Pittsburgh, Providence–Fall River–Pawtucket, Rochester, St. Louis, Washington, DC.

Source: United States Census, via IPUMS-USA.

of symbolic analysts and low-wage service-oriented workers increased quite significantly at both central and suburban locations in metropolitan areas between 2000 and 2010, while production workers declined across the board. These observations are consistent with the broad arguments presented above about the restratification of urban society in general, and the deepening but still less than total gentrification of central cities. The second two columns of Table 8.2 present parallel but significantly refined information. Here, the units of observation are restricted to metropolitan areas with populations greater than one million (and where data are available) lying in the Northeast of the United States. This second view is presented because many metropolitan areas outside the Northeast have unusually extended central cities that include wide stretches of suburban or quasi-suburban land, and this state of affairs might well bias our results in unwarranted ways. Cities in the Northeast, by contrast, are typified by relatively restricted central cities that are usually more clearly distinguishable from suburban areas. In the Northeast, then, the number of symbolic analysts living in central cities grew by 19.2 percent between 2000 and 2010 (in contrast to the lower 14.7 percent growth rate for central cities in the United States as a whole), while those living outside central cities grew by only 8.2 percent (in contrast to the higher 14.8 percent for the United States as a whole). The number of low-wage service-oriented workers living in central cities in the Northeast expanded at a rate more or less equal to the corresponding rate for the United States as a whole, but outside central city areas the rate was rather lower. Production workers living inside and outside central cities declined even more markedly in the Northeast than they did in the country as a whole. The data set forth in Table 8.2 indicate that rates of change in the residential populations of symbolic analysts, low-wage service-oriented workers, and production workers, both inside and outside central cities, are very much more extreme than corresponding rates of change for the population as a whole. The clear inference is that internal socio-spatial readjustments in American cities have been much more pronounced in the recent past than aggregate population shifts would suggest.

An echo of these same trends can be found in many other large cities around the world. Instances of gentrification have been reported for cities as far afield as Cairo (Abaza 2001), Istanbul (Islam 2005), Moscow (Badyina and Golubchikov 2005), Santiago (Lopez-Morales 2010), and Seoul (Shin 2009), to mention only a few; though the specific modalities of gentrification obviously differ widely from case to case depending on housing finance arrangements, local government priorities, and general social conditions (Lees 2012). An example of particular interest is presented by the case of Paris, which is all the more apposite in the present context because it is sometimes assumed that North American-style

Table 8.3   Number of workers in selected occupational categories residing in the City of Paris (1999 and 2008)

Occupation	Residents by occupation (15 years or older)		
	1999	2008	Percent change
Executive and professional occupations (*Cadres et professions intellectuelles supérieures*)	393 871	513 027	30.3
Middle management and administrative occupations (*Professions intermédiaires*)	259 408	284 894	9.8
Service, sales, and clerical occupations (*Employés*)	275 446	255 391	−7.3
Production worker occupations (*Ouvriers*)	116 504	98 004	−15.9
All workers	1 191 149	1 103 277	−0.1

Source: Institut National de la Statistique et des Etudes Economiques, Paris.

1999

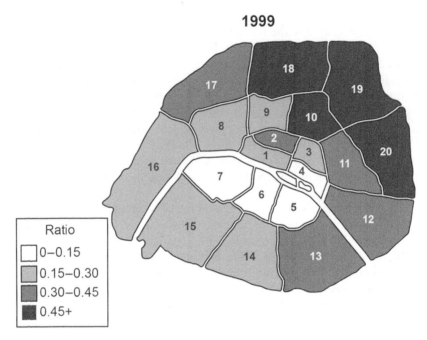

*Figure 8.4   City of Paris: ratio of residents in production worker
               occupations to residents in executive and professional
               occupations, by* arrondissement *(1999)*

gentrification must be limited or nonexistent in continental Europe given
the traditionally high incidence of middle and upper middle class neighborhoods in central city areas. However, Paris *intra-muros* has always
contained dense working-class enclaves providing labor to local workshops and small factories. Indeed, in 1954, production workers constituted
one-third of the city's population (Yankel and Marco 2001), though their
numbers have been declining steadily as a result of gentrification over the
last few decades. As indicated by Table 8.3, the City of Paris continues
to experience significant growth (30.3 percent between 1999 and 2008) in
the number of residents in various kinds of executive, professional, and
managerial occupations, while the number of residents in production
worker occupations has declined sharply (that is, by 15.9 percent between
1999 and 2008). Even the number of individuals in service, sales, and
clerical occupations living in central Paris has been declining. Figures 8.4
and 8.5 sketch out the detailed intra-urban geography of these changes.

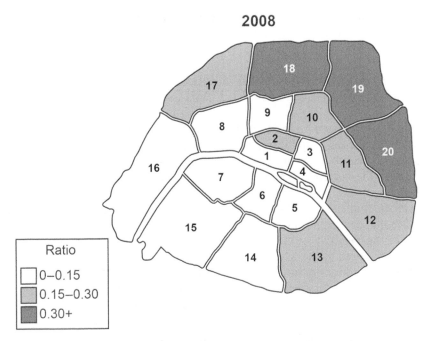

Source: Institut National de la Statistique et des Etudes Economiques, Paris.

Figure 8.5 *City of Paris: ratio of residents in production worker occupations to residents in executive and professional occupations, by* arrondissement *(2008)*

The traditional working-class neighborhoods in the northeast quadrant of the city display notably strong evidence of persistent gentrification, with the number of production workers falling sharply in relation to the number of executive and professional workers between 1999 and 2008 (Clerval 2011).

The large metropolis in the 21st century, just like the fordist metropolis of earlier years, thus has a conspicuously variegated internal social space, modulated by a number of very specific features related to basic changes in the division of labor and structures of human capital in the new economy. In some respects, moreover, socio-spatial segmentation of the city has become more strongly indurated as the incomes of different occupational strata have diverged and as members of the upper tier of the labor force have sought to enhance their seclusion in residential space by forming gated communities (Blakely and Snyder 1997; Le Goix 2005). The right to the city that Lefebvre (1968) saw, correctly, as one of the basic conditions for a renewal of democratic values, social solidarity, and the capacity for *réjouissance* seems as distant as ever.

AESTHETICIZATION OF URBAN SPACE IN COGNITIVE–CULTURAL CAPITALISM

The aestheticization or re-aestheticization of urban space is one of the hallmarks of the new capitalism. The landscapes of cities in capitalism have always been subject to different kinds of aesthetic urges, and in this broad respect, the current situation is one of continuity rather than a radical break with the past. What *is* unique about the current situation is the diversity and extent of these urges and their idiomatic forms of expression reflecting, in part, peculiar commercial and symbolic priorities that spring out of the cognitive–cultural economy. Current rounds of aestheticization are also geared to the selective appropriation, marking out, and recycling of particular kinds of intra-urban territorial complexes. The gentrification of old working-class neighborhoods is one form of aestheticization in the contemporary city, but I want to focus above all here on the upgrading and renovation of non-residential land use. The term "gentrification" is frequently used in the literature to designate operations of this type, but we shall find it useful to distinguish these from gentrification in the strict sense (that is, as originally identified by Glass (1964)). Instead, I shall refer to the conversion of non-residential land use in the central city to higher uses by the awkward but evocative term "aestheticized land use intensification."

By far the most dramatic instances of this process take the form of insistent land use redevelopment at the cores of large metropolitan areas all over the world. In the early 21st century, this type of redevelopment involves the quest for increases in productivity per unit of land while typically giving voice to an architectural ethos that abjures the minimalist forms of the fordist urban skyline and that tends increasingly to express itself in more bombastic formulae. The visible signs of this dynamic are the ever-escalating vertical expansion of large city centers and the revitalization of formerly derelict areas around these centers where large-scale land assemblies can be put together and where vigorous rehabilitation is able to restore dramatically improved value to the land. The long-standing practice of land-use intensification in central-city areas has always, of course, been subject to various forms of aestheticization, but this process has taken on new and greatly enlarged meaning in the current conjuncture as a function of the creative urges and possibilities unleashed by urbanization in the global cognitive–cultural economy (Bontje et al. 2011; Schmid et al. 2011). Among other things, the built structures and landscapes of the central city undergird and reflect the high-level creative, cerebral, and cultural labor processes that now dominate in these areas. In addition, as Sklair (2000; 2010) has pointed out, some of the more ostentatious and self-assertive architectural set-pieces in the cores of major world cities often house global corporations seeking to highlight their international significance. This is an architecture that accords well with the aspirations and ideology of the transnational capitalist class – managers of global corporations, high-level bankers, representatives of the media and other cultural industries, globalizing professionals, international bureaucrats, etc. – linking these places into worldwide networks. At the same time, the corporate spaces of the central city are increasingly integrated with upscale consumer-oriented facilities, or what Sklair (2010) calls "cathedrals of consumption," such as gallerias, shopping malls, upscale retail strips (like Rodeo Drive in Los Angeles, Avenue Montaigne in Paris, or Bond Street in London), music centers, museums, art galleries, conference facilities, sports stadia, public squares, and so on. These facilities are principally at the service of the upper fraction of the labor force, and, by making the central business districts and adjacent areas of large cities yet more enticing to this fraction as places of work, shopping, and leisure, they add their weight to the glamour of the city and further encourage gentrification of surrounding residential neighborhoods.

Aestheticized land use intensification, then, commonly assumes the mantle of spectacular architectural gestures – no matter whether they be monuments to corporate power or shrines to public self-esteem – with the ultimate effect of dramatizing the urban landscape. These sorts of gestures are widely observable in flagship cities of the new global order (Kaika 2010; Zukin 1991) where they not only serve specific corporate interests, but also in part express the ambitions of particular places to function as focal points of reference in the world system and as destinations for inward flows of capital and skilled workers. As such, urban design and architectural built forms are increasingly being enrolled as adjuncts to local economic development strategies. Large-scale iconic architectural gestures play an especially critical role in this respect by virtue of their capacity to serve as urban branding and marketing devices. The point is exemplified by recent megaprojects (often signed by celebrity architects) such as Los Angeles' Disney Hall, London's Docklands, Bilbao's Guggenheim Museum, Kuala Lumpur's Petronas Towers, Shanghai's World Financial Center, and so on. Moreover, it is precisely the new digital technologies of cognitive–cultural capitalism that make it possible to achieve the characteristically complex topological forms that typify so many of these projects. In these and other ways, the physical landscape of the city functions more and more as a trump card in the global inter-city contests for status, inward investment, mega-events (such as the Olympic Games), and tourist dollars that recur at ever shorter intervals of time in the contemporary world. Recycled formerly derelict areas of the city, as in the cases of the Harborplace mall in Baltimore, the Parc de la Villette in Paris, and the Zürich West development, play much the same role. Similar kinds of initiatives can be found in Britain in Manchester's Northern Quarter and Sheffield's Cultural Industries Quarter with their aspirations to develop as dynamic hubs for small creative enterprises such as recording studios, electronic media labs, fashion designers, and so on. In Los Angeles, to cite another example of upgraded industrial land use, a new Fashion District just to the south of the central business district has recently been created in what was originally a dispiriting cluster of grimy clothing factories. This project, with its renovated buildings and colorful street scenes, expresses the rising status of the Los Angeles clothing industry as a global center of designer fashions, and helps to proclaim the new-found ambitions of many local producers to compete in high-end markets. In parallel with initiatives like these, local authorities in cities all over the world are insistently pursuing projects that involve the conversion of neglected and abandoned facilities to serve a diversity of cultural purposes, as in the case of Amsterdam's Westergasfabriek or parts of the Ruhr region of Germany where efforts to rebuild a decaying industrial landscape have been aggressively under way for some time and where old industrial and coal mining properties are being converted into restaurants, museums, art galleries, and so on (Prossek 2011).

This is all of a piece with the social and economic mood of cognitive–cultural capitalism generally. In these ways, and in contrast with the sharp and often incompatible contrasts between production space and residential space that typified much of the urbanism of earlier capitalist eras, a sort of continuity or balance seems now to be spreading over privileged segments of the metropolis where work, shopping, leisure, and residential activities interpenetrate with one another in relatively smooth mutual interdependencies. A new kind of harmony appears to be emerging as these spaces become more spatially interwoven and less mutually repellent in terms of their social functions and needs. Even parts of suburbia display a similar syndrome, as represented by verdant industrial parks with sleek buildings housing technology-intensive firms and office complexes alongside the sweeping residential estates and gated communities of upper-income denizens of the urban periphery. Still, the paradox of the large metropolis in cognitive–cultural capitalism lies in the contrast between the dazzle and glamour of much of its immediate outward form and the lugubriousness of its underbelly, for beyond the allure of the more privileged portions of the city, there remain large swaths of less visible, or at any rate, less mediatized urban squalor where the lower-tier denizens of metropolitan society pass the greater part of their lives. The paradox assumes particularly striking proportions in the large metropolitan areas of the Global South where high-level international financial and corporate activities exist within a stone's throw of some of the world's most disquieting slums.

APPENDIX: LAND USE INTENSIFICATION

Suppose that the economic rent *per unit of output* is $r(d)$, at distance d from the city center. Spatially invariant production costs can be expressed as c per unit of output, and spatially varying costs as $c(d)$. The latter costs include transport costs on inputs and commuting costs (embodied in wages) paid to workers, and we can assume schematically that these costs in aggregate increase as we move away from the city center. The market price of the product is p. We then have:

$$r(d) = p - c - c(d).$$

Assume, at the outset, that the quantity of output from any given unit area of land is x, where density is for the moment taken to be constant over space. Rent *per unit area of land* at distance d from the city center is, then:

$$R(d) = x[p - c - c(d)].$$

A graph of this equation is given in Figure A8.1.

Now suppose that we are in a position to increase total production by building more floor space at any given location, d. As a consequence, output at d will rise from from x to Δx, and the spatially invariant unit costs of production will rise from c to Δc. For simplicity, we shall assume that no changes occur in the (market-determined) price, p, or in the spatially-varying cost function $c(d)$. Land rent at our chosen location will now become:

$$R^*(d) = (x + \Delta x)[p - (c + \Delta c) - c(d)].$$

The relationship of $R^*(d)$ to $R(d)$ will vary depending on the values of Δx and Δc. However because the slope of $R^*(d)$ will always be greater than the slope of $R(d)$ relative to d it will always intersect the latter curve from above for any given value of d. Figure A8.1 shows a case where the two curves intersect in the positive quadrant of the graph. Clearly, intensification will tend to occur at locations where an augmentation of land rent can

Rent per
unit of land

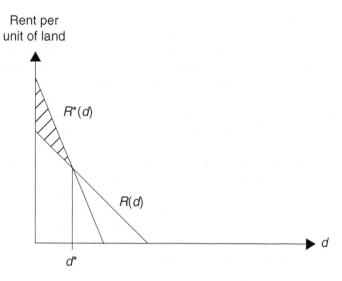

Notes: The line R(*d*) shows rent per unit of land before land use intensification; the line
R*(*d*) shows possible values of rent per unit of land as a result of land use intensification.
No intensification will occur beyond the point *d**.

Figure A8.1   Land rent as a function of distance from the city center

be obtained (that is, at locations where *d* is less than *d** in Figure A8.1),
and the most desirable – that is, rent-maximizing – location will be right
at the city center.

Obviously, this schema is oversimplified, and, among other amendments
needed to make it more realistic, we should to add a temporal dimension
in order to take account of the timing of land redevelopment decisions.
As it is, the schema helps us to understand something of how land rent
and property development dynamics are intertwined with one another in
central city areas. In particular, it suggests a basic mechanism explaining why land use intensification tends to coincide with the most central
(that is, accessible) locations in intra-urban space. The adaptation of this
schema to the case of residential gentrification would entail appropriate
restatement of the land rent equations to take account of the increased
consumer evaluation and the cost of any property after upgrading.

NOTE

1.   However, Jameson himself was never directly associated with the LA School as such.

9. Interstitial geographies: the cultural economy of landscape

BEYOND METROPOLIS

Just as large metropolitan regions are undergoing far-reaching transformation in this historical moment of capitalism, so, too, are many of the interstitial spaces between them. The spaces that I have in mind here do not concern the endless tracts of industrial agriculture or the desolate wastes that make up much of the earth's land surface. Rather, my focus in this chapter is on those non-metropolitan areas comprising rural expanses and associated networks of small towns that participate in the new cognitive–cultural economy by means of their specialized forms of agricultural and craft production, their symbolic assets and traditions, and the appeal of their natural landscapes. As such, these areas are articulated with major metropolitan areas around the world both as production locales that export distinctively marked local outputs to urban markets and as places that offer *in situ* experiences to visitors. Obvious examples abound: specialized agricultural regions like the Napa Valley and Burgundy with their vintage wines; many different parts of France and Italy with their picturesque landscapes and historical scenes; archeological sites all around the shores of the Mediterranean; areas of Botswana, Brazil, and Costa Rica where ecological tourist sites are developing rapidly; and any number of out-of-the-way locations in both the Global North and the Global South where traditional arts and crafts are undergoing commercialization for wider markets. Large numbers of small urban settlements are also participating in this trend by reinventing themselves as theme towns that capitalize on their inherited idiosyncrasies and other specialized resources (Bell and Jayne 2009). These burgeoning new rural spaces and the small urban centers that they encompass owe much of their success to the rising affluence of contemporary society, and to the expansion of a middle stratum of society with strong predilections for goods and services that combine a kind of authenticity with unique experiential encounters (MacCannell 1976).

DIFFUSE RURAL ASSEMBLAGES IN COGNITIVE–CULTURAL CAPITALISM

All over the world today new economic currents are penetrating peripheral spaces in a manner that brings them into ever closer articulation with the overall system of cognitive–cultural capitalism (cf. Ward and Brown 2009) but without any concomitant drive to large-scale urbanization. As Ray (1998) has suggested, development of this sort, with its focus on the countryside and small towns, can typically be characterized in terms of: (a) a territorial base; (b) a set of symbolic signifiers; and (c) a structure of economic synergies. On these bases, enormous re-mobilization of assets in peripheral areas is occurring at the present time as new opportunities multiply within the orbit of the cognitive and cultural economic order. Ray (1998, p. 3) goes on to describe this re-mobilization in terms of its roots in both cultural and natural heritage – for example:

> . . . traditional foods, regional languages, crafts, folklore, local visual arts and drama, literary references, historical and prehistorical sites, landscape systems and their associated flora and fauna.

Various combinations of these heritage phenomena form integrated spatial complexes subject to both endogenous developmental dynamics and extra-local influences. Their market value is founded on the recreational, aesthetic, and semiotic pleasures that they induce. As such, they are rarely consumed in their pristine forms but are staged and packaged in various ways so as to make them more accessible and palatable to external audiences. The growing numbers of food festivals, musical events, art exhibitions, and other thematic presentations in rural areas and small towns are testimony to this point, as is the accompanying development of local tourist accommodations to serve floating populations of temporary visitors. The marketing of these assets is frequently consolidated by the branding of local products and by publicity campaigns that create conventionalized images of particular localities.

Place-based systems of these types can be seen as unique spatial assemblages of cultural and economic activities similar in certain respects to industrial agglomerations in that they are characterized by numerous internal synergies and spillover effects, though with the signal difference that they are not necessarily concentrated around a dominant center. More often than not, these assemblages assume the guise of scattered but regionalized congeries of miscellaneous activity with occasional and minor spatial bunching effects in villages and towns. We can describe them as extensive, non-metropolitan, and emphatically fragile residues of common-pool resources (Ostrom 2008; Palermo 2008) forming unique regional conglomerates, or compages.[1] As such, Marshallian concepts of regional development often have some pertinence to the economic dynamics of areas like these, though with major qualifications. Thus, collective synergies emanating out of internal economic linkages, local labor markets, and information flows may well be important, but we should not expect these variables to play as insistent a role in inducing spatial polarization as they do in classical industrial agglomerations. Clearly, joint publicity and marketing activities also represent important sources of competitive advantage. However (and in opposition to the generally positive dynamic of Schumpeterian creative destruction that underpins the success of many different kinds of industrial agglomerations in large metropolitan areas), any vigorous process of this type in the kinds of spatial systems under scrutiny in this chapter will be apt to have severely negative impacts on many facets of local life and may therefore threaten overall economic viability.

In short, there is a continual tension within these systems between the search for local prosperity and the preservation or enhancement of those regional attributes that are the very bases of their competitive advantages. This is essentially a political problem calling for collective adjudication between demands for the protection of common pool resources on the one hand, and free-riders who threaten the viability of those resources on the other. There is a clear echo here of the dilemmas that run through urban agglomerations but with very different kinds of stakes. Of course, these dilemmas are more easily stated in abstract terms than they can be resolved in practice, for in places where tradition counts for much, they inevitably raise thorny issues like authenticity versus debasement, or preservation versus modernization, and there are likely to be varying opinions on these matters by different constituencies. Figure 9.1 puts this general argument into more elaborate form. Here, a schematic view is offered of some of the main ingredients of a hypothetical rural assemblage whose basic assets comprise a physical and symbolic landscape and a traditional store of know-how. These assets then serve as the basis of a small-scale local production system that is subject to a constantly changing complex of human perceptions and projects that come and go as the locality evolves through time. Three principal groups of socio-economic actors, differentiated according to specific sets of interests, are designated in Figure 9.1, namely residents, producers of goods and services, and visitors (though any individual may embody more than one set of interests). All three groups of actors are continually involved in consumption of the local landscape and its products, in various interpretations of these materials, and in the pursuit of specific undertakings related to their interests. In other

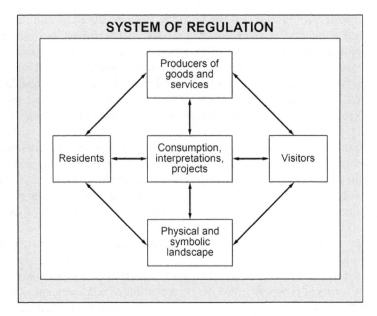

Figure 9.1   Some structural elements of a diffuse rural assemblage in the cognitive–cultural economy

words, residents, producers, and visitors are all variously caught up in the tensions of preserving and transforming the locality as a focus of cultural and economic significance.

One way in which this transformation operates is by means of an evolutionary process of symbolic change based on the accumulation of new cultural meanings on the landscape as existing cultural endowments are reinterpreted and recycled and further meanings are created. For example, a particular locale may be chosen as a site for location filming due to its unique background scenery and symbolic atmosphere. The film that is subsequently released creates new cinematic images of that locale and these are then assimilated back into its distinctive landscapes and products. In this manner, a deepening sedimentation of aesthetic and semiotic references may accumulate in any given locale, offering opportunities for the further development of indigenous cultural and economic values and the transformation of the locale as a spatially concentrated sign system (Hudson and Brent Ritchie 2006; Riley, Baker, and Van Doren 1998; Tooke and Baker 1996). However, market failures and socially colliding visions of future developments mean that successful social reproduction of any such locale over time necessitates a regulatory framework composed of public and semi-public bodies dealing with tasks of overall coordination and management. In rural contexts, the decision-making processes embedded in these frameworks will no doubt usually be marked by an overarching caution that puts a high premium on conservation of the physical and symbolic heritage, even if the same caution may dampen down internal regional dynamism by ensuring that little can be done to compromise the inherited stock of resources that are the foundation of the local economy.

DEVELOPMENTAL EXPERIENCES AND POSSIBILITIES

As Williams (1973) has written, there are many traditional economic and cultural tensions – real or imagined – between the city and the country. The city is often seen as a domain of sophistication, fashion, and the rapid accumulation of wealth; the country is more often thought of as a bucolic realm of relative quietude and backwardness. Bunce (1994) adds the gloss that the Industrial Revolution accentuated these contrasts by giving birth to the bustling capitalist metropolis with its sharp separation from so much that might be categorized under the rubric of "Nature." All that being said, the rise of the cognitive–cultural economy now heralds a state of affairs where the city and the country seem to be set on a path of reconvergence toward one another. This is not simply a matter of the spatially widening influence of the city as a consequence of extended commuting fields, or the spread of second homes, or the near-universal intrusiveness of the media, but is more fundamentally related to the ways in which the new economy is penetrating into so many of the far recesses of the rural environment. The proximate causes of this shift reside partly in rising demands in large cities for things like organic agricultural produce and traditional artifacts, and partly in the growing requirements of members of the upper tier of the labor force for leisure-time escape into worlds promising experiences that contrast with the round of workaday life in the nerve-centers of the cognitive–cultural economy – that is, worlds that offer relaxation, tranquility, participation in nature, outdoor activities, and communion with residues of the past. There is, indeed, an astonishing and rapidly increasing diversity of these possibilities in the 21st century, as illustrated by the following six brief sketches, all of which capture something of the ways in which rural areas and small towns are coming to function more and more as specialized adjuncts of the cognitive–cultural economy of large cities:

1. Encounters with the natural world nowadays form an important segment of the modern tourist industry. They are focused not only

on dramatic scenery and physical challenges, but also on flora and fauna in unique ecological settings. Activities like climbing, hiking, cycling, boating, and so on, are often pursued in tandem with these encounters, sometimes in the context of special parks and reservations. Some of the most spectacular of the natural attractions that are being exploited in this way are to be found in the Global South, as exemplified by the ecological tourist center of Bonito in the Mato Grosso of Brazil (Camargo et al. 2011), the Goo-Moremi area in Botswana with its scenic gorge (Mbaiwa 2011), or the Sariska Tiger Reserve, India (Sekhar 2003). Many areas of special natural beauty are now protected by UNESCO as World Heritage Sites, as in the cases of Yosemite National Park in the United States, Ha Long Bay in Vietnam, and the Victoria Falls in Zimbabwe. Such protection allows for tourist access while ensuring that basic conservation principles are observed.

2. Another important facet of modern tourism is the heritage industry focused on commercializing physical relics of the past such as old landscape artifacts, architectural monuments, and archeological remains (Philo and Kearns 1993). Rural areas and small towns often have especially attractive assets of these kinds, and all the more so where these fit into the local milieu to generate a strong sense of place identity. In some cases, too, former industrial and mining landscapes have been successfully brought into service as tourist attractions, as illustrated in the study by Conradson and Pawson (2009) of the old resource periphery along the West Coast of South Island, New Zealand, constituting what they call a "cultural economy of marginality." To be sure, these physical relics of the past are rarely consumed in their raw state, but are usually transformed by processes of commodification and staging, including ideological framings that project specific interpretative readings (Johnson 1999; MacCannell 1976). Like many areas of special natural interest, more and more historical and archeological remains are now being designated as World Heritage Sites by UNESCO, as in the case of major tourist foci like Stonehenge, Angkor Wat, and the Semmering Railway in Austria.

3. A major trend in the agricultural economy is the increasing output of locally-specialized and organically-grown products, and the use of brands or AOC certifications (*appellations d'origine contrôlée*) to proclaim their individuality and enhance their marketability (Bell and Jayne 2010; Marsden and Smith 2005; Moran 1993). From this perspective, intellectual property is becoming as much a part of the new rural economy as it is of the urban economy with its active patenting and copyrighting in sectors like advanced technology or the media

(Moran 1993). Intellectual property in the rural economy derives from both traditional methods of production and the subtle qualities of topography, soil, and microclimate that endow certain kinds of agricultural regions with unique and highly valued qualities. A locality that commands competitive advantages like these is often referred to as a *terroir*, a term that was originally used to designate a tract of countryside marked by a rustic economy and culture, but that is now often extended to designate an agricultural area with specific physical and human resources enabling producers to earn monopoly rents related to the quality of final products, such as wine, olive oil, cheese, cream, butter, poultry, or tea. Bowen (2011) for example, writes about *terroir* as manifest in the taste of place, and then goes on to illustrate the point by reference to *comté* cheese made in the Jura region of France. Nel et al. (2007) provide another illustration of *terroir* in their account of Rooibos tea production in the Western Cape Province of South Africa. Many of these areas of specialized intensive agriculture around the world are prospering today not only on the basis of formal geographical indications and brands, but also intensifying social capital in the form of production, processing and marketing cooperatives and collaborative supply chains (Marsden 2010).

4.   Small towns and the countryside around them are frequently repositories of distinctive culinary memories, in many cases expressed in recipes for the preparation of locally-grown agricultural products. Local restaurants often offer menus based on these recipes, and many of these restaurants are starred in tourist guides. To an increasing degree, especially in Europe, high-quality gastronomic restaurants with celebrity chefs are opening up in small towns and rural areas where the pleasures of eating can be combined with relaxation in a low-stress milieu. Many small towns hold periodic food fairs where local specialties like jams, dried fruits, sausages, cured meats, and pickled vegetables are on display. Policy-makers are increasingly recognizing the value of regional food and cuisine in the wider rural economy, as in the case of Le Haut Plateau de l'Aubrac in the Massif Central of France where a strategy of promoting heritage and gastronomy has been pressed into the service of local economic development (Bessière 1998). We should also note, in this context, the more than 140 towns around the globe that have joined the *CittàSlow* movement – an international organization closely allied to the Slow Food movement – dedicated to the preservation of local produce, aesthetic traditions, and cuisine in unhurried, unpolluted, small urban milieux (Knox 2005).

5.   Areas lying outside large metropolitan areas often have rich traditions

of arts and crafts, many of which are now being repackaged for export markets or restaged for the tourist trade. Illustrative instances are Caltagirone pottery from Sicily (Santagata 2002), *Shamisen* folk music in the Tsugaru district of northwest Honshu, Japan (Rausch 2010), and Balinese dance (Wall 1996), among the multitude of examples that might be cited here. Policy-makers in many regions have recognized the useful role that arts and crafts can play in local economic development, and in cases where these have declined or are extinct, active efforts of resuscitation have sometimes been put into effect. Even where historical traditions of these sorts are lacking, many rural areas and small towns have nonetheless succeeded in building reputations as foci of art galleries, museums, gardens, open-air sculptures, antique shops, and so on (Douglas 2002). Artists' colonies, like Marfa in West Texas or Taos in New Mexico also contribute significantly to economic development in otherwise marginal, isolated areas.

6. Additional forms of development in small towns are often initiated on the basis of some local historical or geographical idiosyncrasy. American theme towns like Solvang, CA, otherwise known as "Little Denmark" (Linde-Laursen 1999), or Lindsborg, KS, otherwise known as "Little Sweden" (Schnell 2003), exemplify this trend. However, as Engler (2000) observes in her account of the theme towns strung out along Interstate 80 in Iowa, these staged recreations frequently dispense with a strict respect for veracity and due measure. Among the more remarkable instances of modern theme towns are the numerous second-book centers that have sprung up from the United States through Finland to Japan in imitation of the original success of the small Welsh market town of Hay-on-Wye whose first foray into the second-hand book market dates from the early 1960s (Seaton 1996; Vik and Villa 2010). Hay-on-Wye is also the annual venue for a major literary festival. Indeed, there is now a profusion of periodic festivals in small towns across the world, ranging from the International Festival of Geography in Saint-Dié-des-Vosges, France, to the Country and Western Music Festival in Tamworth, Australia (Gibson and Davidson 2004).

These six vignettes are testimony to the point that while the new cognitive–cultural economy is predominantly concentrated in major cities, it is far from being confined to large urban areas, and is, in fact, making its presence increasingly felt in a diversity of interstitial spaces. In what now follows, I shall elaborate further on this matter by means of a synthetic discussion of one specific space, namely the English Lake District, that exemplifies dramatically a number of the arguments made above. This area has been a privileged locus of landscape appreciation for more than two centuries, and in the 21st century it is moving into a very special position as a unique geographic formation within the global cognitive–cultural economy.

THE CULTURAL ECONOMY OF LANDSCAPE: THE CASE OF THE ENGLISH LAKE DISTRICT

The Making of a Romantic Landscape: The Genesis of an Evolutionary Process

The Lake District is situated in the county of Cumbria[2] in the far northwest corner of England, and since 1951 the region has been designated as a National Park (see Figure 9.2). It is an area of mountains and fells, valleys and lakes, offering stirring vistas and numerous recreational opportunities. The region is also marked by many literary and artistic associations, and its scenery has been widely celebrated in poetry and painting over the course of the last two centuries. The rich natural and symbolic landscape that emerges out of these sundry elements constitutes the foundation of a now-vibrant cultural economy.

Over the second half of the 18th century and the first half of the 19th, a series of highly influential travel books and guides were published, in which the Lake District was romantically portrayed as a paragon of sublime and picturesque scenery. These publications helped to initiate a fashion for visiting the region and for viewing its dramatic landscapes and panoramas (Nicholson 1955). Wordsworth's widely-circulated *Guide to the Lakes* (1810) did much to consolidate the reputation of the region as a supreme exemplar of the picturesque and to boost yet further the influx of fashionable visitors (Whyte 2000). In conjunction with these developments through the 18th and 19th centuries, the Lake District was also acquiring a wider cachet as a center of literary and artistic production. In 1817, an article in the *Edinburgh Review* identified Wordsworth, Coleridge and Southey as forming a so-called "Lake School" of poetry. De Quincy, who had gone to live in the region in 1809, is also usually counted as a member of the School. Other celebrated literary figures who spent time in the region in the first half of the 19th century were Byron, Hazlitt, Keats, and Shelley. Harriet Martineau, the writer and philosopher, lived at Ambleside from 1846 until her death in 1876. In 1871, Ruskin took up residence at Brantwood on Coniston Water where he continued to produce a stream of writing. Ruskin's influence was also partly felt in the formation of a small outpost of the Arts and Crafts Movement in the Lake District from

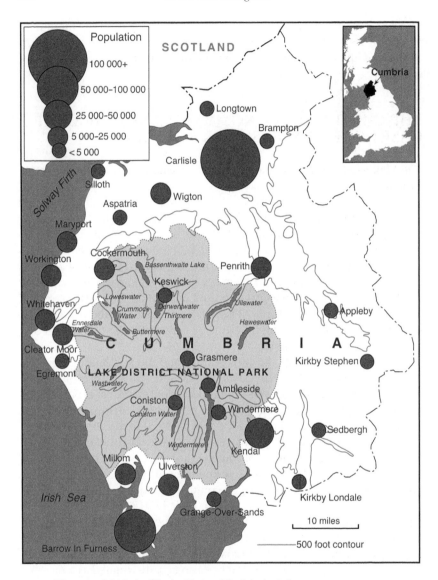

Note: The area of the Lake District National Park is shaded.

Figure 9.2   Cumbria and the Lake District, with principal urban settlements

the 1880s to the 1920s (Brunton 2001; Haslam 2004). Beatrix Potter first visited the Lakes in 1882, and later settled at Hill Top Farm near the village of Sawrey (Squire 1993).

The lives and works of these writers have left imprints throughout the Lake District, both in regard to the places where they dwelt and the topographic features that they commemorated in their work. The reputation of the Lake District as a center of aesthetic creation was further reinforced by the numerous painters who found inspiration in the ever-varying forms and moods of the landscape. In particular, Constable and Turner travelled to the region at the turn of the 19th century and left striking visual records of their visits.

The Tourist Experience

By far the greater part of the economy in the area of the National Park is based on the tourist trade, but even in the remainder of Cumbria, tourism makes a significant contribution to local income levels. For example, Carlisle's medieval cathedral and castle attract many visitors. The small town of Sedbergh, in the far southeast of the region, was designated as a book town in 2006, and is a center for writers, book designers, publishers, and booksellers.[3] Similarly, Cockermouth (lying to the northwest just outside the National Park) was admitted to the international *CittàSlow* network in 2008.

In the Lake District proper, the ideal tourist experience is preeminently one that entails self-locomotion, tranquillity, and visual contemplation. According to the Lake District National Park Authority, the leading reasons given by surveyed individuals for visiting the Park in 2001 were walking (48 percent), sightseeing (22 percent), climbing (7 percent), and cycling (4 percent).[4] In short, tourism in the Lake District is focused primarily on engagement with the landscape through various forms of physical exertion and by internalizing its natural and symbolic attributes via the sense of sight. As Urry (1992; 1995) suggests, it is the primacy of the visual that regulates so much of the tourist's experience in general, and in the Lake District this feature is paramount. The experience is intensified by the literary and artistic traditions of the region, and the ways in which they surge through the natural landscape in the guise of locales and vistas associated with this or that writer or painter, thus endowing local topographic and other natural features with rich symbolic value (Lindop 1993). The houses where different writers and painters lived (including Wordsworth's birthplace in Cockermouth) are also important elements of this landscape. The historical accumulation of literary and artistic materials within and around the region persists in a more or less unbroken line down to the present day. Several influential living writers continue to add to this record, and Cumbrian authors over the last few decades have done much to publicize the county's charms and points of interest to the rest of the world. In recent years, indeed, an avalanche of books about the region has been published by writers of every stripe. The regular flow of novels, guidebooks, works of natural history, photographic albums, collections of poetry, memoirs, local historical studies, dialect stories, and so on, celebrating various aspects of the Lake District and its life, has done much to draw wide attention to the region.

Just as writing in and about the Lake District is marked by a long tradition, so too a large body of work produced by painters and photographers of the region's landscapes and panoramas has built up over the last two centuries. Since Turner and Constable created their paintings and sketches of the area, successions of visual artists over the 19th and 20th centuries have generated a copious record of the views and changing moods of the Lake District. In recent years, the record has become, if anything, increasingly dense and complex. Of modern Lakeland painters, Sheila Fell (1931–1979) and William Heaton Cooper (1903–1995) are perhaps the best known, the former for her brooding landscapes, and the latter for his impressionistic watercolors. William Heaton Cooper's old studio and art shop in Grasmere continues as a family tradition. This is but one of the many galleries spread out across the region providing outlets for the work of local artists.

In addition to diverse literary and arts shows, the Lake District is the site of numerous sporting events (including local pursuits such as Cumberland wrestling and fell running), as well as exhibitions devoted to different aspects of regional history, geography, and folk-life. Two performing arts festivals have risen to some significance of late, and have engendered echoes that have spread well beyond the borders of the Lake District as such. One is the Lake District Summer Music Festival, founded in 1984, which entails a series of ambitious musical events in different locales around the region over the month of August. The other is the Words by the Water Festival, a literary gathering, initiated in 2002, and held annually in Keswick over a 10-day period in March. Successful events like these no doubt contain the seeds of new rounds of cultural and economic dynamism, portending yet more local arts initiatives in the region over the coming years.

Food and Cuisine

In regional complexes outside major metropolitan areas, significant development potentials are frequently to be found in local food traditions, and in customary craft activities more generally. Food has a special meaning in this context because it is so deeply intertwined both functionally and symbolically with landscape (Vergunst et al. 2009). In these matters, the Lake District has advanced to a perhaps surprising degree over the last few decades, given that there is little in the region by way of gastronomic traditions and achievements that can match those of, say, Italy or France.

All the same, one of the more remarkable recent changes in the region has been the definite if uneven upgrading that has occurred in the sphere of food and cuisine, both in terms of direct exports and catering to the tourist trade. Farming is today only a small segment of the local economy, but the farms that remain are increasingly capable of turning out high quality specialized products, and many are resorting to organic farming as demand by local residents and restaurateurs rises upward. Farm products from the Lake District that are now aggressively entering both local and non-local markets include butter, eggs, game, and lamb of the local Herdwick variety. Among other things, these trends work in the direction of improved local sustainability and the reinvigoration of rural communities that would otherwise be under greatly intensified threat. Local sourcing of food products and the revival of traditional cuisine, moreover, help to reinforce the authenticity of the tourist experience, and to underline the cachet of the region as an iconic and multifaceted travel destination.

Local culinary products that have seen a resurgence as tourism to the region has grown include (in the characteristically rough-edged local vocabulary) Cumberland sausage, sticky toffee pudding, Cumberland rum nicky, apple tansey, Kendal mint cake, Grasmere gingerbread, and Cumberland rum butter, to mention only a few. We should also include in this list various preserves and cured foodstuffs, above all damson jams from the Kendal area where the growing of damson plums is concentrated. In addition, a wide spectrum of specialty beers is being produced in the 23 micro-breweries currently in existence in Cumbria as a whole. The region is, indeed, starting to earn a modest reputation as a center of specialty food products and culinary enterprise. In 2009, for example, the *Good Food Guide* listed 23 different restaurants in Cumbria (19 of them in the area of the National Park) of which 11 are assigned a score of 4 or more.[5] The number of these restaurants is certainly not overwhelming, but by any standards, this must be seen as a striking change from the situation as it was a few decades ago when a single pioneering restaurant, Sharrow Bay by Ullswater, struck out with cuisine that aspired to something more than a purely local standard of performance. Three restaurants in the region currently hold one Michelin star apiece, namely Sharrow Bay, L'Enclume in Cartmel, and Holbeck Ghyll at Windermere.

Collective Order

Many governmental agencies and other public bodies participate in one way or another in managing the diverse environmental, social, and economic issues that continually intrude into the public sphere in the Lake District and surrounding areas. Some of the more important of these agencies are the Cumbria County Council, the Northwest Regional Development Agency (soon to be phased out in favor of a system of local economic partnerships), the Lake District National Park Authority, and the Forestry Commission. Two significant non-governmental organizations are the National Trust (Canon Hardwicke Rawnsley, one of its three founders, was a local philanthropist and writer) and the Friends of the Lake District.

All of these organizations, and others, have played a decisive role in guiding the path-dependent trajectory of evolution in the region. They have achieved this feat by correcting market failures, by providing forums of public debate and decision-making, and by taking strategic initiatives to foster continued development without unduly threatening to undermine the region's romantic heritage. As such, they have helped to maneuver the region through a developmental course that has consistently veered to the conservative side but that has warded off many potential pitfalls including more obtrusive forms of development of the type sometimes described as "disneyfication" (Relph 1976; Terkenli 2006) or analogous spectacles that Eco (1986) refers to as "hyper-reality." In fact, the Lake District lies for the most part at the opposite end of the spectrum from phenomena like these. By the same token, the region's institutional infrastructure has succeeded against numerous odds in helping to imbue the Lake District label with powerful brand-like resonances that have contributed greatly to its success as a tourist destination. In 2006, a partnership of several local and national organizations voted to proceed with a bid to UNESCO to declare the region a World Heritage Site. Obviously, if eventually successful, this bid will consolidate yet further the region's developmental pathway as a unique reserve of environmental and symbolic capital forming the basis of a high-quality cultural economy.

COGNITIVE–CULTURAL COUNTRYSIDE?

The reflections set forth in this chapter suggest that that some important shifts are occurring in the economic and cultural character of many of the interstitial spaces that lie between the large global city-regions of the contemporary era. These shifts consist above all of a revalorization of many of the traditional resources that exist in these areas, together with the creation of new kinds of assets that play predominantly on expanding global demands for organic products, recreational opportunities, traditional designs, and contact with the natural milieu. Many of the economic and cultural features of the interstitial spaces or compages discussed in these pages precede the rise of the cognitive–cultural economy as such, but have taken on renewed importance and intensity, as well as new interpretative meanings, as the changing production possibilities and consumption habits of 21st century society have deepened and widened. Not the least of these changes is the vast increase in the provision and consumption of tourist services in rural environments and small towns all around the world.

One consequence of developments of this sort is the currently surging academic and policy interest in "creative regions" – that is, extended territorial systems with distinctive competitive advantages based on unique, place-specific resources (Cooke and Schwartz 2007). Tuscany, for example, has been described by Lazzeretti et al. (2010) as a creative region that has successfully preserved and enhanced many of its traditional assets in art and food while at the same time promoting a growing tourist trade. We might say that regions like Tuscany and the English Lake District function nowadays as creative geographic areas in the overall system of cognitive–cultural capitalism. In a nutshell, the viability of these regions' cultural economies depends on an overall atmosphere – and a facilitating grid of recreational resources – that is endemically conducive to experiential encounters on the part of those who take the time and trouble to become acquainted with their unique fund of natural and symbolic endowments and who allow these endowments to work on their faculty for "fancy, fantasy, and wishful thinking" (Shields 1991, p. 14). Still, very similar provisos can be raised with respect to the creative region idea that was raised earlier regarding creative cities. Above all, creativity is not an open-ended process of unlimited scope or potential, but is always situated in concrete historical and geographical circumstances. Equally, the transformative powers of policy-makers in any given region are strictly limited, not only by the current configuration of its concrete assets, but also by the alignment of the political forces in play. Policy-makers in both rural and urban contexts are probably well advised to abandon the currently fashionable focus on "creativity" as such, with all the tempting but misleading innuendoes that accompany the term, and to set their sights more carefully on concrete tasks of preservation and redevelopment relative to real local threats, opportunities, and possibilities with regard to economic and cultural development.

NOTES

1. The term "compage," although obsolete, is particularly apposite with regard to present purposes, for it conveys directly the sense of a system of formally conjoined elements. The compage idea was first introduced in geography by Whittelsey (1954) who used it to designate a unique but open-ended assemblage of regional *relata*, though few subsequent scholars have pursued this notion further.
2. The current county of Cumbria was formed in 1974 by amalgamating the old counties of Cumberland and Westmorland together with the Furness and Cartmel Districts of Lancashire and a small area of Yorkshire around Sedbergh.
3. Sedbergh is actually located in the Yorkshire Dales National Park, but is nonetheless contained within the county of Cumbria.
4. www.lake-district.gov.uk
5. The *Good Food Guide* defines a score of 4 as a "dedicated, focused approach to cooking, good classical skills, and high-quality ingredients."

10. Cosmopolis

A NEW GEOMETRY OF SPACE

The geographic realities now emerging around us are preeminently – though as we have just seen, not uniquely – constituted by an urban world, one in which some of the more dynamic and diversified forms of economic and social life are concentrated above all in large city-regions. These same city-regions make up the principal nodes of the global networks of spatial flows and interconnections that also typify this world. At the same time, we must not lose sight of the other geometries and topologies that characterize the contemporary condition, and in particular, the different spatial scales at which life is played out, not only at the local level but simultaneously at many more spatially extensive levels as well (Badie 1995; Brenner 2009; Jessop et al. 2008).

In recent years there have been calls, notably by Marston et al. (2005), to abandon the notion of scale altogether and to view reality in terms of a "flat ontology" in which the world becomes just a multiplicity of co-equal sites of social activity lacking any principle of spatial, juridical or functional ordering. This advocacy has the merit of correcting exaggerated views of the world as being composed of unidirectional top-down hierarchies, as for instance in the bare proposition that the forces of globalization determine the constitution and logic of local economic systems. It posits, instead, a world in which different socio-spatial assemblages interact with one another in complex relationships of antagonism and cooperation, producing "localized expressions of endo-events and exo-events" (Marston et al. 2005, p. 426). However, it suffers from the signal deficiency that in repudiating any kind of underlying systematic order it reduces social action and outcomes to an endlessly chaotic swirl of bodies (Woodward et al. 2012). This is fair enough at the level of everyday news reporting or story-telling about the world, but it fails totally to deal with the durable, repetitive structures that are an endemic element of social reality. The relations of authority and subordination that frequently run through the connective tissue of organized life, such as the interconnections between federal, state and local governments, are just one illustration of this point. Relations of this sort are not necessarily or invariably one-way, like the brain's control of the fingers, or all-encompassing like a nested series of Russian dolls, but they do nonetheless constitute a form of hierarchy. Clearly, decisions taken at one level of authority can frequently be renegotiated by countervailing powers at lower levels; and we may even find that some overarching organizations are actually less powerful than their component elements, as in the case of the relationship between multi-nation blocs like the EU or NAFTA and the individual countries that make them up. As it is, and in practice, the geography of the contemporary world can be described by neither the one extreme nor the other (that is, purely vertical interactions on the one side or invariable flatness on the other). Rather, it is made up by tangled networks of relationships sometimes in tiered configurations, sometimes in heterarchical arrays, and sometimes in convoluted hybrid forms.

As globalization moves forward, the manifold complexities of this geography across many different scales, territorial orbits, and topological conjunctions have become ever more marked, and their political expressions increasingly finely-grained (Allen and Cochrane 2010). Among the numerous phenomena making their historical and geographical appearance within this landscape, one of the more insistent in terms of its potent impacts at every level of spatial resolution is the large city-region. Indeed, the city-region, or something like it, has been seen in some accounts as a possible eventual challenge to the integrity of the nation state itself (Courchene 2001; Ohmae 1995; Peirce 1994).

COSMOPOLIS IN CONTEXT: FROM INTERNATIONALISM TO MULTISTRUCTURED GLOBALISM

Capitalism and the competitive markets that sustain it are based in essential ways on private decision-making and behavior – that is, on the individual conduct of firms and households. Utopian libertarians would claim that capitalist society can only achieve its ultimate capacities for efficient functioning and democratic order when civil society is released from all collective control, with the possible exception of a few residual governmental functions focused on essential public goods like national defense and the money supply. This claim is utopian in the pejorative sense of the term because it is, in the strictest possible manner, impossible. In other words, the continuation of capitalist society depends not only on individual action coordinated by markets, but also on wider institutions with the capacity and legitimacy to deal with the multiple breakdowns, failures, and lost opportunities that would inevitably undermine the viability of capitalism if individual decision-making and action alone were to prevail. This argument includes but goes far beyond the usual "market failure" idea, and invokes three interrelated social imperatives. The first is that markets cannot exist, in any case, in the absence of legal and political infrastructures guaranteeing orderly exchange and reliable enforcement of contracts. The second is that smooth social reproduction can never be assured by markets alone, not just because of common-pool resource issues (which, as we have seen, are legion), but also because unfettered markets are apt to give rise to many different kinds of corrosive outcomes, from child labor, through trade in toxic substances, to national and international financial crises. The third is that markets are unable in the long run to dissolve away the endemic political collision between capital and labor over the distribution of the surplus into profits and wages because for any given size of the total pie, as the whole of classical political economy from Smith through Ricardo to Marx makes abundantly clear, increases on the one side must always be accompanied by decreases on the other side. More generally, markets cannot resolve political conflicts, whatever their basis (with the exception, perhaps, of disputes that are susceptible to private settlement by means of compensation). These simple observations mean that apparatuses of political order, capable of both administrative regulation of the economy and the management of agonistic social tensions, are an indispensable element of any viable capitalist system. In brief, political apparatuses in capitalism are neither historical accidents not gratuitous irrationalities, but a basic imperative without which continued economic development and social viability would falter. By their very nature, they are also always subject to irregular twists and turns as different socioeconomic factions fight for their interests in diverse forums of political expression and representation.

In fordism, the preeminent institution of collective political order was the sovereign national state. The strongly national flavor of capitalism in the fordist era, extending roughly from the First World War to the mid-1970s, was reinforced by the existence of large mass production or growth-pole industries, functioning as national champions, and driving economic prosperity in each individual country of the economically developed world at that time. As shown earlier, this era was one in which two overarching policy priorities came steadily to account for increasing shares of governmental activity – that is, regulation of the boom and bust cycle, and maintenance of the social reproduction of the blue-collar working class. After the Second World War, these priorities were systematically consolidated in various versions of national keynesian economic policy and welfare-statist social policy throughout North America and much of Western Europe. As the Cold War deepened, the major capitalist societies became linked together in an international coalition in the interests of orderly trade and national defense. In this manner, the First World came into being as an economic and political bulwark against the Second World. The political geometry of the Cold War period was further complicated by the rivalry between the First and Second Worlds as they jockeyed for positions of influence with regard to the inchoate but pervasively impoverished set of countries designated as the Third World. In this tripartite world, the system of sovereign states seemed, as Waltz (1979) suggested, to resemble an anarchical collection of billiard balls colliding with and bouncing off one another; though on closer examination we ought not to overemphasize the pertinence of this metaphor or the strict territorial impermeability of the fordist state. True enough, the great economic and military crises of the 20th century had encouraged a retreat of the state back into its territorial shell, especially as compared with the situation that prevailed in the late 19th century. However, as capitalism recovered from the Second World War, at least some of the billiard balls began to display increasingly evident symptoms of economic and political porosity (Agnew 1994; Rosecrance 1986), and this state of affairs has intensified down to the present day. At the same time, each individual fordist state embodied a system of local governmental arrangements, functioning both as relay posts for the implementation of centrally-coordinated keynesian welfare-statist policies and as political decision-making centers in their own right focused on the idiosyncrasies of their individual territorial jurisdictions (Brenner 2004b).

With the ending of the Cold War and the steady globalization of capitalism, this dynamic of increasing inter-state porosity and local devolution has proceeded apace, together with the spread of capitalist economic arrangements to formerly peripheral territories (most forcefully in Asia, as Arrighi (2007) has shown). One rather apposite definition of globalization, indeed, is that it represents a steadily deepening though markedly uneven process of mutual osmosis on the part of national capitalisms. Still, far from leading to a monolithic translation of state authority into some supranational center of power, this osmosis is finding expression in the formation of labyrinthine, overlapping structures of regulation, some of them coinciding with formal governmental organizations, some with civil associations of many different kinds, and some with hybrid private–public institutions (Allen and Cochrane 2007; Hardt and Negri 2000). By the same token, the political geography of the world has also become increasingly multifarious and multitiered. Thus, as nation states progressively restructure, some regulatory functions are increasingly being consolidated at the inter-state level, as represented, for example, by organizations like the European Union, the North American Free Trade Agreement, the

G8/G20, the World Trade Organization, and the International Monetary Fund. Some functions, too, are consolidating at the sub-state level where many new predicaments have come into being as globalization proceeds. Thus, local and regional governmental organizations in various parts of the world have been asserting a diversity of independent lines of decision-making and action as national states find themselves unwilling or unable to cater to all the needs of their subjacent territorial units. Among these needs, some of the most urgent stem from the difficulties that localities face as global competition puts stress on their developmental prospects.

All that being said, the nation state unquestionably remains the privileged political entity of the 21st century world, and, as the current economic crisis of Europe so forcefully indicates, is the continuing focus of powerful nationalist sentiment. It is nonetheless the case that the economic and political geography of the world since the great crisis of fordism in the 1970s has been evolving from a condition of internationalism based on self-assertive national economies and nation states to a multistructured globalism reflecting many different and interacting lines of spatial convergence, interpenetration, and relationality. Threading through this labyrinth are two critical units of economic and political agency that have become especially prominent in recent decades. On the one hand, multinational corporations play a critical role as midwives of global capitalism, and these entities now account for huge cross-border flows, with as much as 48.6 percent of US goods imports consisting of intra-firm trade in 2010.[1] On the other hand, NGOs, private–public partnerships, and other civil associations are proliferating on all sides at the present time, and these perform important functions at all levels of geographic scale by filling regulatory absences and taking responsibility for collective action needs neglected by other institutions of governance.

NEW REGIONALISM AND THE CITY

Keating et al. (2009) suggest that we might well have expected, as modernity advanced over the course of the 20th century, to see a steady erosion of the region as a distinctive expression of social and political life, and a corresponding integration of local interests into nation-wide collectivities (see also Paasi 2011). Nothing like this has actually come to pass. Rather, the emerging world of the 21st century is one in which regions appear in practice to be asserting ever more forcefully their significance as elements of national and global space.

In fordist capitalism, the region, as both an economic and a political entity, lay decidedly toward the bottom end of a hierarchy of administrative relationships. A rough sort of parallel to this hierarchy could also be observed in the world of business where the great corporate entities at the head of the mass production system ruled over a panoply of manufacturing facilities whose differentiated tiers of productive activity powered the heartland regions of fordist capitalism. After the crisis of the 1970s, deep shifts in these arrangements started to become evident. The first symptom of this change was a significant withdrawal of the state from the keynesian and welfare-statist policies that had helped to propel fordism forward after the Second World War; and over the 1980s and 1990s, this withdrawal spread from one country to another. A second symptom was the rise of the postfordist economy and the formation of new industrial spaces scattered over many formerly peripheral and semi-peripheral areas (Scott 1988). Along with postfordism came a flattening of the multinational corporation, as individual branch operations were largely transformed into profit centers in their own right, and as a rising tide of vertical disintegration of production relationships occurred. The rounds of urban expansion unleashed by these and related developments, in combination with the spread of neoliberalism, set the scene for the emergence of a so-called new regionalism, and, in particular, a new city-centric regionalism marked by the widening global reach (but also vulnerability) of individual localities and increasing levels of local political autonomy.

   Regions, of course, have always been important foci of life throughout the history of capitalism, whether as simple administrative subdivisions of national space or as geographically distinctive elements of the landscape, such as areas of specialized agriculture or manufacturing. In fordist capitalism there was commonly a strong link between the policy objectives of the nation at large and those of its component geographic units. In conformity with keynesian welfare-statist principles, the state not only played an important role in protecting and enhancing the interests of these units, but was also actively concerned in efforts to redistribute income from richer to poorer regions and to enhance overall spatial equity. As the retreat from keynesian welfare-statism took deeper and deeper hold, this link was greatly relaxed. In 1975, for example, the federal government of the United States made direct monetary transfers to cities amounting to 9.8 percent of aggregate city receipts, whereas by 1992 the percentage had dropped markedly to 3.6 percent, even though a shift of responsibility for many kinds of social services from upper to lower tiers of government was simultaneously forcing local governments into higher levels of expenditure (US Department of Commerce 1997). Cutbacks in intergovernmental transfers were especially drastic in the country's three largest cities, namely New York, Los Angeles, and Chicago, which, respectively, over the period from 1975 to 1992, experienced a decline in combined federal and state subsidies from 52.6 percent to 32.1 percent, from 24.0 percent to 6.2 percent, and from 28.3 percent to 18.2 percent of total revenues. As shown in Figure 10.1, the retreat of the US federal government from financial support of local governments was especially severe over the decade from 1980 to 1990. Since then it has leveled out at an average of about 2.4 percent of local government receipts per annum, but it has never again attained the levels reached in the last years of fordism. In a world of shrinking support from the central state, major cities in many of the advanced capitalist countries, and in some less advanced capitalist countries too, can thus no longer count to the degree that they had earlier on the national government coming to their aid in times of economic stress, or promoting their growth when latent developmental prospects make their appearance on the horizon. On the contrary, and in view of the ever-expanding globalization of capitalism, with its multiple threats and opportunities, cities are now increasingly finding that they need to take much of the initiative themselves with regard to their developmental fortunes, or suffer the consequences of inaction. Harvey (1989) has pointed out that by the end of the 1980s, these conditions were provoking a marked evolution in the character of urban policy apparatuses, away from managerial and toward entrepreneurial governance – that is, away from concerns with distribution and equity, and toward more aggressive concentration on issues of local economic development.

In parallel with these trends, and in the context of the widespread market-opening measures of the 1980s and 1990s, vigorous bursts of re-agglomeration were now occurring in a wide global swath of metropolitan areas. Many of these metropolitan areas, as we have seen, represent the pioneer fringe of the new cognitive–cultural economy, and are now emerging as the focal points of a world-wide city-centric capitalism. According to the World Bank (2009), as much as 16 percent of global economic output today is produced in the world's top 30 cities, and over 75 percent of world output originates in urban areas at large. Moreover, as was already pointed out in Chapter 2, cities account for just over 50 percent of the world's population today. The large city-regions that have come into existence as these trends have moved ahead assume the form of overgrown and often coalescent metropolitan areas with large hinterland areas that themselves usually harbor subsidiary urban centers (Courchene 2001; Hall 2001; Sassen 2001; Ward and Jonas 2004), and, as such, they now constitute the core building blocks of the global urban system.

There can be no hard and fast line of functional demarcation around these city-regions – for their external relationships extend asymptotically outward to an indefinite extent – though we can often make a putative identification of a composite city-region by tracing out an approximate

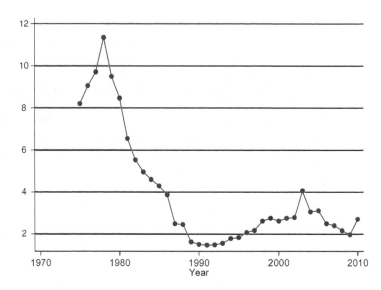

Notes: Grants-in-aid are shown as a percentage of total local government receipts.

Source: US Department of Commerce, Bureau of Economic Analysis, http://www.bea. gov.

Figure 10.1   Federal grants-in-aid to local governments in the United States (1975–2010)

gravitational field of interaction (for example, economic synergies, com-muting patterns, or potential efficiencies in service provision), linking the core city or cities to adjacent hinterland areas. As city-regions continue to emerge, the more intensely interconnected spaces that comprise their basic arena of operation sometimes also begin to take on definite administrative/ institutional identity. In fact, we can observe in many different countries today a slow and uncertain but nonetheless quite evident process in which city-regions are in various stages of emergence as identifiable, if fuzzy, functional and spatial entities. In this manner, the emerging city-regions of the contemporary world are starting to function as important nodes of the cosmopolitan system of "Empire" that Hardt and Negri (2000) have iden-tified as the decentered and uncoordinated network of institutions that is coming to characterize the global condition, and that they claim will one day transcend the Westphalian system of sovereign states.

PLANNING AND POLICY ISSUES IN GLOBAL CITY-REGIONS

The Imperative of Collective Action

Scholars like Allen et al. (1998) and Amin and Thrift (2002) have written about contemporary cities as being fundamentally composed out of relationships to a purely external world. In a certain way, this notion has much to recommend it, for urban areas today are deeply imbricated in relationships that span the entire globe and that help to sustain much of the internal activity of the city. By itself, however, the notion is signally inadequate. It makes no reference to what it is that holds cities together as spatially-concentrated clusters of economic and social activity; and, by the same token, it evades the critical question as to why municipal systems of regulation should invariably come into being as integral elements of these same clusters. In particular, the external relationships of the individual units of social action that comprise the city – such as firms and households – are always complemented by networks of intra-urban interaction that in turn account for the co-location of these units around a common center of gravity. In part, these networks consist of purely privatized transactions, and in part they are constituted by the massive systems of regional synergies and joint interests that underpin urban agglomerations as going concerns. Furthermore, urban governance structures come into existence not just as an arbitrary lower administrative tier for the relay of national policy directives, but as necessary guarantors of social and spatial order in these localized cauldrons of potential disarray and social irrationality.

From the very beginning of capitalism, urban areas have been sites of endless endogenously-generated problems and predicaments (Benevolo 1971). Much of this condition derives from the joint generation of positive and negative outcomes in the urban arena outside any established system of property rights or market mediation. Agglomeration economies and diseconomies represent a major component of these outcomes, but, in addition, many other sources of inefficiency and breakdown can be identified, including spatial and temporal misallocation of resources, underinvestment in needed public services, land use conflicts, free-rider problems with regard to property development, and so on. Moreover, the quandaries that revolve around these issues are exacerbated by the endemic social conflicts that exist over access to infrastructures of collective consumption in the city (Castells 1976; Preteceille 1986). In the era of keynesian welfare-statism, urban planners and policy-makers were relatively (though never fully) responsive to these threats to overall urban performance and were on occasion even prepared to deal with them in order to promote redistributive welfare. By comparison, in large city-regions today, enveloped as they are in a dominantly neoliberal policy environment with its dampening effect on public spending, problems like these are often pushed to one side by policy-makers. Conversely, certain urban policy questions that were relatively subdued at an earlier period of time have now come much more firmly onto the agenda. These revolve primarily around economic pressures on cities due to globalization and the concomitant search (more or less intense depending on political circumstances) for institutions capable of boosting local competitive advantages, not only in a static sense, but also in the sense of being able to steer the urban economy away from adverse path selection and ensuring that there is sufficient system resilience so that the city can rebound rapidly from external shocks. The quest for improved economic performance at the level of the individual city is central here (Cox 2011; Logan and Molotch 1987), even though this quest is apt to be at least partially vitiated by the heritage of municipal fragmentation that almost always characterizes the internal spaces of large cities. This heritage is often a source of inefficiency and social bias in the provision of urban public goods and services, just as it is also a very real impediment to achieving effective coordination of policy and planning activities focused on building up city-region competitive advantages.

Administrative Consolidation and Political Prospects

Many city-regions all over the world are now struggling to come to terms with the dilemmas and tensions engendered by this internal splintering of governance structures, and to create a more rational and inclusive managerial order. In view of the increasing pressures to which city-regions are subject, actual progress in this matter has perhaps been slower than might have been expected, possibly in large degree because of the entrenched vested interests that reside in inherited patterns of municipal fragmentation. Still, numerous experiments in cross-municipal administration can now be detected in many different countries. Toronto, London, Tokyo, and Hong Kong, for example, have all instituted one version or another of extended metropolitan governance. The specific solutions that have been implemented in different instances take on assorted forms, varying from overall municipal federations, through multi-tiered jurisdictions, to region-wide special-purpose districts with authority over specific issues such as water supply, utilities, or air quality management. The latter approach is strongly in evidence in the greater Los Angeles region. As Vogel et al. (2010) have intimated, China offers some particularly revealing instances of this hunt for overarching administrative command of city-regions. The steady advance of capitalism in that country has been attended by precipitously rising levels of inter-municipal competition, a phenomenon that was unknown in the period of state socialism. This turn of events has set in motion a drive to establish city-region governmental structures, both as a way of securing higher levels of operating efficiency, and as a mechanism for building more effective local economic development policies. The most impressive instance of this trend is the current move to amalgamate Shanghai and the adjacent provinces of Jiangsu and Zhejiang into a giant city-region of 90 million people. As the urge to consolidation moves forward in country after country across the globe, city-regions are beginning to function in important ways as political actors and economic motors on the world stage. To put the matter in more general terms, considerable effort is currently being expended in attempts to build new institutions of collective management and coordination at the level of the city-region, and this effort is intensifying as global competition grows stronger and as the protective umbrella of the national state becomes more selective. That said, the view of Ohmae (1995) to the effect that a sort of new city-state system is now in the process of emerging, is almost certainly an exaggeration.

The search for some measure of city-region governance appears to be especially strong in metropolitan areas with a high quotient of cognitive–cultural economic activity, for besides the market failures and political predicaments that are prevalent in dense agglomerations, the cultivation of advanced forms of production and employment based on high-level human capital calls for careful regulation of the urban milieu so as to ensure that the built environment and local social life conform to standards that are consonant with this vocation. Governance structures that overlie the fragmented municipalities and other local administrations that almost always make up the individual city-region are well positioned to deal with these multiple issues, for overarching administrative arrangements of this type are in principle able to develop coherent policy approaches for handling the numerous collective action needs that reverberate across any major urban area. Such arrangements are especially important in dealing with issues like common pool resources, infrastructural investments, pollution control, and transportation in their full deployment over urban space. Local economic development issues, in particular, are very susceptible to treatment at the city-region level given that competitive advantage resides to such a large extent in regionally-specific inter-firm networks, labor markets, and information systems.

Certainly, competitiveness has become one of the principal watchwords of urban administrations in the United States and other countries in recent decades as manifest in Harvey's arguments about the emergence of aggressively entrepreneurial mayors and city councils. In the same way, there has been a proliferation of different kinds of regional economic development agencies (funded by local governments, business associations, private–public partnerships, and so on) focused on strategies for promoting technological development, skills, and business acumen. The Third Italy has been notably successful in setting up organizations of this sort (see for example Bianchi 1992), but counterparts can be found in virtually every country in the advanced capitalist world, and in many less economically advanced countries too. Similarly, national urban policy has in numerous cases more or less consistently turned away from old fordist-era strategies of locational decentralization while encouraging individual cities and regions to develop their own growth potentials on the basis of their individual resources and capabilities. The rationale underlying this policy shift is partly founded on the renewed innovativeness of localized industrial clusters in an economic environment where the cognitive and cultural assets of the labor force play an ever-augmenting role in the development process. The Regional Development Agencies of England (to be succeeded by Local Enterprise Partnerships and other successor bodies in March 2012) are an example of this approach to local economic growth. Perhaps nowhere is this shift more evident than in France, where one of the latest substitutes for the old decentralization policy mania of the fordist era can be found in the ambitious *Pôles de Compétitivité* program initiated in 2004, with its emphasis on advanced technology-intensive and creative industries (Darmon and Jacquet 2005; Guillaume 2008; Pecqueur 2008), as exemplified by the Aerospace Valley linking Bordeaux and Toulouse, the Lyonbiopôle with its focus on biotechnology and medicine, or the Grenoble technopole specializing in microelectronics and micromechanics. However, effective institution-building and other programmatic interventions to build local competitive advantage take considerable time to come to fruition, hence the Achilles heel of many local economic development initiatives today is frequently to be found in the typically curtailed capacity of the political process, especially at the local level, to sustain durable policy commitments over a time horizon that extends well beyond one or two electoral cycles (Scott 1995; 2001).

Economic development is a key policy challenge facing global city-regions. Another key challenge revolves around the deepening social and economic divide that separates symbolic analysts and low-wage service workers in urban areas. The politically problematical nature of this divide is magnified by the massive absorption of ethnically and racially distinctive immigrant groups into the underbelly of the cognitive–cultural economy of leading city-regions today, and it is becoming all the more acute in the context of the anti-welfare policy regimes that prevail all over the world at the present time. A significant corollary of these circumstances is the rapidly diminishing levels of enfranchisement and democratic incorporation of large segments of the population caught up in the lower reaches of urban society. There are no simple technocratic solutions to the indurated social problems highlighted by these remarks, particularly in view of the political resistances that can be expected to materialize from those who reap advantage from the existing state of things. It is one thing to propose remedial programs focused on reforms like subsidized housing or a more equitable local system of taxation and redistribution, not to mention higher wages, improved benefits, and better working conditions for members of the servile class. But it is altogether another thing to generate political support for such programs, and in the absence of a considerably more forceful level of political contestation than is the case in most of the world's great city-regions today the prospects of major restructuring in the interests of more equitable income distribution and democratic inclusion would seem to be rather limited.

Nonetheless, there is surely a point at which the tensions and inequities of urban life might be expected to tip the balance in favor of greatly increased political activism on the part of those who toil at or close to the bottom end of the urban economy, and there are signs that the neoliberal political practices that have accompanied the rise of the cognitive–cultural economy over the last few decades are now approaching exhaustion as instruments of socio-economic regulation. The rising tide of poverty and marginalization in large cities is just one symptom of this failure, as are the fiscal crises currently raging at every level of government today. If correct, these remarks mean that prospects for a new progressive political opening may be on the horizon, bringing with it new projects of urban reform that enlarge the role of the city as a center of democratic and communal life (cf. Lefebvre 1968). If not correct, one likely alternative is the steady deterioration of the city as a locus of community, conciliation, and conviviality, together with a continued widening of the gulf between the rich and the poor. Certainly there is a real tension today in major cities all around the world between the steady privatization of urban space on the one side, and demands for its democratization on the other side; and a further stress point is the deteriorating levels of accessibility between home and work for many of the less privileged denizens of the city. These irrationalities can be observed in the increasing spread of gated communities, in the concomitant deepening of urban social segregation, in the development of privileged and highly controlled enclaves for elite shopping and leisure pursuits, and in the increasing ejection of low-wage workers from inner city neighborhoods to peripheral urban locations that are today often far distant from relevant employment opportunities.

COSMOPOLIS REDUX

City-regions represent an advanced form of urbanization – namely, super-cluster development – based on the resurgence of agglomeration tendencies in the contemporary economy combined with the ever-deepening functional integration of urban areas with one another across the globe. As such, city-regions are caught up with one another in world-wide relations of competition and collaboration. Each individual city-region represents an interlocking system of local and global relationships, which, in successful cases, is structured by a path-dependent dynamic of agglomeration $\rightarrow$ market extension $\rightarrow$ growth $\rightarrow$ agglomeration $\rightarrow$ . . . $\rightarrow$ etc., as captured in the theoretical ideas laid out in Chapter 2. Growth, in turn, is dependent not only on the joint competitive advantages generated within the economy of the city-region as a whole, but also, and increasingly, on appropriate institutions of planning and coordination, capable of maintaining order in the social and economic functions of the city region, and above all of effective management of its collective assets.

With the globalization of capitalism, increasing numbers of metropolitan areas are graduating to the status of city-regions. The overall result is an emerging cosmopolitan network of gigantic urban centers, each representing a major concentration of economic muscle and political influence. As such, city-regions are steadily taking their place as one of the more potent and visible elements of the new world order.

NOTE

1. As reported by the US Census Bureau of Statistics, Related Part Database, http://www.census.gov/foreign-trade/Press-Release/2010pr/aip/related_party/rp10.pdf.

11. Brave new world?

In the final years of fordism, it was not uncommon for marxist scholars, like Mandel (1975) for example, to refer to the world around them as having entered the phase of "late capitalism," a term that carries with it the more or less open implication that the end is nigh. The economic crises of the 1970s and the devastation that was visited on the major manufacturing regions of North America and Western Europe at this time lent an air of credibility to this manner of viewing the world. The emergence of post-fordism and postmodernism over the 1980s was taken in other quarters as a further indication of impending doom, the former being interpreted as a morbid and opportunistic means of shoring up a crumbling economic system (Pollert 1991), and the latter being seen as a passionless, irrational substitute for a waning cultural modernity (Hicks 2011).

However, capitalism, like nature, is vastly more cunning than most of the analysts who subject it to scrutiny. The "late capitalism" of the 1970s and early 1980s was not followed by systemic collapse, but by a significant reconfiguration of the technological and organizational arrangements underlying the production system, and – of special importance in the present context – by big shifts in the geographic outlines of economic development. These shifts are manifest, above all, in two main outcomes. One is represented by the relative and absolute transfer of routinized manufacturing and service activities from older geographic centers of capitalist growth into new industrial spaces in low-wage countries, followed by subsequent upgrading, and, in some instances, by significant further development of these spaces. The other is represented by the efflorescence of the cognitive–cultural economy and its concentration in major city-regions, most notably in North America, Western Europe, and the Asia-Pacific region. Something of the first trend is captured in the changing terminology of development studies over the last few decades, in which the conception of a stubbornly underdeveloped Third World gives way to the proposition that some parts of the Third World should more appropriately be treated as newly industrializing countries or NICs, and then, in turn, to the notion that what were referred to as NICs eventually evolve into "tiger economies," BRICs, and other manifestations of relatively advanced economic development. In the light of all these comments, we should probably acknowledge that capitalism, so far from being in or close to a late stage of evolution, is in all likelihood still in the early stages of historical development.

Certainly, the vast majority of the world's population, and above all, more and more of the world's cities, have now been brought directly within the ambit of capitalism. Above all, the very largest metropolitan areas of both the Global North and the Global South function ever more intensely as economic and political nerve-centers of the world system, and most notably as the main hubs of the cognitive–cultural economy. In addition, they are linked together in complex networks of competition and collaboration marked by abundant inter-urban flows of goods and services as well as technological know-how, information, finance, and labor. These circumstances underpin the formation of what I identified in Chapter 5 as a third wave of urbanization, coinciding above all with the global mosaic of large metropolitan areas or city-regions. This mosaic intersects with purely national systems of urban development and extends over the Global North, and, to a lesser but rapidly growing extent, the Global South. To be sure, any reference to the South raises the further issue of those dramatic points of suture where modern urbanization processes and the peculiar socio-economic circumstances of the world's poorer countries encounter one another within the megacity; that is, where pockets of advanced capitalism come into being cheek-by-jowl with the slums, destitution, environmental toxicity, and other social problems that so acutely accompany urbanization processes in many less economically developed countries (Robinson 2006; Roy 2011). My account in this book has largely glossed over the latter issues, not because I consider them unimportant, but because my chief concern here has been to elucidate another basic facet of the urban problematic, namely the impacts of the dynamic leading edges of capitalism on spatial development, and, most dramatically of all, the concomitant emergence of a globally-interconnected system of city-regions. Of course, we must acknowledge that these impacts are always filtered through the inherited milieu of each individual city (cf. Kloosterman 2010). For this and other reasons, my arguments about a third wave of urbanization are far from insinuating that the great cities of the contemporary world are converging toward some sort of universal norm. We do not need to declare, along with Dick and Rimmer (1998), that cities are becoming more substantively alike – for, in certain senses, and especially in the context of the new economy, cities are actually becoming more diverse – but only that a common theoretical language can be brought to bear on the kaleidoscopic reality of the city in the 21st century.

In this book, I have tried to work out some of this theoretical language by paying special attention to the interrelations between capitalism and urbanization with special reference to the rise of the cognitive–cultural economy and ways in which it is taking root, unequally but definitely, in large urban areas. As it does so, many far-reaching shifts in the social and physical structure of cities can be observed: changes in their productive activities and capacities, restructuring of local labor markets, renewal of urban physical and symbolic landscapes, and so on. The discussion in Chapter 9 has also indicated that the expansion of the new economy has done much to accelerate the continuing erosion of the opposition between the urban and the rural as distinctive realms of social life. In the 21st century, increasingly large expanses of rural territory, or better yet, the interstices between major urban concentrations, are being colonized by segments of the new economy and are being brought within its system of aesthetic and semiotic production. As this occurs, these interstitial areas start to form one of the constituent facets of a complex web of alternating high-density and low-density spaces, each of them, in their different ways, harboring specialized clusters and assemblages of cognitive–cultural economic activity and human capital.

These developments are all part of the massive geographical reconstruction that is currently going on as the new economy and its subjacent production and employment systems spread across the globe and intensify their hold on selected places. This reconstruction can be described in terms of a threefold spatial logic of convergence, differentiation, and multiplicity. Convergence is represented above all by the centripetal forces that are everywhere reinforcing agglomeration and its expression in the world-wide resurgence of large metropolitan areas or city-regions (in contrast to the metropolitan decay characteristic of late fordism). Spatial differentiation is occurring in conjunction with convergence because the emerging global system of chamberlinian competition is making it increasingly possible, and indeed imperative, for individual cities to specialize in specific market niches. Convergence and differentiation are in turn accompanied by spatial multiplicity in the sense that the organization of economic and political activity is marked by many overlapping, interpenetrating, and spatially assorted layers of systemic order from the local to the global. This multiplicity means that today we are all caught up simultaneously in sundry local, national, and supranational relationships. What is more, rapidly rising levels of population mobility mean that our allegiances in these matters frequently undergo significant modification at intervals over our lifetimes as more and more of us periodically move our work-places and residence-places from one location to another around the globe. The result is that increasing numbers of individuals today are eligible to carry two and sometimes three or more passports. At the same time, the advancing pace of globalization is evidently not, as some had thought, leading to a monolithic hierarchy of planetary order with some form of world government at its peak; rather, the expanding multiplicity of political collectivities and networks means that a much more ambiguous situation prevails with many different, and at best only loosely coordinated, forms of political organization occurring at many different geographic scales.

Despite this multiplicity, the nation state still represents the central pivot of global order and the most decisive focus of political power in the modern world. As Sassen (2008) justly indicates, the global, in the end, is endogenous to the national. To put this point another way, the global (including multination blocs) emerges out of a controlled reallocation of regulatory functions upward from the nation state to plurinational institutions; though clearly, important modifications of state functions and authority tend to come about as this reallocation proceeds. Concurrently, we can observe a converse drift of functions downward from the nation state to major urban areas, many of which are increasingly acting in independent ways in order to ensure their own economic and social well-being. Moreover, these urban areas are coming to function as the heartlands of a new cosmopolitanism as ever-augmenting flows of the world's capital and labor wash around and through these peculiar islands of productive activity and social life. The principal nodes of this new cosmopolitan landscape are the great global city-regions, most notably in view of their significance as instruments through which the escalating convergence, differentiation, and multiplicity of the new world order is preeminently being ushered in. They are, by the same token, coming to play a visible role as unique laboratories of political experimentation.

The new cognitive–cultural capitalism is in part driving these developments forward while at the same time infusing them with multifaceted political predicaments. Some of these predicaments stem from increasing economic inequality between and within individual places; some result from the deepening divide in the opportunities and life chances that different social groups are able to secure for themselves; yet others can be traced to the resurgent economic competition and volatility that threaten economic well-being in many different places. Each version of capitalism comes with its own in-built tendencies to crisis, but the new capitalism, especially given the insistent financialization of so many of its core functions, appears to have unleashed unprecedented forces of destabilization, as manifest in the prolonged economic crash of recent years. The state's retreat from robust forms of regulation under the aegis of neoliberalism has greatly exacerbated this state of affairs. Probably the worst case scenario that might be envisaged for the future in political terms is the further extension and deepening of the neoliberalism that has prevailed locally, nationally, and internationally over the last few decades. Among other things, continued reluctance of governmental apparatuses to engage in more effective social and economic regulation will almost certainly be the occasion of further widening of the income gap between upper and lower segments of urban society, of continued if not aggravated uneven development across geographic space, and of rapidly alternating episodes of financial boom and bust in the macro-economy. If this diagnosis is on target, it means that one of the central imperatives of policy in the current conjuncture must be to build institutional frameworks that will secure meaningful redistribution and redress regional inequalities while ensuring steady and widespread economic growth. Notwithstanding the endless spate of right-wing ideology to the effect that social equity and economic growth are mutually exclusive goals, the call for more progressive forms of capitalism is far from being a utopian illusion. Indeed, quite apart from the theoretical justification of collective action in the sphere of the economy as laid out in earlier chapters of this book, the social market alternatives that have been established in some countries already demonstrate in practice that they are capable of robust management of capitalism, and specifically of securing high levels of prosperity combined with social equity.

To be sure, it is one thing to express opinions about desirable political goals, but an altogether different thing to bring those goals to fruition. The pursuit of political goals, in other words, depends critically upon social mobilization in the context of an organizational framework capable of maintaining a disciplined focus on practical results. There is no scarcity of contestatory causes in today's world, ranging from Occupy Wall Street, through the Chinese Democracy Movement, to the Arab Spring, not to mention the myriad campaigns in virtually every city of the world focused on local social justice issues and on securing wider democratic rights. Many of these causes have made significant gains, and some, like the Arab Spring, are full of large-scale transformational potential. At the same time, the rise of the Internet has added a new dimension to the tasks of political mobilization by making it possible for huge numbers of individuals to connect with one another instantaneously and to strategize about their goals. The Internet has also enabled local political movements to reach out globally and thus to build wide political momentum much more rapidly than was ever the case in the past. In many respects, indeed, the urge to engage in political protest seems nowadays to be running ahead of any effort to build systematic and progressive conceptual guidelines in which ordinary people can see something of their own lives and predicaments in meaningful and actionable ways. This lacuna is especially noticeable in the USA, where many grass-roots movements can be found all across the country, but where the overall terms of national debate appear for the most part to have been hammered out between an increasingly conservative right wing and a technocratic center. It is perhaps not surprising to find that at least some of these movements, in spite of their grass-roots origins, have taken to expressing their multiple dissatisfactions in terms of a hard-edged conservative rhetoric. The Tea Party is a noteworthy example of this curious turn of events.

In this context, it is evident that one of the enormous questions that haunts the politics of the current era derives from the ways in which consciousness and authority are becoming ever more intimately caught up in a system of biopolitical order. This is a system in which the regulation and normalization of life are in important ways secured by means of internal acquiescence of the subject without any compulsion or external constraint. The genesis of this biopolitical order can be traced back to the first half of the 20th century as the real subsumption of labor to the needs and purposes of capitalism starts to gather momentum. This trend then becomes steadily more assertive over the course of the 20th century, and, through a series of stages, begins to take on an even more dramatic complexion in the guise of the real subsumption of social life – that is, a state of affairs in which the needs and purposes of capitalism are reflected in the entire social context of the subject. The burgeoning cognitive–cultural economy has unquestionably contributed significantly to this process, and all the more so in light of the manner in which it intertwines with intellect and affect on both the supply side and the demand side (Moulier Boutang 2007; Vercellone 2007). In this connection, Hardt and Negri (2009, p. 251) have claimed that "today, finally, the biopolitical city is emerging." This state of affairs poses crucial questions for future research. Precisely how, we might ask, does the cognitive–cultural economy, as both production system and mode of consumption, operate on psycho-social outcomes? What are its ideological functions and how are they maintained? What is the wider political meaning of these phenomena? And perhaps most urgently of all, what effects does the intimate convergence of economy and culture in today's world have on the forms of critical consciousness that are the key to all rational collective life? These questions indicate that, above and beyond the issues of urbanization, regional development, and globalization that are the main focus of this book, we must also resolutely turn our attention to concerns about just what forms of human subjectivity, cultural awareness, and social interaction are being shaped in capitalism today and what this means for public life. Does the new capitalism signify that the gloomy predictions of the Frankfurt School philosophers are finally about to be realized (Adorno 1991; Horkheimer and Adorno 1972)? Or that some sort of dystopia à la Huxley is in the offing? Or are there identifiable openings toward a more progressive set of outcomes?

There can be no decisive answer to this last question in the abstract, for any concrete response needs to be worked out in the arena of practical politics. In the 21st century, progressive political action must not only continue to focus on fundamental issues of distribution in the widest possible sense of the term, but also on dominant processes of intellectual and affective habituation. Above all, it must display a willingness to confront, through public debate, the opportunistic and philistine proclivities in so much of contemporary social and economic life. There is, to be sure, much that responds to genuinely human needs and values in the offerings of the new cognitive–cultural order, but there is also much that is problematical, from its involvement in high-technology weapons production, through its tendency to generate increasingly contrived financial instruments with potentially disastrous social costs, to its active propagation of commercial culture of the most intellectually debased variety. The politics of these issues, like the politics of income distribution, stands urgently in need of recovery.

References

Abaza, M. 2001. Shopping malls, consumer culture and the reshaping of public space in Egypt. *Theory, Culture & Society*, 18 (5): 97–122.

Acs, Z. J. 2002. *Innovation and the Growth of Cities*. Cheltenham: Edward Elgar.

Adorno, T. W. 1991. *The Culture Industry: Selected Essays on Mass Culture*. London: Routledge.

Aglietta, M. 1976. *Régulation et Crises du Capitalisme*. Paris: Calmann-Lévy.

Agnew, J. A. 1994. The territorial trap: the geographical assumptions of international relations theory. *Review of International Political Economy*, 1:53–80.

Allen, J., and A. Cochrane. 2007. Beyond the territorial fix: regional assemblages, politics and power. *Regional Studies*, 41:1161–1175.

Allen, J., and A. Cochrane. 2010. Assemblages of state power: topological shifts in the organization of government and politics. *Antipode*, 42:1071–1089.

Allen, J., D. Massey, and A. Cochrane. 1998. *Rethinking the Region*. London: Routledge.

Amin, A., ed. 1994. *Post-Fordism: A Reader*. Oxford: Blackwell.

Amin, A., and J. Roberts. 2008. Knowing in action: beyond communities of practice. *Research Policy*, 37:353–369.

Amin, A., and N. Thrift. 2002. *Cities: Reimagining the Urban*. Cambridge: Polity.

Amin, S. 1973. *Le Développement Inégal; Essai sur les Formations Sociales du Capitalisme Périphérique*. Paris: Les Éditions de Minuit.

Anderson, G. 1974. *Networks of Contact: The Portuguese in Toronto*. Waterloo: Wilfred Laurier University Press.

Andreff, W. 2009. Outsourcing in the new strategy of multinational companies: foreign investment, international subcontracting, and production relocation. *Papeles de Europa*, 18:5–34.

Appelbaum, E., and J. Schmitt. 2009. Low wage work in high-income countries: labor market institutions and business strategy in the US and Europe. *Human Relations*, 62:1907–1934.

Arrighi, G. 2007. *Adam Smith in Beijing: Lineages of the Twenty-First Century*. London: Verso.

Asheim, B. T., and L. Coenen. 2005. Knowledge bases and regional innovation systems: comparing Nordic clusters. *Research Policy*, 34:1173–1190.

Attewell, P. 1987. The deskilling controversy. *Work and Occupations*, 14:323–346.

Autor, D. H., L. F. Katz, and M. S. Kearney. 2006. The polarization of the US labor market. *American Economic Review*, 96:189–194.

Autor, D. H., F. Levy, and R. J. Murnane. 2003. The skill content of recent technological change: an empirical exploration. *Quarterly Journal of Economics*, 118:1279–1333.

Bacolod, M., B. S. Blum, and W. C. Strange. 2009. Urban interactions: soft skills versus specialization. *Journal of Economic Geography*, 9:227–262.

Badie, B. 1995. *La Fin des Territoires*. Paris: Fayard.

Badyina, A., and O. Golubchikov. 2005. Gentrification in central Moscow – a market process or a deliberate policy? Money, power and people in housing regeneration in Ostozhenka. *Geografiska Annaler Series B-Human Geography*, 87B (2):113–129.

Bagnasco, A. 1977. *Tre Italie: la Problematica Territoriale dello Sviluppo Italiano*. Bologna: Il Mulino.

Becattini, G. 1987a. Introduzione: il distretto industriale Marshalliano: cronaca di un ritrovamento. In *Mercato e Forze Locali: Il Distretto Industriale*, ed. G. Becattini. Bologna: Il Mulino, pp. 7–34.

Becattini, G., ed. 1987b. *Mercato e Forze Locali : Il Distretto Industriale*. Bologna: Il Mulino.

Bell, D. 1973. *The Coming of Post-Industrial Society; A Venture in Social Forecasting*. New York: Basic Books.

Bell, D., and M. Jayne. 2009. Small Cities? Towards a Research Agenda. *International Journal of Urban and Regional Research*, 33 (3):683–699.

Bell, D., and M. Jayne. 2010. The creative countryside: policy and practice in the UK rural cultural economy. *Journal of Rural Studies*, 26 (3):209–218.

Benevolo, L. 1971. *The Origins of Modern Town Planning*. Cambridge, MA: MIT Press.

Benjamin, W. 1969. *Illuminations: Essays and Reflections*. New York: Schocken.

Berry, C. R., and E. L. Glaeser. 2005. The divergence of human capital levels across cities. *Papers in Regional Science*, 84:407–444.

Bessière, J. 1998. Local development and heritage: traditional food and cuisine as tourist attractions in rural areas. *Sociologia Ruralis*, 38:21–34.

Bianchi, P. 1992. Levels of policy and the nature of postfordist competition.

In *Pathways to Industrialization and Regional Development*, eds M. Storper, and A. J. Scott. London: Routledge, pp. 303–315.

Blackaby, F., ed. 1978. *De-Industrialization*. London: Heinemann.

Blakely, E. J., and M. G. Snyder. 1997. *Fortress America: Gated Communities in the United States*. Washington, DC: Brookings Institution Press.

Blaut, J. M. 1976. Where was capitalism born. *Antipode*, (8):1–11.

Bluestone, B., and B. Harrison. 1982. *The Deindustrialization of America*. New York: Basic Books.

Bontje, M., S. Musterd, and P. Pelzer. 2011. *Inventive City-Regions: Path Dependence and Creative Knowledge Strategies*. Farnham: Ashgate.

Borrus, M., L. D. Tyson, and J. Zysman. 1986. Creating advantage: how government policies shape international trade in the semiconductor industry. In *Strategic Trade Policy and the New International Economics*, ed. P. Krugman. Cambridge: The MIT Press, pp. 91–114.

Bowen, S. 2011. The importance of place: re-territorializing embeddedness. *Sociologia Ruralis*, 51:325–348.

Boyer, R. 1986. *La Théorie de la Régulation: Une Analyse Critique*. Paris: Algalma.

Brenner, N. 2004a. *New State Spaces: Urban Governance and the Rescaling of Governance*. Oxford: Oxford University Press.

Brenner, N. 2004b. Urban governance and the production of new state spaces in Western Europe, 1960–2000. *Review of International Political Economy*, 11:447–488.

Brenner, N. 2009. A thousand leaves: notes on the geographies of uneven spatial development. In *Leviathan Undone? Towards a Political Economy of Scale*, eds R. Keil, and R. Mahon. Vancouver: UBC Press, pp. 27–49.

Brown, A., J. O'Connor, and S. Cohen. 2000. Local music policies within a global music industry: cultural quarters in Manchester and Sheffield. *Geoforum*, 31:437–451.

Brown, E., B. Derudder, C. Parnreiter, W. Pelupessy, P. J. Taylor, and F. Witlox. 2010. World city networks and global commodity chains: towards a world-systems integration. *Global Networks – A Journal of Transnational Affairs*, 10 (1):12–34.

Brown, J. S., and P. Duguid. 1991. Organizational learning and communities of practice: toward a unified view of working, learning, and innovation. *Organization Science*, 2:40–57.

Brunton, J. 2001. *The Arts and Crafts Movement in the Lake District: A Social History*. Lancaster: University of Lancaster, Centre for North-West Regional Studies.

Brusco, S. 1982. The Emilian model: productive decentralization and social integration. *Cambridge Journal of Economics*, 6:167–180.

Bunce, M. 1994. *The Countryside Ideal: Anglo-American Images of Landscape.* London: Routledge.

Cairncross, F. 1997. *The Death of Distance: How the Communications Revolution Will Change our Lives.* Boston: Harvard Business School Press.

Camagni, R., ed. 1991. *Innovation Networks: Spatial Perspectives.* London: Pinter.

Camagni, R. P. 1995. The concept of innovative milieu and its relevance for public policies in European lagging regions. *Papers in Regional Science,* 74:317–340.

Camargo, L. J. J., C. M. J. Camargo, E. V. Rondon, H. P. B. Queiroz, S. R. d. Santos, and M. A. Mercante. 2011. Anályse da sustentabilidade do turismo ecológico no município de Bonito, Mato Grosso do Sul na promoção desenvolvimento regional. *Sociedade & Natureza,* 23:65–75.

Carney, J., R. Hudson, and J. Lewis, eds. 1980. *Regions in Crisis: New Perspectives in European Regional Theory.* New York: St Martin's Press.

Castells, M. 1972. *La Question Urbaine.* Paris: Maspéro.

Castells, M. 1976. Crise de l'état, consommation collective et constradictions urbaines. In *La Crise de l'Etat,* ed. N. Poulantzas. Paris: Presses Universitaires de France, pp. 179–208.

Cenzatti, M. 1993. *Los Angeles and the L.A. School: Postmodernism and Urban Studies.* Los Angeles: Los Angeles Forum for Architecture and Urban Design.

Chen, Y., and S. S. Rosenthal. 2008. Local amenities and life-cycle migration: do people move for jobs or fun? *Journal of Urban Economics,* 64:519–537.

Childe, V. G. 1950. The urban revolution. *Town Planning Review,* 21:3–17.

Christaller, W. 1933. *Die Zentralen Orte in Süddeutschland.* Jena: Gustav Fischer.

Clark, T. N. 2004. Introduction: taking entertainment seriously. In *The City as an Entertainment Machine,* ed. T. N. Clark. Amsterdam: Elsevier, pp. 1–18.

Clark, T. N., R. Lloyd, K. K. Wong, and P. Jain. 2002. Amenities drive urban growth. *Journal of Urban Affairs,* 24:493–515.

Clerval, A. 2011. Les dynamiques spatiales de la gentrification à Paris. *Cybergéo: Revue Européenne de la Géographie,* http://cybergeo.revues. org/.

Cochrane, A. 2007. *Understanding Urban Policy: A Critical Approach.* Oxford: Blackwell.

Coe, N. M., M. Hess, H. W. C. Yeung, P. Dicken, and J. Henderson. 2004. Globalizing regional development: a global production networks perspective. *Transactions of the Institute of British Geographers*, 29 (4):468–484.

Condit, C. W. 1964. *The Chicago School of Architecture: A History of Commercial and Public Building in the Chicago Area, 1875–1925*. Chicago: University of Chicago Press.

Conradson, D., and E. Pawson. 2009. New cultural economies of marginality: revisiting the West Coast, South Island, New Zealand. *Journal of Rural Studies*, 25:77–86.

Cooke, P., and L. Lazzeretti. 2007. Creative cities: an introduction. In *Creative Cities, Cultural Clusters and Local Economic Development*. Cheltenham: Edward Elgar, pp. 1–24.

Cooke, P., and A. Piccaluga, eds. 2006. *Regional Development in the Knowledge Economy*. New York: Routledge.

Cooke, P., and D. Schwartz. 2007. Creative regions: an introduction. In *Creative Regions: Technology, Culture and Knowledge Entrepreneurship*, eds P. Cooke, and D. Schwartz. London: Routledge, pp. 1–20.

Courchene, T. J. 2001. Ontario as a North American region-state, Toronto as a global city-region: responding to the NAFTA challenge. In *Global City-Regions: Trends, Theory, Policy*, ed. A. J. Scott. Oxford: Oxford University Press, pp. 158–190.

Cox, K. R. 2011. Institutional geographies and local economic development. In *Handbook of Local and Regional Development*, eds A. Pike, A. Rodríguez-Pose, and J. Tomaney. London: Routledge, pp. 272-282.

Cranford, C. J. 2005. Networks of exploitation: immigrant labor and the restructuring of the Los Angeles janitorial industry. *Social Problems*, 52:379–397.

Currid, E. 2007. *The Warhol Economy: How Fashion, Art and Music Drive New York City*. Princeton: Princeton University Press.

Cusumano, M. A. 1985. *The Japanese Automobile Industry: Technology and Management at Nissan and Toyota*. Cambridge, MA: Harvard University Press.

Cuthbert, A. R. 2006. *The Form of Cities: Political Economy and Urban Design*. Oxford: Blackwell.

Darmon, D., and N. Jacquet. 2005. *Les Pôles de Compétitivité: Le Modèle Français*. Paris: La Documentation Française.

Davis, M. 1990. *City of Quartz: Excavating the Future in Los Angeles*. London: Verso.

Dear, M. 2000. *The Postmodern Urban Condition*. Oxford: Blackwell.

Dear, M., and S. Flusty. 1998. Postmodern urbanism. *Annals of the Association of American Geographers*, 88: 50–72.

De Berranger, P., and M. C. R. Meldrum. 2000. The development of intelligent local clusters to increase global competition and local cohesion:

the case of small businesses in the creative industries. *Urban Studies*, 37:1827–1835.

De Boeck, F. 2012. Spectral Kinshasa: building the city through an architecture of words. In *Urban Theory Beyond the West*, eds T. Edensor, and M. Jayne. London: Routledge, pp. 311–328.

De Boeck, F., M. F. Plissart, and J. P. Jacquemin. 2005. *Kinshasa: Récits de la Ville Invisible*. Tervuren: Musée Royal de l'Afrique Centrale.

DeFilippis, J., N. Martin, A. Bernhardt, and S. McGrath. 2009. On the character and organization of unregulated work in the cities of the United States. *Urban Geography*, 30:63–90.

De Geer, S. 1927. The American Manufacturing Belt. *Geografiska Annaler*, 27:233–259.

Dick, H. W., and P. J. Rimmer. 1998. Beyond the Third World city: the new urban geography of South-East Asia. *Urban Studies*, 35 (12):2303–2321.

Dosi, G. 1982. Technological paradigms and technological trajectories. *Research Policy*, 11:147–162.

Douglas, A., ed. 2002. *On the Edge: Culture and the Arts in Remote and Rural Locations*. Aberdeen: Faculty of Design, The Robert Gordon University.

Drennan, M. P. 2002. *The Information Economy and American Cities*. Baltimore: Johns Hopkins University Press.

Duranton, G., and D. Puga. 2004. Micro foundations of urban agglomeration economies. In *Handbook of Regional and Urban Economics, Vol. 4*, eds J. V. Henderson, and J. F. Thisse. Amsterdam: Elsevier, pp. 2065–2118.

Durkheim, E. 1893. *De la Division du Travail Social*. Paris: Félix Alcan.

Dyer, S., L. McDowell, and A. Batnitzky. 2008. Emotional labour/body work: the caring labours of migrants in the UK's National Health Service. *Geoforum*, 39 (6):2030–2038.

Eco, U. 1986. *Travels in Hyper-Reality*. London: Picador.

Ellis, M., R. Wright, and V. Parks. 2007. Geography and the immigrant division of labor. *Economic Geography*, 83:255–281.

Emmanuel, A. 1969. *L'Échange Inégal*. Paris: Maspéro.

Engels, F. 1845 [1950]. *The Condition of the Working Class in England in 1844*. London: Allen and Unwin.

Engler, M. 2000. Drive-thru history: theme towns in Iowa. In *Take The Next Exit: New Views Of The Iowa Landscape*, ed. R. F. Sayre. Ames: University of Iowa Press, pp. 255-276.

Escobar, A. 2005. Economics and the space of modernity: tales of market, production and labour. *Cultural Studies*, 19 (2):139–175.

Farías, I., and T. Bender, eds. 2010. *Urban Assemblages: How Actor–Network Theory Changes Urban Studies*. London: Routledge.

Feenstra, R. C. 1998. Integration of trade and disintegration of production in the global economy. *Journal of Economic Perspectives*, 12 (4):31–50.

Fernandez, R. M., and I. Fernandez-Mateo. 2006. Networks, race, and hiring. *American Sociological Review*, 71 (1):42–71.

Fine, J. 2005. Worker centers: organizing communities at the edge of the dream. Economic Policy Institute, briefing paper, available at: www.epi. org/publications/entry/bp159.

Florida, R. 2002. *The Rise of the Creative Class*. New York: Basic Books.

Fortunati, L. 2007. Immaterial labor and its machinization. *Ephemera: Theory and Politics in Organization*, 7:139–157.

Fortuny, K., R. Capps, and J. S. Passel. 2007. *The Characteristics of Unauthorized Immigrants in California, Los Angeles County, and the United States*. Washington, DC: The Urban Institute.

Frank, A. G. 1978. *Dependent Accumulation and Underdevelopment*. London: Macmillan.

Franke, S., and E. Verhagen. 2005. *Creativity and the City: How the Creative Economy Changes the City*. Rotterdam: NAi Publishers.

Freeman, L. 2005. Displacement or succession? Residential mobility in gentrifying neighborhoods. *Urban Affairs Review*, 40 (4):463–491.

Fröbel, F., J. Heinrichs, and O. Kreye. 1980. *The New International Division of Labor*. Cambridge: Cambridge University Press.

Fuerst, S. 2010. Global value chains and local cluster development: a perspective on domestic small enterprises in the 3D-animation industry in Colombia. *Revista Ad-Minister*, 16:89–102.

García, M. I., Y. Fernández, and J. L. Zofío. 2003. The economic dimension of the culture and leisure industry in Spain: national, sectoral and regional analysis. *Journal of Cultural Economics*, 27:9–30.

Garofoli, G. 1987. Il modello territoriale di sviluppo degli anni '70–'80. *Note Economiche*, 1:156–176.

Gatta, M., H. Boushey, and E. Appelbaum. 2009. High-touch and here-to-stay: future skills demands in US low wage service occupations. *Sociology – The Journal of the British Sociological Society*, 43:968–989.

Gereffi, G., J. Humphrey, and T. Sturgeon. 2005. The governance of global value chains. *Review of International Political Economy*, 12:78–104.

Gereffi, G., and M. Korzeniewicz, eds. 1994. *Commodity Chains and Global Capitalism*. Westport: Greenwood Press.

Gertler, M. S. 2003. Tacit knowledge and the economic geography of context, or, the undefinable tacitness of being (there). *Journal of Economic Geography*, 3:75–99.

Gibson, C., and D. Davidson. 2004. Tamworth, Australia's country music capital: place-marketing, rurality, and resident reactions. *Journal of Rural Studies*, 20:387–404.

Giedion, S. 1948. *Mechanization Takes Command: A Contribution to Anonymous History*. New York: Oxford University Press.

Glaeser, E., and J. Gottlieb. 2006. Urban resurgence and the consumer city. *Urban Studies*, 43:1275–1299.

Glaeser, E. L. 2011. *The Triumph of the City*. New York: Penguin.

Glaeser, E. L., J. Kolko, and A. Saiz. 2001. Consumer city. *Journal of Economic Geography*, 1:27–50.

Glaeser, E. L., and D. C. Maré. 2001. Cities and skills. *Journal of Labor Economics*, 19:316–342.

Glass, R. 1964. Aspects of change. In *London: Aspects of Change*, ed. Centre for Urban Studies. London: MacGibbon and Kee, pp. xiii-xlii.

Gouldner, A. 1979. *The Future of Intellectuals and the Rise of the New Class*. New York: Seabury.

Grabher, G. 2001a. Ecologies of creativity: the village, the group, and the heterarchic organization of the British advertising industry. *Environment and Planning A*, 33:351–374.

Grabher, G. 2001b. Locating economic action: projects, networks, localities, institutions. *Environment and Planning A*, 33:1329–1331.

Grabher, G. 2004. Temporary architectures of learning: knowledge governance in project ecologies. *Organization Studies*, 25:1491–1514.

Gramsci, A. 1975. *Quaderni del Carcere*. Turin: Einaudi.

Grant, J. L., and K. Kronstal. 2010. The social dynamics of attracting talent in Halifax. *Canadian Geographer*, 54 (3):347–365.

Grant, R., and J. Nijman. 2004. The re-scaling of uneven development in Ghana and India. *Tijdschrift Voor Economische en Sociale Geografie*, 95 (5):467–481.

Greenwood, M. J., and G. L. Hunt. 1989. Jobs versus amenities in the analysis of metropolitan migration. *Journal Of Urban Economics*, 25:1–16.

Guillaume, R. 2008. Des systèmes productifs locaux aux pôles de compétitivité: approches conceptuelles et figures territoriales du développement. *Géographie, Economie, Société*, 10:295–309.

Haase, A., S. Kabisch, A. Steinführer, S. Bouzarovski, R. Hall, and P. Ogden. 2010. Emergent spaces of reurbanisation: exploring the demographic dimension of inner-city residential change in a European setting. *Population Space And Place*, 16 (5):443–463.

Hall, P. 1998. *Cities in Civilization*. New York: Pantheon.

Hall, P. 2001. Global city-regions in the twenty-first century. In *Global City-Regions: Trends, Theory, Policy*, ed. A. J. Scott. Oxford: Oxford University Press, pp. 59–77.

Hall, P. 1962. *The Industries of London since 1861*. London: Hutchinson.

Hall, P., and D. Soskice, eds. 2001. *Varieties of Capitalism: The Institutional Foundations of Comparative Advantage*. New York: Oxford University Press.

Hamnett, C., and D. Whitelegg. 2007. Loft conversion and gentrification in London: from industrial to postindustrial land use. *Environment and Planning A*, 39:106–124.

Hardt, M., and A. Negri. 2000. *Empire*. Cambridge, MA: Harvard University Press.

Hardt, M., and A. Negri. 2009. *Commonwealth*. Cambridge, MA: Belknap Press.

Harris, A. 2008. From London to Mumbai and back again: gentrification and public policy in comparative perspective. *Urban Studies*, 45:2407–2428.

Harris, C. D., and E. L. Ullman. 1945. The nature of cities. *Annals of the American Academy of Political and Social Science*, 242:7–17.

Harvey, D. 1973. *Social Justice and the City*. London: Edward Arnold.

Harvey, D. 1982. *The Limits to Capital*. Oxford: Blackwell.

Harvey, D. 1989. From managerialism to entrepreneurialism – the transformation in urban governance in late capitalism. *Geografiska Annaler, Series B – Human Geography*, 71:3–17.

Haslam, S. E. 2004. *John Ruskin and the Lakeland Arts Revival, 1880–1920*. Cardiff: Merton.

Hayek, A. F. 1944. *The Road to Serfdom*. Chicago: Chicago University Press.

Heckscher, E. F., and B. Ohlin. 1991. *Heckscher–Ohlin Trade Theory*. Translated by H. Flam, and M. J. Flanders. Cambridge, MA: MIT Press.

Henderson, J. W., and A. J. Scott. 1987. The growth and internationalisation of the American semiconductor industry: labour processes and the changing spatial organisation of production. In *The Development of High Technology Industries: An International Survey*, eds M. J. Breheny, and R. McQuaid. London: Croom Helm, pp. 37-79.

Herrigel, G., and J. Zeitlin. 2010. Inter-firm relations in global manufacturing: disintegrated production and its globalization. In *The Oxford Handbook of Comparative Institutional Analysis*, eds G. Morgan, J. Campbell, C. Crouch, O. K. Pedersen, and R. Whitley. Oxford: Oxford University Press.

Hicks, S. R. C. 2011. *Explaining Postmodernism: Skepticism and Socialism from Rousseau to Foucault*. Love's Park, IL: Ockham's Razor.

Hirschman, A. O. 1958. *The Strategy of Economic Development*. New Haven: Yale University Press.

Hirst, P., and G. Thompson. 1996. *Globalization in Question*. Cambridge: Polity Press.

Hochschild, A. 1989. *The Second Shift: Working Parents and the Revolution at Home*. New York: Penguin.

Holzer, H. J. 1994. Black-employment problems – new evidence, old questions. *Journal of Policy Analysis and Management*, 13 (4):699–722.

Hoover, E. M., and R. Vernon. 1959. *Anatomy of a Metropolis*. Cambridge, MA: Harvard University Press.

Horkheimer, M., and T. W. Adorno. 1972. *Dialectic of Enlightenment*. New York: Herder and Herder.

Hoyt, H. 1939. *The Structure and Growth of Residential Areas in American Cities*. Washington, DC: Federal Housing Administration.

Hudson, S., and J. R. Brent Ritchie. 2006. Film tourism and destination marketing: the case of *Captain Corelli's Mandolin*. *Journal of Vacation Marketing*, 12:256–268.

Hutton, T. A. 2008. *The New Economy of the Inner City: Restructuring, Regeneration, and Dislocation in the Twenty-First Century Metropolis*. London: Routledge.

Islam, T. 2005. Outside the core: gentrification in Istanbul. In *Gentrification in a Global Context: The New Urban Colonialism*, eds R. Atkinson, and G. Bridge. London: Routledge, pp. 121–136.

Jacobs, J. 1969. *The Economy of Cities*. New York: Random House.

Jaffe, A. B., M. Trajtenberg, and R. Henderson. 1993. Geographic localization of knowledge spillovers as evidenced by patent citations. *Quarterly Journal of Economics*, 108:577–598.

Jameson, F. 1984. Postmodernism, or the cultural logic of late capitalism. *New Left Review*, 146:53–92.

Jayet, H. 1983. Chômer plus souvent en région urbaine, plus souvent en région rurale. *Economie et Statistique*, 153:47–57.

Jessop, B., N. Brenner, and M. Jones. 2008. Theorizing socio-spatial relations. *Environment and Planning D: Society and Space*, 26:389–401.

Johnson, N. C. 1999. Framing the past: time, space and the politics of heritage tourism in Ireland. *Political Geography*, 18:187–207.

Judd, D. R., and D. Simpson. 2011. *The City, Revisited: Urban Theory from Chicago, Los Angeles, and New York*. Minneapolis: University of Minnesota Press.

Kaika, M. 2010. Architecture and crisis: re-inventing the icon, re-imag(in)ing London and rebranding the City. *Transactions of the Institute of British Geographers*, 35:453–474.

Kain, J. F. 1968. The distribution and movement of jobs and industry. In *The Metropolitan Enigma*, ed. J. Q. Wilson. Cambridge, MA: Harvard University Press, pp. 1–40.

Kain, J. F. 1992. The spatial mismatch hypothesis: three decades later. *Housing Policy Debate*, 3:371–460.

Kang, M. 2003. The managed hand: the commercialization of bodies and emotions in Korean immigrant-owned nail salons. *Gender and Society*, 17:820–839.

Kaplinsky, R., O. Memedovic, M. Morris, and J. Readman. 2003. *The Global Wood Furniture Value Chain: What Prospects for Upgrading by Developing Countries?* Vienna: United Nations Industrial Development Organization.

Keating, M., P. Cairney, and E. Hepburn. 2009. Territorial policy communities and devolution in the UK. *Cambridge Journal of Regions, Economy and Society*, 2:51–66.

Kessler, J. A. 1999. The North American Free Trade Agreement, emerging apparel production networks and industrial upgrading: the Southern California/Mexico connection. *Review of International Political Economy*, 6:565–608.

Klepper, S. 2010. The origin and growth of industry clusters: the making of Silicon Valley and Detroit. *Journal of Urban Economics*, 67 (1):15–32.

Klink, J. J. 2001. *Cidade-Região: Regionalismo e Reestruturação no Grande ABC Paulista*. Rio de Janeiro: Lamparina Editora.

Kloosterman, R. C. 2010. This is not America: embedding the cognitive–cultural urban economy. *Geografiska Annaler: Series B, Human Geography*, 92B (2):131–143.

Knox, P. L. 2005. Creating ordinary places: slow cities in a fast world. *Journal of Urban Design*, 10:1–11.

Krugman, P. 1991. *Geography and Trade*. Leuven, Belgium: Leuven University Press.

Kunzmann, K. R. 2009. The strategic dimensions of knowledge industries in urban development. *Disp*, 45 (2):40–47.

Landry, C., and F. Bianchini. 1995. *The Creative City*. London: Demos.

Lazzarato, M., and A. Negri. 1991. Travail immatériel et subjectivité. *Futur Antérieur*, 6:86–89.

Lazzeretti, L., F. Capone, and T. Cinti. 2010. The regional development platform and "related variety": some evidence from art and food in Tuscany. *European Planning Studies*, 18:27–45.

Lees, L. 2012. The geography of gentrification: thinking through comparative urbanism. *Progress in Human Geography*, 36:155–171.

Lees, L., T. Slater, and E. Wyly. 2008. *Gentrification*. London: Routledge.

Lefebvre, H. 1968. *Le Droit à la Ville*. Paris: Editions Anthropos.

Lefebvre, H. 1970. *La Révolution Urbaine*. Paris: Gallimard.

Le Goix, R. 2005. Gated communities: sprawl and social segregation in southern California. *Housing Studies*, 20 (2):323–343.

Levy, F., and R. J. Murnane. 2004. *The New Division of Labor: How Computers are Creating the Next Job Market*. New York: Russell Sage Foundation.

Ley, D. 1996. *The New Middle Class and the Remaking of the Central City*. Oxford: Oxford University Press.

Linde-Laursen, A. 1999. "Unsettled" Solvang, Danish capital of America: a photoessay. *South Atlantic Quarterly*, 98 (4):781–799.

Lindop, G. 1993. *A Literary Guide to the Lake District*. London: Chatto and Windus.

Lipietz, A. 1986. New tendencies in the international division of labor: regimes of accumulation and modes of social regulation. In *Production, Work, Territory: The Anatomy of Industrial Capitalism*, eds A. J. Scott, and M. Storper. Boston: Allen and Unwin, pp. 16-40.

List, F. 1841 [1977]. *National System of Political Economy*. Fairfield, NJ: A. M. Kelley.

Lloyd, R. 2002. Neo-Bohemia: art and neighborhood development in Chicago. *Journal of Urban Affairs*, 24:517–532.

Logan, J. R., and H. L. Molotch. 1987. *Urban Fortunes: The Political Economy of Place*. Berkeley: California University Press.

Loo, B. P. Y. 2012. *The E-Society*. Hauppauge, NY: Nova Science Publishers.

Lopez-Morales, E. 2010. Gentrification by ground rent dispossession: the shadows cast by large-scale urban renewal in Santiago de Chile. *International Journal of Urban and Regional Research*, 35 (2): 330–357.

Lösch, A. 1940. *Die räumliche Ordnung der Wirtschaft*. Jena: G. Fischer.

Lowry, G., and E. McCann. 2011. Asia in the mix: urban form and global mobilities – Hong Kong, Vancouver, Dubai. In *Worlding Cities: Asian Experiments in the Art of Being Global*, eds A. Roy, and A. Ong. Oxford: Blackwell, pp. 182–204.

MacCannell, D. 1976. *The Tourist: A New Theory of the Leisure Class*. New York: Schocken Books.

Maillat, D., and J. Y. Vasserot. 1986. *Les Milieux Innovateurs: le Cas de l'Arc Jurassien Suisse*, ed. P. Aydalot. Paris: GREMI, pp. 217-246.

Mandel, E. 1975. *Late Capitalism*. London: NLB.

Markusen, A., P. Hall, and A. Glasmeier. 1986. *High Tech America: The What, How, Where and Why of the Sunrise Industries*. Boston: Allen and Unwin.

Markusen, A., G. H. Wassall, D. DeNatale, and R. Cohen. 2008. Defining the creative economy: industry and occupational approaches. *Economic Development Quarterly*, 22:24–45.

Marsden, T. 2010. Mobilizing the regional eco-economy: evolving webs of agri-food and rural development in the UK. *Cambridge Journal of Regions, Economy and Society*, 3:225–244.

Marsden, T., and E. Smith. 2005. Ecological entrepreneurship: sustainable development in local communities through quality food production and local branding. *Geoforum*, 36 (4):440–451.

Marshall, A. 1890. *Principles of Economics*. London, New York: Macmillan.

Marshall, A. 1919. *Industry and Trade; A Study of Industrial Technique and Business Organization*. London: Macmillan.

Marston, S. A., J. P. Jones, and K. Woodward. 2005. Human geography without scale. *Transactions of the Institute of British Geographers*, 30:416–432.

Marx, K. 1852 [1935]. *The Eighteenth Brumaire of Louis Bonaparte*. New York: International Publishers.

Marx, K. 1856 [1935]. *Value, Price and Profit*. New York: International Publishers.

Massey, D. 1984. Introduction; geography matters. In *Geography Matters! A Reader*, eds D. Massey, and J. Allen. Cambridge: Cambridge University Press, pp. 1-11.

Massey, D., and R. Meegan. 1982. *Anatomy of Job Loss: The How, Why, Where, and When of Employment Decline*. London: Methuen.

MasterCard Worldwide. 2008. *Worldwide Centers of Commerce Index*. http://www.mastercard.com/us/company/en/insights/pdfs/2008/ MCWW_WCoC-Report_2008.pdf.

Mbaiwa, J. E. 2011. Cultural commodification and tourism: the Goo-Moremi community, central Botswana. *Tijdschrift Voor Economische En Sociale Geografie*, 102 (3):290–301.

McDowell, L. 2009. *Working Bodies: Interactive Service Employment and Workplace Identities*. Chichester: Wiley-Blackwell.

McFarlane, C. 2011. Assemblage and critical urban theory. *City;* 15:204–224.

McGee, T. G. 1967. *The Southeast Asian City: A Social Geography of the Primate Cities of Southeast Asia*. London: Bell.

McKinnish, T., R. Walsh, and T. K. White. 2010. Who gentrifies low-income neighborhoods? *Journal Of Urban Economics*, 67 (2): 180–193.

McRobbie, A. 2004. Making a living in London's small-scale creative sector. In *Cultural Industries and the Production of Culture*, eds. D. Power and A. J. Scott. London: Routledge, pp. 130–143.

Milkman, R. 2006. *L.A. Story: Immigrant Workers and the Future of the US Labor Movement*. New York: Russell Sage Foundation.

Moran, W. 1993. The wine appellation as territory in France and

California. *Annals Of The Association Of American Geographers*, 83 (4):694–717.

Moulier Boutang, Y. 2007. *Le Capitalisme Cognitif, Comprendre la Nouvelle Grande Transformation et ses Enjeux*. Paris: Editions Amsterdam.

Myrdal, G. 1959. *Economic Theory and Under-Developed Regions*. London: Gerald Duckworth & Co.

Nel, E., T. Binns, and D. Beck. 2007. Alternative foods and community-based development: Rooibos tea production in South Africa's coast mountains. *Applied Geography*, 27:112–129.

Nicholson, N. 1955. *The Lakers: The Adventures of the First Tourists*. London: Robert Hale.

Niedomysl, T., and H. K. Hansen. 2010. What matters more for the decision to move: jobs versus amenities. *Environment and Planning A*, 42 (7):1636–1649.

Norton, R. D., and J. Rees. 1979. The product cycle and the spatial decentralization of American manufacturing. *Regional Studies*, 13:141–151.

Nowlan, D. M. 1977. The land market: how it works. In *Public Property?* eds L. B. Smith, and M. Walker. Vancouver: Fraser Institute, pp. 3–37.

O'Brien, R. O. 1992. *Global Financial Integration: the End of Geography*. London: Royal Institute of International Affairs.

Ohmae, K. 1995. *The End of the Nation State*. New York: The Free Press.

Ostrom, E. 2008. The challenge of common-pool resources. *Environment*, 50:8–20.

Paasi, A. 2011. The region, identity and power. *Procedia Social and Behavioral Sciences*, 14:9–16.

Palermo, P. C. 2008. Thinking over urban landscapes: interpretations and courses of action. In *Urban Landscape Perspectives*, ed. G. Maciocco. New York: Springer, pp. 27-41.

Park, R. E., E. W. Burgess, and R. D. McKenzie. 1925. *The City*. Chicago: University of Chicago Press.

Partridge, M. D. 2010. The duelling models: NEG vs amenity migration in explaining US engines of growth. *Papers in Regional Science*, 89 (3):513–536.

Peck, J. 1996. *Work-Place: The Social Regulation of Labor Markets*. New York: Guilford Press.

Peck, J., and N. Theodore. 2001. Contingent Chicago: restructuring the spaces of temporary labor. *International Journal of Urban and Regional Research*, (25):471–496.

Pecqueur, B. 2008. Pôles de compétitivité et spécificité de la ressource technologique: une illustration grenobloise. *Géographie, Economie, Société*, 10:311–326.

Peirce, N. R. 1994. *Citistates: How America Can Prosper in a Competitive World*. Santa Ana: Seven Locks Press.

Peters, M. A., R. Britez, and E. Bulut. 2009. Cybernetic capitalism, informationalism, and cognitive labor. *Geopolitics, History, and International Relations*, 1:11–39.

Philo, C., and G. Kearns. 1993. Culture, history, capital: a critical introduction to the selling of places. In *Selling Places: The City as Cultural Capital, Past and Present*, eds G. Kearns, and C. Philo. Oxford: Pergamon Press, pp. 1–32.

Piketty, T., and E. Saez. 2003. Income inequality in the United States, 1913–1998. *Quarterly Journal of Economics*, 118 (1):1–39.

Pine, B., and J. Gilmore. 1999. *The Experience Economy: Work is Theatre and Every Business a Stage*. Boston: Harvard Business School.

Piore, M., and C. Sabel. 1984. *The Second Industrial Divide: Possibilities for Prosperity*. New York: Basic Books.

Pollard, J. 2004. Manufacturing culture in Birmingham's jewelry quarter. In *Cultural Industries and the Production of Culture*, eds. D. Power, and A. J. Scott. London: Routledge, pp. 169–187.

Pollard, S. 1981. *Peaceful Conquest: The Industrialization of Europe, 1760–1970*. Oxford, New York: Oxford University Press.

Pollert, A. 1991. The orthodoxy of flexibility. In *Farewell to Flexibility?* ed. A. Pollert. Oxford: Blackwell, pp. 3–31.

Porter, M. E. 1985. *Competitive Advantage*. New York: The Free Press.

Power, D. 2002. Cultural industries in Sweden: an assessment of their place in the Swedish economy. *Economic Geography*, 78:103–127.

Power, D., and D. Hallencreutz. 2002. Profiting from creativity? The music industry in Stockholm, Sweden and Kingston, Jamaica. *Environment and Planning A*, 34:1833–1854.

Pratt, A. C. 1997. The cultural industries production system: a case study of employment change in Britain, 1984–91. *Environment and Planning A*, 29:1953–1974.

Prebisch, R. 1959. Commercial policy in the underdeveloped countries. *American Economic Review: Papers and Proceedings*, 44:251–273.

Preteceille, E. 1986. Collective consumption, urban segregation, and social classes. *Environment and Planning D: Society and Space*, 4 (2):145–154.

Prossek, A. 2011. Redesigning the metropolis: purpose and perception of the Ruhr district as European capital of culture 2010. In *Cities and Fascination: Beyond the Surplus of Meaning*, eds H. Schmid, W.-D. Dietrich, and J. Urry. Farnham: Ashgate, pp. 147–168.

Ramirez, H., and P. Hondagneu-Sotelo. 2009. Mexican immigrant gardeners: entrepreneurs or exploited workers? *Social Problems*, 56:70–88.

Rantisi, N. M. 2004. The ascendance of New York fashion. *International Journal of Urban and Regional Research*, 28 (1):86–106.

Rauch, J. E. 1993. Productivity gains from geographic concentration of human capital: evidence from the cities. *Journal of Urban Economics*, 34:380–400.

Rausch, A. S. 2010. *Cultural Commodities in Japanese Rural Revitalization: Tsugaru Lacquerware and Tsugaru Shamisen*. Leiden: Brill.

Ray, C. 1998. Culture, intellectual property and territorial rural development. *Sociologia Ruralis*, 38:3–20.

Reich, R. 1992. *The Work of Nations*. New York: Vintage.

Relph, E. 1976. *Place and Placelessness*. London: Pion.

Ricardo, D. 1817 [1971]. *Principles of Political Economy and Taxation*. Harmondsworth: Penguin Books.

Riley, R., D. Baker, and C. S. Van Doren. 1998. Movie induced tourism. *Annals of Tourism Research*, 25:919–935.

Robinson, J. 2006. *The Ordinary City: Between Modernity and Development*. London: Routledge.

Rodríguez-Pose, A., and J. Tomaney. 1999. Industrial crisis in the centre of the periphery: stabilisation, economic restructuring and policy responses in the São Paulo metropolitan region. *Urban Studies*, 36:329–343.

Rosecrance, R. 1986. *The Rise of the Trading State*. New York: Basic Books.

Roy, A. 2011. Slumdog cities: rethinking subaltern urbanism. *International Journal of Urban and Regional Research*, 35:223–238.

Rubino, S. 2005. A curious blend? City revitalisation, gentrification and commodification in Brazil. In *Gentrification in a Global Context: The New Urban Colonialism*, eds. R. Atkinson and G. Bridge. London: Routledge, pp. 225–239.

Rullani, E. 2000. Le capitalisme cognitif: du déjà vu? *Multitudes*, 2: 87–94.

Russo, M. 1985. Technical change and the industrial district: the role of interfirm relations in the growth and transformation of ceramic tile production in Italy. *Research Policy*, 14:329–343.

Salomon, R. M., and J. M. Shaver. 2005. Learning by exporting: new insights from examining firm innovation. *Journal of Economics and Management Strategy*, 14:431–460.

Salway, S. 2008. Labour market experiences of young UK Bangladeshi men: identity, inclusion and exclusion in inner-city London. *Ethnic and Racial Studies*, 31:1126–1152.

Sanders, J., V. Nee, and S. Sernau. 2002. Asian immigrants' reliance on social ties in a multiethnic labor market. *Social Forces*, 81:281–314.

Santagata, W. 2002. Distretto culturale e gestione dei diritti di proprietà:

la ceramica di Caltagirone. Turin: University of Turin, EBLA Working papers, No 200206.

Sassen, S. 2001. Global cities and global city-regions: a comparison. In *Global City-Regions: Trends, Theory, Policy*, ed. A. J. Scott. Oxford: Oxford University Press, pp. 78–95.

Sassen, S. 2008. *Territory, Authority, Rights: From Medieval to Global Assemblages*. Princeton: Princeton University Press.

Sassen-Koob, S. 1982. Recomposition and peripheralization at the core. *Contemporary Marxism*, (5):88–100.

Saunders, P. 1981. *Social Theory and the Urban Question*. London: Unwin Hyman.

Saxenian, A. 1994. *Regional Advantage: Culture and Competition in Silicon Valley and Route 128*. Cambridge, MA: Harvard University Press.

Saxenian, A. 2002. Transnational communities and the evolution of global production networks: the cases of Taiwan, China and India. *Industry and Innovation*, 9:183–202.

Saxenian, A. 2005. From brain drain to brain circulation: transnational communities and regional upgrading in India and China. *Studies in Comparative International Development*, 40 (2):35–61.

Schmid, H., W.-D. Dietrich, and J. Urry, eds. 2011. *Cities and Fascination: Beyond the Surplus of Meaning*. Farnham: Ashgate.

Schmitz, H. 2007. Regional systems and global chains. In *Development on the Ground: Clusters, Networks and Regions in Emerging Economies*, eds A. J. Scott, and G. Garofoli. London: Routledge, pp. 322–339.

Schmitz, H., and P. Knorringa. 2000. Learning from global buyers. *Journal of Development Studies*, 37:177–204.

Schnell, S. M. 2003. Creating narratives of place and identity in "Little Sweden, U.S.A." *Geographical Review*, 93:1–29.

Schonhardt-Bailey, C. 1996. *Free Trade: The Repeal of the Corn Laws*. Bristol: Thoemmes Press.

Schumpeter, J. A. 1942. *Capitalism, Socialism and Democracy*. New York: Harper and Row.

Scott, A. J. 1980. *The Urban Land Nexus and the State, Research in Planning and Design; No. 8*. London: Pion.

Scott, A. J. 1988a. *Metropolis: From the Division of Labor to Urban Form*. Berkeley: University of California Press.

Scott, A. J. 1988b. *New Industrial Spaces: Flexible Production Organization and Regional Development in North America and Western Europe*. London: Pion.

Scott, A. J. 1995. The electric vehicle industry and local economic development: prospects and policies for Southern California. *Environment and Planning A*, 27:863–875.

Scott, A. J. 2001. Industrial revitalization in the ABC municipalities, São Paulo: diagnostic analysis and strategic recommendations for a new economy and a new regionalism. *Regional Development Studies*, 7:1–32.

Scott, A. J. 2002. Competitive dynamics of Southern California's clothing industry: the widening global connection and its local ramifications. *Urban Studies*, 39:1287–1306.

Scott, A. J. 2005. *On Hollywood: The Place, The Industry*. Princeton: Princeton University Press.

Scott, A. J. 2008a. The resurgent metropolis: economy, society and urbanization in an interconnected world. *International Journal of Urban and Regional Research*, 32:548–564.

Scott, A. J. 2008b. *Social Economy of the Metropolis: Cognitive–Cultural Capitalism and the Global Resurgence of Cities*. Oxford: Oxford University Press.

Scott, A. J. 2009. Human capital resources and requirements across the metropolitan hierarchy of the United States. *Journal of Economic Geography*, 9:207–226.

Scott, A. J. 2010a. Cultural economy and the creative field of the city. *Geografiska Annaler: Series B, Human Geography*, 92 (2):115–130.

Scott, A. J. 2010b. Jobs or amenities? Destination choices of migrant engineers in the USA. *Papers of the Regional Science Association*, 89:43–63.

Scott, A. J. 2010c. Space–time variations of human capital assets in the American economy: profiles of abilities and skills across metropolitan areas, 1980 to 2000. *Economic Geography*, 86:233–249.

Scott, A. J., and D. P. Angel. 1987. The U.S. semiconductor industry: a locational analysis. *Environment and Planning A*, 19:875–912.

Scott, A. J., and A. Mantegna. 2009. Human capital assets and structures of work in the US metropolitan hierarchy (an analysis based on the O*NET information system). *International Regional Science Review*, 32:173–194.

Scott, A. J., and N. Pope. 2007. Hollywood, Vancouver and the world: employment relocation and the emergence of satellite production centers in the motion picture industry. *Environment and Planning A*, 39:1364–1381.

Scott, A. J., and E. Soja, eds. 1996. *The City: Los Angeles and Urban Theory at the End of the Twentieth Century*. Berkeley and Los Angeles: University of California Press.

Scott, A. J., and J. M. Zuliani. 2007. L'industrie de l'informatique à Toulouse: développement, structure, enjeux. *Revue d'Economie Régionale et Urbaine*, 3:1–26.

Seaton, A. V. 1996. Hay on Wye, the mouse that roared: book towns and rural tourism. *Tourism Management*, 17:379–382.

Sekhar, N. U. 2003. Local people's attitudes towards conservation and wildlife tourism around Sariska Tiger Reserve, India. *Journal of Environmental Management*, 69 (4):339–347.

Sheppard, E. 2012. Trade, globalization and uneven development: entanglements of geographical political economy. *Progress in Human Geography*, 36 (1):44–71.

Shields, R. 1991. *Places on the Margin: Alternative Geographies of Modernity*. London: Routledge.

Shin, H. B. 2009. Property-based redevelopment and gentrification: the case of Seoul, South Korea. *Geoforum*, 40 (5):906–917.

Simmel, G. 1903 [1950]. The metropolis and mental life. In *The Sociology of Georg Simmel*, ed. K. H. Wolff. New York: Free Press, pp. 409–424.

Simon, C. J., and C. Nardinelli. 2002. Human capital and the rise of American cities, 1900–1990. *Regional Science and Urban Economics*, 32:59–96.

Singer, H. W. 1950. The distribution of gains between investing and borrowing countries. *American Economic Review: Papers and Proceedings*, 40:473–485.

Sklair, L. 2000. *The Transnational Capitalist Class*. Oxford: Blackwell.

Sklair, L. 2010. Iconic architecture and the culture-ideology of consumerism. *Theory, Culture and Society*, 27:135–159.

Slater, T. 2006. The eviction of critical perspectives from gentrification research. *International Journal of Urban and Regional Research*, 30:737–757.

Smith, N. 1982. Gentrification and uneven development. *Economic Geography*, 58:139–155.

Smith, N. 1986. Gentrification, the frontier, and the restructuring of urban space. In *Gentrification of the City*, eds N. Smith, and P. Williams. London: Allen and Unwin, pp. 15–34.

Soja, E. W. 1980. The socio-spatial dialectic. *Annals of the Association of American Geographers*, 70:207–225.

Soja, E. W. 1989. *Postmodern Geographies: The Reassertion of Space in Social Theory*. London: Verso.

Soja, E. W. 1996. *Thirdspace: Journeys to Los Angeles and Other Real-and-Imagined Places*. Oxford: Blackwell.

Soja, E. W. 2000. *Postmetropolis: Critical Studies of Cities and Regions*. Oxford: Blackwell.

Soja, E. W. 2010. *Seeking Spatial Justice*. Minneapolis: University of Minnesota Press.

Soja, E. W., and A. J. Scott. 1986. Los Angeles: capital of the late twentieth century. *Environment and Planning D: Society and Space*, 4:249–254.

Squire, S. J. 1993. Valuing countryside: reflections on Beatrix Potter tourism. *Area*, 25:5–10.

Srivastava, S., and N. Theodore. 2006. Offshoring call centers: the view from Wall Street. In *Developments in the Call Centre Industry*, eds J. Burgess, and J. Connell. Abingdon: Routledge, pp. 19–35.

Standing, G. 2011. *The Precariat: The New Dangerous Class*. London: Bloomsbury.

Stare, M., and L. Rubalcaba. 2009. International outsourcing of services: what role for Central and East European countries? *Emerging Markets Finance and Trade*, 45 (5):31–46.

Stedman Jones, G. 1984. *Outcast London: A Study in the Relationship between Classes in Victorian Society*. London: Penguin.

Stoll, M. A. 1999. Spatial job search, spatial mismatch, and the employment and wages of racial and ethnic groups in Los Angeles. *Journal of Urban Economics*, 46 (1):129–155.

Stolper, W. F., and P. A. Samuelson. 1941. Protection and real wages. *Review of Economic Studies*, 9:58–73.

Storper, M. 1997. *The Regional World: Territorial Development in a Global Economy*. New York: Guilford Press.

Storper, M., and A. J. Scott. 1990. Work organization and local labor markets in an era of flexible production. *International Labour Review*, 129:573–591.

Storper, M., and A. J. Venables. 2004. Buzz: face-to-face contact and the urban economy. *Journal of Economic Geography*, (4):351–370.

Struyk, R. J., and F. J. James. 1975. *Intrametropolitan Industrial Location: The Pattern and Process of Change*. Lexington, MA: Lexington Books.

Sturgeon, T. J. 2002. Modular production networks: a new American model of industrial organization. *Industrial and Corporate Change*, 11 (3):451–496.

Sunley, P., S. Pinch, S. Reimer, and J. Macmillen. 2008. Innovation in a creative production system: the case of design. *Journal of Economic Geography*, 8 (5):675–698.

Terkenli, T. S. 2006. Landscapes of a new cultural economy of space: an introduction. In *Landscapes of a New Cultural Economy of Space*, eds T. S. Terkenli, and A. M. d'Hauteserre. Dordrecht: Springer, pp. 1–18.

Thompson, J. E., and S. D. Krasner. 1989. Global transactions and the consolidation of sovereignty. In *Global Changes and Theoretical Challenges*, eds E. O. Czempiel, and J. N. Rosenau. Lexington: Lexington Books.

Tooke, N., and M. Baker. 1996. Seeing is believing: the effect of film on visitor numbers to screened locations. *Tourism Management*, 17:87–94.

United Nations. 2007. *World Urbanization Prospects*. New York: United Nations.

United Nations. 2009. *World Urbanization Prospects*. http://esa.un.org/unpd/wup/index.htm.

Urry, J. 1992. The tourist gaze and the environment. *Theory, Culture and Society*, 9:1–26.

Urry, J. 1995. *Consuming Places*. London: Routledge.

US Department of Commerce. 1997. *City Government Finances*. Washington, DC: Bureau of the Census.

Vercellone, C. 2007. From formal subsumption to general intellect: elements for a Marxist reading of the thesis of cognitive capitalism. *Historical Materialism*, 15:13–36.

Vergunst, J., A. Árnason, R. Macintyre, and A. Nightingale. 2009. Using environmental resources: networks in food and landscape. In *Comparing Rural Development: Continuity and Change in the Countryside of Western Europe*, eds A. Árnason, M. Shucksmith, and J. Vergunst. Farnham: Ashgate, pp. 143–170.

Vik, J., and M. Villa. 2010. Books, branding and boundary objects: on the use of image in rural development. *Sociologia Ruralis*, 50 (2):156–170.

Vogel, R. K., H. V. Savitch, J. Xu, A. G. O. Yeh, W. P. Wu, A. Sancton, P. Kantor, P. Newman, T. Tsukamoto, P. T. Y. Cheung, J. F. Shen, F. L. Wu, and F. Z. Zhang. 2010. Governing global city regions in China and the West. *Progress in Planning*, 73:1–75.

Wacquant, L. 2008. Relocating gentrification: the working class, science and the state in recent urban research. *International Journal of Urban and Regional Research*, 32:198–205.

Walker, R. A. 1981. A theory of suburbanization: capitalism and the construction of urban space in the United States. In *Urbanization and Urban Planning in Capitalist Society*, eds M. Dear, and A. J. Scott. London: Methuen, pp. 383–430.

Wall, G. 1996. Perspectives on tourism in selected Balinese villages. *Annals of Tourism Research*, 23:123–137.

Wallerstein, I. 1979. *The Capitalist World Economy*. Cambridge: Cambridge University Press.

Waltz, K. N. 1979. *The Theory of International Politics*. Reading, MA: Addison-Wesley.

Ward, K., C. Fagan, L. McDowell, D. Perrons, and K. Ray. 2010. Class transformation and work–life balance in urban Britain: the case of Manchester. *Urban Studies*, 47 (11):2259–2278.

Ward, K., and A. E. G. Jonas. 2004. Competitive city-regionalism as a politics of space: a critical reinterpretation of the new regionalism. *Environment and Planning A*, 36 (12):2119–2139.

Ward, N., and D. L. Brown. 2009. Placing the rural in regional development. *Regional Studies*, 43:1237–1244.

Wheeler, C. H. 2007. Do localization economies derive from human capital externalities? *Annals of Regional Science*, 41:31–50.

Whittlesey, D. 1954. The regional concept and the regional method. In *American Geography, Inventory and Prospect*, eds P. E. James, and C. F. Jones. Syracuse: Syracuse University Press, pp. 21–68.

Whyte, I. 2000. William Wordsworth's *Guide to the Lakes* and the geographic tradition. *Area*, 32:101–106.

Whyte, W. H. 1956. *The Organization Man*. New York: Simon and Schuster.

Williams, R. 1973. *The Country and the City*. London: Chatto and Windus.

Williamson, O. E. 1975. *Markets and Hierarchies: Analysis and Antitrust Implications*. New York: The Free Press.

Wirth, L. 1938. Urbanism as a way of life. *American Journal of Sociology*, 44:1–24.

Woodward, K., J. P. Jones, and S. A. Marston. 2012. The politics of autonomous space. *Progress in Human Geography*, 36:204–224.

World Bank. 2009. *Reshaping Economic Geography*. Washington, DC: World Development Report.

Wright, R., M. Ellis, and V. Parks. 2010. Immigrant niches and the intra-metropolitan spatial division of labour. *Journal of Ethnic and Migration Studies*, 36:1033–1059.

Wyly, E., K. Newman, A. Schafran, and E. Lee. 2010. Displacing New York. *Environment and Planning A*, 42 (11):2602–2623.

Yankel, F., and O. Marco. 2001. Urbanisme embourgeoisement et mixité sociale à Paris. *Mouvements*, 13:9–21.

Yu, F. L. T. 2009. Taiwan's entrepreneurs and international coordination: evolution of global production network in electronics and IT industries. *Global Economic Review*, 38 (1):49–62.

Zukin, S. 1982. *Loft Living: Culture and Capital in Urban Change*. Baltimore: John Hopkins University Press.

Zukin, S. 1991. *Landscapes of Power: From Detroit to Disney World*. Berkeley: University of California Press.

Index